PAUL SELIGSON
CAROL LETHABY

2nd edition

English
ID

Student's
Book
1

ID Language map

	Question syllabus	Vocabulary	Grammar	Speaking & Skills
1				
1.1	Are you Canadian?	Countries & nationalities Adjectives and a / an + noun	Verb be – ➕ ➖ Yes / No ❓ Subject pronouns	Introduce yourself & greetings Ask & answer about countries & nationalities Give opinions about people and places
1.2	How do you spell your last name?	The alphabet Numbers 11–100		Spell words & your name Say your age & where you're from
1.3	What's your email address?	Personal objects / plurals	Verb be – Wh- ❓ Demonstrative pronouns	Ask for & give personal information Ask about & identify objects
1.4	Are these your glasses?	Adjectives & colors	Possessive adjectives	Talk about possessions Describe objects
1.5	What's your full name?			Complete a form
	How are you?	Greetings & responses		Meeting people & social interaction
Writing 1: A social media profile		**ID Café 1: Role-play a class reunion**		
2				
2.1	When do you get up?	Activities & days of the week Time expressions	go activities	Describe routine Ask & answer about routine Ask & answer about sleeping habits
2.2	What do you do in the mornings?	Morning routine	Simple present ➕ ➖ Prepositions of time	Talk about & compare morning routines
2.3	Who do you live with?	Family	Simple present ❓	Describe family Question intonation Ask and answer simple present questions
2.4	When do you check your phone?	Cell phone expressions	Frequency adverbs	Talk about cell phone habits Do a survey about phone use
2.5	How old are you?			Role-play an interview
	How do you celebrate your birthday?	Special occasions		Use celebratory expressions
Writing 2: A personal email		**ID Café 2: Talk about reviews and reports**		**Review 1** p.30
3				
3.1	What's the weather like?	Weather	It's + adjective	Describe weather Ask & answer about weather
3.2	Are you busy at the moment?	Everyday actions (1) Months & seasons	Present continuous ➕ ➖	Talk about what's happening now Talk about months & seasons
3.3	What are you doing these days?	Technology problems	Present continuous ❓	Ask & answer about what's happening now Discuss technology problems
3.4	What do you do after school / work?	Everyday actions (2) Verbs for emotion, senses or mental states Future time expressions	Simple present vs. present continuous	Talk about what people are doing now and what they usually do Talk about celebrity activists
3.5	Why are you learning English?		need to / have to	Analyze your English
	Are you thirsty?	Adjectives (feelings)	Informal English	Make offers
Writing 3: A language profile		**ID Café 3: Discuss photography**		
4				
4.1	Do you like tennis?	Sports	Definite article the	Talk about sports Pronunciation of the
4.2	Can you drive a tractor?	Abilities	Can: Yes / No ❓ / short answers	Ask and answer about ability Rank items that can change the world
4.3	What languages can you speak?	Talents	Can: ➕ ➖ and Wh- ❓ Adverbs	Ask and answer about ability & talents Role-play a job interview
4.4	Are you an organized person?	Clothes	Possessive pronouns Possessive s	Talk about what people are wearing Talk about ownership Talk about being messy / tidy
4.5	Do you like spas?	Spa facilities		Read for details Describe a perfect spa day
	What shoe size are you?	Shopping expressions	Punctuation	Shop for clothes
Writing 4: A job application		**ID Café 4: Design and present a superhero**		**Review 2** p.56
5				
5.1	Is there a mall in your area?	Public places	There is / there are ➕ ➖ ❓	Describe a town / neighborhood
5.2	What are your likes and dislikes?	Free-time activities Household chores	like / love / hate / enjoy / not mind + verb + -ing	Talk about likes and dislikes Sentence stress
5.3	What do you like doing on vacation?	Vacation	Comparative adjectives	Talk about vacations and vacation activities Describe a perfect vacation
5.4	How often do you leave voice messages?	House sitting	Object pronouns Imperatives Comparatives / superlatives	Talk about house sitting Give instructions
5.5	What's a staycation?			Give and understand instructions
	Do you live near here?	Giving directions		Give and follow directions
Writing 5: A city brochure		**ID Café 5: Talk about personal technology**		**Mid-term review** p.70

	Question syllabus		Vocabulary	Grammar	Speaking & Skills
6	6.1	What's in your refrigerator?	Food & drink	Countable vs. uncountable nouns	Talk about food & drink Describe what's in your refrigerator
	6.2	What do you eat for lunch and dinner?	Food portions & containers	Quantifiers: *some* and *any*	Talk about morning food & healthy eating
	6.3	How often do you eat chocolate?	Food and nutrition	Quantifiers: *a little*, *a few*, *a lot of*	Use quantifiers to talk about activities you like / don't like
	6.4	How many meals do you cook a week?	Food Cognates	*How much* vs. *how many*	Talk about food and nutrition Take a class survey
	6.5	Are you hungry?	Menu food		Scan a menu Order food from a menu
		What would you like for lunch?	Restaurant phrases		Order food in a restaurant
	Writing 6: A food diary		**ID Café 6:** Role-play a restaurant situation		**Review 3** p.84
7	7.1	Do you live in a house?	Rooms & furniture	Past of *be*: *there was / there were*	Describe your home Compare a home then and now
	7.2	Where were you last night?	Party items Past time expressions	Past of *be*: ⊕ ⊖ ❓ / short answers	Talk about a party Ask & answer about last week
	7.3	Where were you last New Year's Eve?	New Year's Eve celebrations	Prepositions of place	Describe New Year's Eve celebrations Describe positions of objects
	7.4	Was your hometown different 10 years ago?	Dates Places in a city	*there is / there are* & *there was / there were*	Talk about changes to cities Compare your hometown in the past and now
	7.5	Do you enjoy weddings?			Predict from context Describe a special event
		How about a barbecue on Sunday?			Make invitations
	Writing 7: An online review		**ID Café 7:** Describe a party		
8	8.1	When did you start school?	Life events Past time expressions	Simple past regular verbs ⊕ ⊖	Talk about past events Write a biography Pronunciation of past tense verbs
	8.2	Did you go out last weekend?	Ordinal numbers & dates Simple past irregular verbs	Simple past irregular verbs ⊕ ⊖	Talk about what you did yesterday / last birthday Pronunciation of past irregular verbs
	8.3	Where did you go on your last vacation?	Vacations	Simple past ❓ / short answers	Ask and answer about your last vacation / Pronunciation of *Did you*
	8.4	When do you listen to music?	Everyday activity verbs	Subject questions vs. object questions	Do a pop quiz Write questions for a class quiz
	8.5	Can I use your phone?	Phone phrases		Understand a story Tell a story
		Could you help me, please?	Phrases to make requests		Ask for favors and respond
	Writing 8: A vacation message		**ID Café 8:** Call a friend for help		**Review 4** p.110
9	9.1	How did you get here today?	Transportation	*How do / did you get to …?*	Ask & answer about personal transportation Describe transportation problems
	9.2	What do you do?	Jobs	Articles + jobs	Talk about occupations & dream jobs Talk about commuting & keeping in shape
	9.3	Where are you going to be in 2025?	Future plans	*going to* for future	Talk about future plans Make predictions Pronunciation of *going to* / *gonna*
	9.4	What are you going to do next year?	Life changes	Present continuous for future *going to* vs. present continuous	Talk about intentions and plans Write New Year's resolutions
	9.5	Would you like to be a nurse?	Jobs		Make connections Discuss occupations in the future
		Could I borrow your pen?			Ask for permission
	Writing 9: A reply to a blog post		**ID Café 9:** Speculate about life in the future		
10	10.1	Do you look like your mom?	The body & face Adjectives (appearance)		Talk about parts of the body Describe physical appearance
	10.2	Are you like your dad?	Adjectives (character)	Comparatives with *-er* & *more* *Like* as verb & preposition	Talk about a timeline Make comparisons
	10.3	Who's the most generous person in your family?	Personality types Adjectives (character)	Superlatives with *-est* & *most*	Describe personality and places
	10.4	What's the best place in the world?	Geographical features	Comparatives & superlatives	Sentence stress Talk about surprising facts
	10.5	What's your blood type?	Parts of the body		Understand facts
		Is your English better than a year ago?			Make choices
	Writing 10: A family profile		**ID Café 10:** Talk about making changes to physical appearance		**Review 5** p.136

Grammar p. 138   Sounds and usual spelling p. 158   Audioscript p. 160

Welcome to English ID!

Finally, an English course you can understand!

Famous **song lines** illustrate language from lessons.

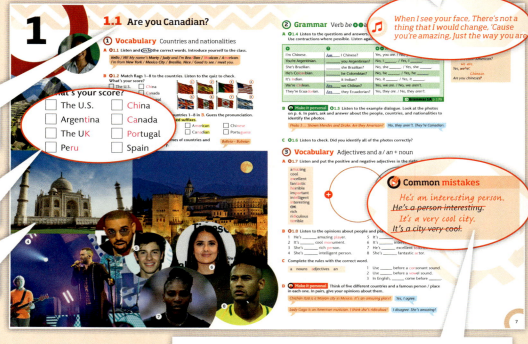

Lesson titles are questions to help you engage with the content.

Word stress in pink on new words.

Contextualized Picture Dictionary to present and review vocabulary.

Focus on **Common mistakes** accelerates accuracy.

ID Skills: extra reading and listening practice.

ID in Action: communication in common situations.

Authentic videos present topics in real contexts.

ID Café: sitcom videos to consolidate language.

Reviews systematically recycle language.

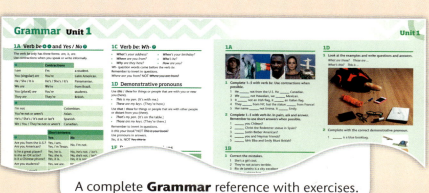

A complete **Grammar** reference with exercises.

Welcome

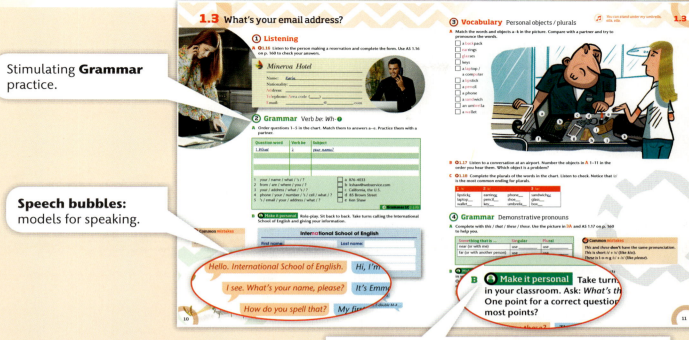

Stimulating **Grammar** practice.

Speech bubbles: models for speaking.

Make it personal: personalized speaking tasks to help you express your identity in English.

Audio script activities to consolidate pronunciation.

Pictures to present and practice **Pronunciation**.

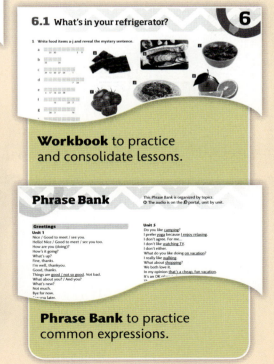

Workbook to practice and consolidate lessons.

Phrase Bank to practice common expressions.

- Teachers and students can find all their resources in one place.
- **Richmond Test Manager** with interactive and printable tests.
- Activity types including pronunciation, common mistakes and speaking.

Learn to express your identity in English!

1

1.1 Are you Canadian?

1 Vocabulary Countries and nationalities

A ▶1.1 Listen and circle the correct words. Introduce yourself to the class.

Hello / Hi! My name's Marty / Judy and I'm Brazilian / Mexican / American. I'm from New York / Mexico City / Brasilia. Nice / Good to see / meet you.

B ▶1.2 Match flags 1–8 to the countries. Listen to the quiz to check. What's your score?

- ☐ The U.S.
- ☐ China
- ☐ Argentina
- ☐ Canada
- ☐ The UK
- ☐ Portugal
- ☐ Peru
- ☐ Spain

C ▶1.3 Match the nationalities to countries 1–8 in **B**. Guess the pronunciation. Listen to check. Notice the unstressed suffixes.

- ☐ Peruvian
- ☐ Spanish
- ☐ American
- ☐ Chinese
- ☐ Argentinian
- ☐ British
- ☐ Canadian
- ☐ Portuguese

D 🔴 **Make it personal** Say the names of countries and nationalities near your country.

Bolivia – Bolivian

2 Grammar Verb *be* ➕➖ and *Yes / No* ❓

🎵 *When I see your face, There's not a thing that I would change, 'Cause you're amazing, Just the way you are.* 1.1

A ▶1.4 Listen to the questions and answers. Complete the grammar box. Use contractions where possible. Listen again to check.

➕	❓	➕➖ Short answers
I'm Chinese.	**Am** I Chinese?	Yes, you *are*. / No, you're not.
You're Argentinian.	_____ you Argentinian?	No, I _____. / Yes, I _____.
She's Brazilian.	_____ she Brazilian?	No, she _____. / Yes, she _____.
He's Colombian.	_____ he Colombian?	No, he _____. / Yes, he _____.
It's Indian.	_____ it Indian?	No, it _____. / Yes, it _____.
We're Chilean.	**Are** we Chilean?	Yes, we *are*. / No, we *aren't*.
They're Ecuadorian.	**Are** they Ecuadorian?	Yes, they *are*. / No, they *aren't*.

→ Grammar 1A p. 138

⚠️ **Common mistakes**

~~Are you~~
~~You are~~ Latin American?
   we are.
Yes, ~~we're~~.
          Chinese
Are you ~~chineses~~?

B 👤 Make it personal ▶1.5 Listen to the example dialogue. Look at the photos on p. 6. In pairs, ask and answer about the people, countries, and nationalities to identify the photos.

> Photo 5 ... Shawn Mendes and Drake. Are they American?   No, they aren't. They're Canadian.

C ▶1.6 Listen to check. Did you identify all of the photos correctly?

3 Vocabulary Adjectives and *a / an* + noun

A ▶1.7 Listen and put the positive and negative adjectives in the right place.

amazing
cool
excellent
fantastic
horrible
important
intelligent
interesting
~~OK~~
rich
ridiculous
terrible

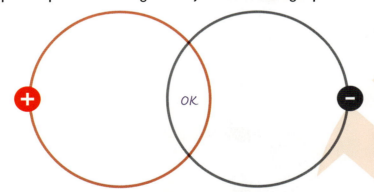

(+)   OK   (−)

⚠️ **Common mistakes**

He's an interesting person.
~~He's a person interesting.~~
It's a very cool city.
~~It's a city very cool.~~

B ▶1.8 Listen to the opinions about people and places. Complete 1–8 with *a / an*.

1 He's _____ amazing player.
2 It's _____ cool monument.
3 She's _____ rich person.
4 She's _____ intelligent person.
5 It's _____ horrible city.
6 It's _____ interesting country.
7 He's _____ excellent teacher.
8 She's _____ fantastic actor.

C Complete the rules with the correct word.

> a   nouns   adjectives   an

1 Use _____ before a consonant sound.
2 Use _____ before a vowel sound.
3 In English, _____ come before _____.

D 👤 Make it personal Think of five different countries and a famous person / place in each one. In pairs, give your opinions about them.

> Chichén Itzá is a Mayan city in Mexico. It's an amazing place!   Yes, I agree.

> Lady Gaga is an American musician. I think she's ridiculous!   I disagree. She's amazing!

1.2 How do you spell your last name?

1 Pronunciation   The alphabet

A ▶1.9 Match the pairs of words to the pictures in **B**. Listen, check, and repeat.

- [ ] a shoe • two
- [ ] a car • a star
- [ ] a pen • ten
- [ ] a nose • a rose
- [1] a plane • a train
- [ ] three • a tree
- [ ] nine • wine

B ▶1.10 Listen to the words and letters in the chart and notice the vowel sounds.

1	2	3	4	5	6	7
eɪ	iː	ɛ	aɪ	oʊ	uː	ɑr
A	B	F ___	I	O	Q	R
H	C	L ___	___		U	
J	D ___	M ___			___	
___	E ___					

⚠ **Common mistakes**

How do you spell that?
~~How can I write?~~

C ▶1.11 Listen to these letters and put them in the correct column in **B**.

G   K   N   P   S   T   V   W   X   Y   Z

D 👤 **Make it personal**   Point to a picture. Ask your partner to say it. Which vowel sound is it? Try to spell the word. Use a dictionary if necessary.

What's that?   It's rain.   How do you spell "rain"?   R-A-I-N   Correct!

2 Vocabulary Numbers 11–100

♪ *It's fun to stay at the Y.M.C.A.*   **1.2**

A ▶1.12 Complete the numbers under the prices. Listen, check, and repeat with the correct stress.

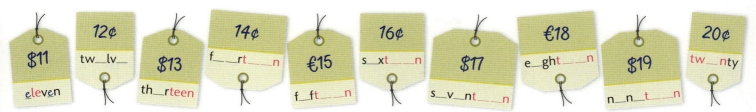

$11 — eleven
12¢ — tw__lv__
$13 — th__rteen
14¢ — f___rt____n
€15 — f__ft____n
16¢ — s__xt____n
$17 — s__v__nt____n
€18 — e__ght____n
$19 — n__n__t____n
20¢ — tw__nty

B ▶1.13 How do you say these numbers? Listen, check, and repeat with the correct stress.

| 30 40 50 60 70 80 90 100 |

Thirty, forty ...

C ▶1.14 Listen to sentences 1–8 and circle the number you hear.

1 18 80 85   3 20 11 12   5 15 50 55   7 06 60 16
2 17 70 73   4 19 90 99   6 14 40 43   8 13 30 33

D 🔵 **Make it personal** Play *Bingo*. Write numbers from 1 to 20 on the card.

One student: Call numbers from 1 to 20 in any order.
Winner: Shout *Bingo!* when you complete a line.

Play again with numbers from 21 to 40, 41 to 60, etc.

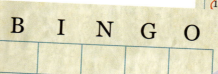

3 Listening

A ▶1.15 Listen to five dialogues and circle the names you hear. Use AS 1.15 on p. 160 to check your answers.

1 **First name:** Jack / Jake   **Last name:** Noore / Moore
2 **Full name:** Peter / Dieter   Queen / Quinn
3 **Name:** Rochelle / Roxalle   Johns / Jones
4 **First name:** George / Jeorge   **Last name:** Wessex / Essex
5 **Full name:** Joy / Joi   Boscombi / Boscombe

B 🔵 **Make it personal** In pairs, practice the dialogues with your own name and names of people you know. Say your age, too.

What's your name, please?   Bruce Wayne.   *How do you spell that?*   B-R-U-C-E W-A-Y-N-E. I'm 18.

Are you British?   No, I'm from Gotham City.

🔵 **Common mistakes**
I'm 18 (years old).
~~I have 18 years.~~

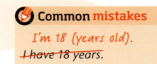

1.3 What's your email address?

1 Listening

A ▶1.16 Listen to the person making a reservation and complete the form. Use AS 1.16 on p. 160 to check your answers.

Minerva Hotel

Name: Karin
Nationality: _____
Address: _____
Telephone: Area code (___) _____
Email: _____@_____.com

2 Grammar Verb *be*: Wh-❓

A Order questions 1–5 in the chart. Match them to answers a–e. Practice them with a partner.

Question word	Verb *be*	Subject
1 What	's	your name?

1 your / name / what / 's / ?   a 876-4033
2 from / are / where / you / ?   b kshaw@webservice.com
3 your / address / what / 's / ?   c California, the U.S.
4 phone / your / number / 's / cell / what / ?   d 85 Brown Street
5 's / email / your / address / what / ?   e Ken Shaw

➔ **Grammar 1C** p. 138

B 🔵 **Make it personal** Role-play. Sit back to back. Take turns calling the International School of English and giving your information.

⚠ Common mistakes

I'm ^a student.

International School of English

First name: _____   Last name: _____
Address: _____
Phone number: _____
Email address: _____

Hello. International School of English.   — Hi, I'm a student.
I see. What's your name, please?   — It's Emma Miranda.
How do you spell that?   — My first name is E-double M-A …

3 Vocabulary Personal objects / plurals

🎵 *You can stand under my umbrella, ella, ella.*   1.3

A Match the words and objects a–k in the picture. Compare with a partner and try to pronounce the words.

- [ ] a **back**pack
- [ ] **ear**rings
- [ ] **gla**sses
- [ ] keys
- [ ] a **lap**top / a com**pu**ter
- [ ] a **lip**stick
- [ ] a **pen**cil
- [ ] a phone
- [ ] a **sand**wich
- [ ] an um**brel**la
- [ ] a **wa**llet

B ▶ 1.17 Listen to a conversation at an airport. Number the objects in **A** 1–11 in the order you hear them. Which object is a problem?

C ▶ 1.18 Complete the plurals of the words in the chart. Listen to check. Notice that /z/ is the most common ending for plurals.

1 /s/	2 /z/		3 /ɪz/
lipstick*s*	earring*s*	phone__	sandwich*es*
laptop__	pencil__	shoe__	glass__
wallet__	key__	umbrella__	box__

4 Grammar Demonstrative pronouns

A Complete with *this / that / these / those*. Use the picture in **3A** and AS 1.17 on p. 160 to help you.

Something that is …	Singular	Plural
near (or with me)	use _____	use _____
far (or with another person)	use _____	use _____

→ Grammar 1D p. 138

⚠️ **Common mistakes**

This and *these* **don't** have the same pronunciation.
This is short /ɪ/ + /s/ (like *kiss*).
These is l-o-n-g /iː/ + /z/ (like *please*).

B 👤 **Make it personal** Take turns to test a partner with the picture in **3A** and objects in your classroom. Ask: *What's this? What's that? What are these? What are those?* One point for a correct question and one point for a correct answer. Who scored the most points?

What are these?   *They're windows.*   *What's that?*   *It's a door.*

1.4 Are these your glasses?

1 Listening

A ▶1.19 Listen to conversations 1–6 and match them to the pictures.

Is this _____ sandwich, Jake?
Are these _____ keys?

That's _____ laptop!

No, they aren't _____ earrings.

Come on, Ed! These are _____ chips!

Are these _____ glasses?

I think it's _____ phone.

I think it's _____ phone.

Hey! Those are _____ potato chips!

B ▶1.19 Complete the sentences in pictures 1–6 with the correct word. Listen again and use AS 1.19 on p. 160 to check.

her   his   my   our   their   your

2 Grammar Possessive adjectives

A ▶1.19 Match the item from **1A** to the owner. Listen to check.

1. potato chips — Ed
2. earrings — Lara
3. glasses — Rosa
4. sandwich — Jake
5. phone — Jake and Rosa
6. laptop

B Complete the grammar box.

Subject	Possessive adjective + noun
I	*my* phone
you	_____ keys
_____	her friend
he	_____ shoes
_____	our house
they	_____ breakfast

➡ Grammar 1E p. 138

Common mistakes

Are these your glasses?
~~Is this your glasses?~~

Common mistakes

her
Lisa's online with ~~your~~ boyfriend.
his
John loves ~~your~~ girlfriend.

C 🔵 **Make it personal** In groups, each person puts one item in a bag. Take the items out in turn. Point and say what the things are using different possessive adjectives.

This is your pen.   This is his phone.   These are her keys.   These are our keys.

3 Vocabulary Adjectives and colors

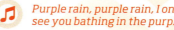
Purple rain, purple rain, I only want to see you bathing in the purple rain.

1.4

A ▶1.20 In pairs, take the quiz. Match the answers to questions a–j and photos 1–10. Listen, check, and repeat the colors.

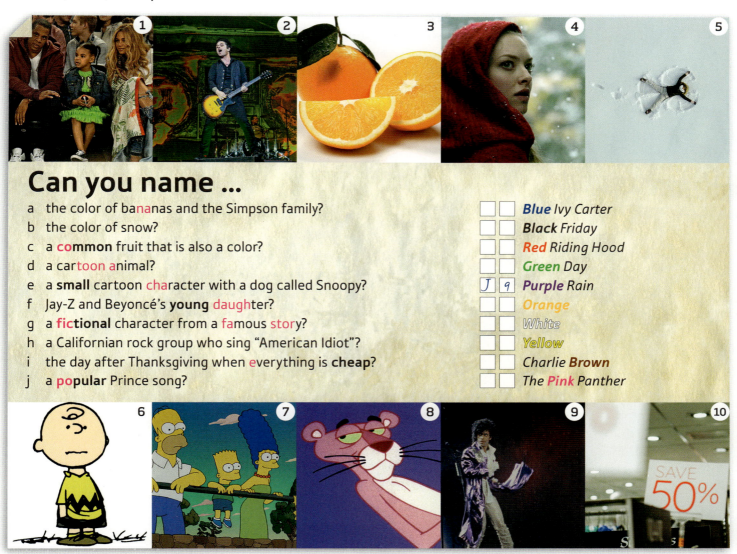

Can you name …

a the color of ba**na**nas and the Simpson family?
b the color of snow?
c a **common** fruit that is also a color?
d a car**toon** a**ni**mal?
e a **small** cartoon cha**rac**ter with a dog called Snoopy?
f Jay-Z and Beyoncé's **young** **daugh**ter?
g a **fic**tional character from a **fa**mous **sto**ry?
h a Californian rock group who sing "American Idiot"?
i the day after Thanksgiving when **ev**erything is **cheap**?
j a **po**pular Prince song?

☐☐ *Blue* Ivy Carter
☐☐ *Black* Friday
☐☐ *Red* Riding Hood
☐☐ *Green* Day
J 9 *Purple* Rain
☐☐ *Orange*
☐☐ *White*
☐☐ *Yellow*
☐☐ Charlie *Brown*
☐☐ The *Pink* Panther

B Underline all the adjectives in the quiz. Circle the correct rules.
Adjectives go **before** / **after** the noun.
Adjectives have **a** / **no** plural form.

C Match the **bold** adjectives in the quiz to their opposites. Test your partner.
1 rare _____
2 expensive _____
3 big _____
4 real _____
5 unpopular _____
6 old _____

What's the opposite of "rare"?   *common*

Common mistakes
blue eyes
My brother has ~~eyes blues~~.

D ▶1.21 Listen to descriptions of five items in the pictures in **1A** on p. 12. Name them after the beep. Then listen to the answer.

E 👥 **Make it personal** In small groups.
A: Describe an object in the room and give an opinion about it.
B and C: Ask questions and guess what the object is.

They're small and black, and they're really cool!   *Are they my glasses?*   *Yes, they are!*

13

1.5 What's your full name?

ID Skills Completing a form

A Read and answer the questions.
1 Match a–f to documents 1–6.
  a a work ID
  b a conference ID
  c a hotel registration form
  d a school registration form
  e a car rental form
  f a passport
2 Who is European?
3 Who is non-European?
4 Who is a teenager?

1 NAME: Amy SEX: F AGE: 18 NATIONALITY: Colombian ADDRESS: Medellín
DESIGN YOUTH CONFERENCE

4 LION COMMUNITY SCHOOL
Name: *Omar Aslam*
Age: *14 yrs 8 mos*
Date: *Sept 1, 2018*
Nationality: *Pakistani*

2
Last name: MARSHALL
First name: Susana
Country of origin: Nigeria
Birthdate: 10/27/1988
Gender: F
Plate number: 6VBV764

3
Full name: *Charles Bouvier*
Date of birth: *5/26/90*
Country of birth: *France*
Current address: *354 Rue de Ville, Nice*
Zip code: *06200*
Date: *8/14/18*

5
UNITED KINGDOM OF GREAT BRITAIN AND NORTHERN IRELAND
Type P Code GBR No. 70125698
Surname (1) MURPHY
Given name(s) (2) GILLIAN JANE
Nationality (3) BRITISH CITIZEN
Date of Birth (4) FEB 15, 1965
Sex (5) F
P<GBRMURHPY<<GILLIAN<<JANE<<<<<<<<<<<<<<<<<<
70125698GBR128963445F18900245<<<<<<<<<<<<<05

6 SunTech
Name: Ken Tran
Place of birth: Ho Chi Minh City, Vietnam
Department: Human Resources
Email address: ktran@suntech.com
Tel: 765-3000 Ext: 145

B Read the documents again and find different ways to refer to:
1 your name (5): *first name*
2 your age (3):
3 where you are from (4):

C ▶ 1.22 Do you know all the countries and nationalities in the documents in **A**? Listen to check.

D ▶ 1.23 Listen to and complete the registration form.

Second International Conference
Telephone registration

Name:		Nationality:	
Address:		Telephone:	
		Email:	
Zip Code:			

⚠ **Common mistakes**
What's your ~~complete~~ *full* name?
My ~~actual~~ *current* address is …

E 👤 **Make it personal** Choose a document from this page. Ask your partner questions to complete it with their data. Change roles. Then present your partner to the class.

This is my friend, Adriana. Her full name is …

1.5 How are you?

Hey, I just met you, And this is crazy, But here's my number, So call me, maybe?

in Action Meeting people

A ▶1.24 Listen to two colleagues and check (✓) the six phrases they say.

Asking	Answering
☐ How are you?	☐ Fine, thanks.
☐ How's it going?	☐ I'm well, thank you.
☐ How are you doing?	☐ Good, thanks.
☐ What about you?	☐ Not much.
☐ What's up?	☐ Things are good.
☐ What's new?	☐ Not bad. And you?

Common mistakes

Thank you.
You're welcome.
~~For nothing.~~

B ▶1.25 Listen to and repeat the other phrases. Which response from **A** is repeated?

C In pairs, practice similar conversations with any possible combination of the phrases in **A**.

> Hi! How are you?   Fine, thanks. What about you? How's it going?   Things are good.

D ▶1.26 Listen to six short dialogues. Write the number of each conversation in the box.

☐ I don't understand.   Oh, sorry.   ☐ See you later!   Bye for now!

☐ Thank you!   You're welcome.   ☐ Excuse me. Can you say that again, please?   Sure …

☐ I'm sorry.   Don't worry about it.   ☐ Excuse me.   Oh, I'm sorry.

E **Make it personal** In pairs, imagine you're the people in photos 1–5. Role-play conversations using appropriate expressions.

Writing 1   A social media profile

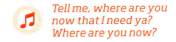

Tell me, where are you now that I need ya? Where are you now?

A Read Cristina's personal profile and complete the form.

e-pals.net

Cristina González
@cristina0330

My name's Cristina González, and I'm 18 years old. I'm Bolivian, from Santa Cruz, but now I live in Toronto, Canada, and I'm a student at Great Lakes High School five days a week. I also work in a local café on weekends. It's popular with students and artists, and the customers are really interesting. Sometimes I don't understand what people say to me, but I'm a fast learner! I don't have a boyfriend at the moment, but I have an amazing best friend called Anya. We go to the gym together. We also go to parties and clubs! Toronto's a fantastic city with an excellent baseball team, the Blue Jays. Anya doesn't like baseball, but I love it. I go alone or with my dad. Please message me: **@cristina0330**.

Profile

Last name:	
First name:	
Age:	
Nationality:	
Country of residence:	
Occupation:	
Username:	

B Read **Write it right!**, then underline the contractions and the connectors in **A**.

> ✓ **Write it right!**
>
> In informal writing, use contractions: *I'm, I don't.*
> Use a variety of connectors: *and, but, or.*

C Find and correct 10 more mistakes in Luís' reply to Cristina.

Messages
LU_PORT:

> Hi, Cristina, my name is Luís, I'm ~~portuguese~~ P and I have 19 years. Wow! You live in Toronto — that is excelent. I live in Porto with my mother and father, and I have a lot of parents here. I too study english, but its very dificult! My brother play baseball, maybe you can meet him, ha-ha! Me, I like the soccer. Pleas email me at luisporto94@e-mates.com and tell me much about Toronto.

D From the texts in **A** and **C**, which questions can we answer about Cristina (C), Luís (L), or both (B)?

1. Where are you from?   _B_
2. How old are you?   ____
3. What's your full name?   ____
4. Where do you live?   ____
5. Who do you live with?   ____
6. What's your email address?   ____
7. Do you go to school?   ____
8. Do you have any brothers or sisters?   ____
9. Do they play sports?   ____
10. Do you have a boyfriend / girlfriend?   ____
11. Do you have a best friend?   ____
12. What are your interests?   ____

E 🎧 **Make it personal**   Write a similar profile of yourself. Write 120–150 words.

Before	Answer questions 1–12 in **D**. Think about extra information, e.g., your opinion about people, places, or things.
While	Use contractions and a variety of connectors. Use adjectives to give your opinion.
After	Check your profile carefully. Show it to a partner before giving it to your teacher.

16

1 An excellent reunion

Café

1 Before watching

A Complete 1–3 with the correct words.
1 This _____ Andrea. She's at _____ class reunion.
2 This _____ her brother. _____ name is August.
3 That's _____ cousin, Genevieve. She _____ Canadian.

B 🅐 **Make it personal** What's your opinion of class, work, family, or old friend reunions? Talk in pairs.

I think class reunions are fun.   *Not me. I think they're boring.*

2 While watching

A Watch the video and circle the correct answer.
1 The party is **in an apartment** / **at a school**.
2 On the wall are some **new pictures** / **class photos**.
3 **August** / **Andrea** remembers where Kitty is from.
4 **Andrea** / **Genevieve** isn't happy at first.
5 **Andrea** / **Genevieve** says, "I'm so glad you're just my cousin."

B Where are they from? Listen and complete the chart.

Classmate	Country / city	Nationality
Manny Vasquez	_____	Peruvian
_____ Findley	England	_____
_____ Jones	_____	Irish
_____ Belucci	_____	American
_____ Jones	_____	British

C Watch and check (✓) all Genevieve's nicknames you hear.
☐ Gen ☐ Gertrude ☐ Gigi ☐ Jenny ☐ Vie-Vie

D Watch and check (✓) all August's nicknames you hear.
☐ Auggie ☐ Augustus ☐ Gigi ☐ Guto ☐ Iggy

E 🅐 **Make it personal** Do you have a nickname? What do your family, friends, and classmates usually call you?

My name's Kathleen, but my friends call me Kathy. What's your nickname?   *Please, call me Fred.*

3 After watching

A True (T) or False (F)?
1 Mrs. Grandby's an old classmate.
2 With Mrs. Grandby, there's never trouble.
3 Ignatius Dansbury's a great guy.
4 Ignatius is in a class above August and Andrea.
5 Joe Bellucci's a rock star.
6 Johnny's Genevieve's old boyfriend.
7 The cute boys from the band are from Canada.

B In pairs, check your answers to **A**. Correct the false statements.

I think number 1 is false.   *Me, too. I think she's their …*

C Complete and match the greetings to speakers 1–5. There's one extra person.
1 Andrea   ☐ Oh, hey! It's Genevieve.
2 August   ☐ _____, Gen. How are you?
3 Ignatius   ☐ Hey, _____, what's up?
4 Genevieve   ☐ I'm so _____ to see you!
5 Joe   ☐ Iggy! What's up?

D In pairs, take turns saying phrases 1–12 with the correct intonation. Who says them, August (A), Andrea (An), Genevieve (G), or Joe (J)?
1 Guess who's over there? ____
2 Isn't that Manny? ____
3 What a horrible guy! ____
4 Forget about it! ____
5 Really? ____
6 Wait, isn't your middle name something with a G? ____
7 That's not the point. ____
8 Don't you say it! ____
9 Get it? ____
10 Stop it, little Guto! ____
11 Don't worry, ladies. ____
12 Geez! Don't drop it! ____

E 🅐 **Make it personal** Role-play a class reunion. Imagine you're old friends. In groups of three, gossip!

Wow, guess who's here? It's Gloria!

No way! Really? Incredible.

That's not Gloria. She's too young. And Gloria's in Mexico.

17

2.1 When do you get up?

1 Vocabulary — Activities and days of the week

A ▶2.1 Listen and match the photos to activities 1–8.
1. go to a café
2. go to church
3. go to the gym
4. go home
5. go to a party
6. go to school
7. go to the grocery store
8. go to work

B Complete rules 1–4 with these expressions.

| go to | go to the | go to a | go |

Use:
1. _____ when we don't know exactly which place it is.
2. _____ when we know exactly which place / there is only one.
3. _____ with *home*.
4. _____ with *school*, *work*, *church*.

> ⚠ **Common mistakes**
> I go ~~to~~ home at about 8 p.m.

C Use the photos to remember the eight *go* activities.

D ▶2.2 Complete the days of the week from these abbreviations. Put them in order, 1 to 7. Listen to check.

- [4] Wed_n_ _e_ _s_ _d_ _a_ _y_
- [ ] Mon__ __ __
- [ ] Sun__ __ __
- [ ] Fri__ __ __
- [ ] Tue__ __ __ __
- [ ] Sat__ __ __ __ __
- [ ] Thu__ __ __ __ __ __

E In pairs, take turns saying the days in order. Who can say them more quickly?

> *Monday, Tuesday, ...*   *Only 10 seconds! Very good!*

F 👤 **Make it personal** When do you do the activities in **A**? Compare with a partner. Are your routines similar?

> *I go to work on Sundays. What about you?*   *I go to work on Saturdays.*

2 Listening

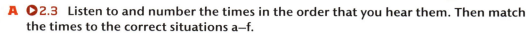

I don't care if Monday's blue. Tuesday's gray and Wednesday too. Thursday I don't care about you.

2.1

A ▶2.3 Listen to and number the times in the order that you hear them. Then match the times to the correct situations a–f.

a at a soccer game   c on TV   e at an airport
b at a party   d at school   f at home

B Write more times for your partner to practice saying.

What time is it?   It's 5:15.

C ▶2.4 Listen to two short interviews and write the days and times.
1 The woman gets up at _____ in the morning. She goes to school at _____. She goes to bed at _____ during the week. She gets _____ hours of sleep a night.
2 The man goes to work at _____ from _____ to _____. He gets home at _____ in the evening. He doesn't work at night or on weekends.

D ▶2.4 Listen again and complete the rules with *on*, *in*, or *at*.
Use:
1 _____ with times and *night*.
2 _____ with days of the week and *weekends*.
3 _____ with the *morning / afternoon / evening*.

E 🧍 Make it personal   In pairs, take turns asking and answering 1–4.
From Monday to Friday, and on weekends, what time do you …
1 get up?   3 go to school / work / university?
2 go to bed?   4 get home from work / school?

I get up at 7 a.m. during the week, but at around 9 on weekends!

I get up early on weekends, around 6:30! I go to work.

⚠ Common mistakes

~~in~~ *at*
I don't work ~~in~~ the night.

~~in~~ *on*
She doesn't go to bed early ~~in~~ weekends.

3 Reading

A Read the report and complete the chart.

On average, how many hours do people in these countries sleep?			
France		Japan	
The U.S.		South Korea	

B 🧍 Make it personal   Do a class survey. Ask:
1 What time do you get up a) on weekdays b) on weekends?
2 What time do you go to bed a) on weekdays b) on weekends?
3 On average, how many hours do people in your class sleep?

The World Sleeps

The Organization for Economic Cooperation and Development asked 18 countries, "How many hours do you sleep?". The French get an average of 8 hours and 50 minutes of sleep a night compared to the U.S. with 8 hours and 38 minutes. The South Koreans only sleep 7 hours and 49 minutes a night, and the Japanese about 8 hours.

2.2 What do you do in the mornings?

1 Vocabulary Morning routine

A Match pictures a–j with phrases 1–10.

1	☐ brush my teeth	5	☐ have breakfast	9	☐ take a shower
2	☐ exercise / work out	6	☐ leave home	10	☐ wake up
3	☐ get dressed	7	☐ make the bed		
4	☐ get up	8	☐ shave		

B ▶ 2.5 Listen to 10 sound effects. Say the phrase before the audio. Were you correct?

C ▶ 2.6 Listen to Jake describe his morning routine. Match the time expressions to his actions in **A**.

☐ 6:30   ☐ for 30 minutes
☐ not immediately   ☐ 8 a.m.

D 🔴 Make it personal Write down your morning routine and the time you do each activity. Compare with a partner. Are your routines similar or different?

I wake up at 6 a.m. You wake up at 7:30 a.m. That's very different!

⚠ **Common mistakes**

do
What time /you get up?

2 Grammar Simple present ⊕ and ⊖

🎵 *Don't forget me, I beg, I remember you said, Sometimes it lasts in love but sometimes it hurts instead.*

2.2

A Look at the man in the photo? What is his morning routine? Put the activities in **1A** on p. 20 in the order you think the man does them.

B ▶2.7 Listen and check your guesses. Any surprises?

C Study the song line above and Common mistakes. Then read and complete the grammar box.

> **a** Complete the sentences with the ⊕ form of the verb in parentheses.
>
> | | Subject | Verb | |
> |---|---|---|---|
> | 1 | I | | home at 7 a.m. (**leave**) |
> | 2 | You | | to school at 7:30 a.m. (**go**) |
> | 3 | My sister | | her bed in the morning. (**make**) |
> | 4 | My dad | | a shower at night. (**take**) |
> | 5 | My brother and I | | up at 6 a.m. (**get**) |
> | 6 | My friends | | breakfast at 10 a.m. (**have**) |
>
> **b** Complete the rules about ⊖ sentences in the simple present.
> *I **don't** watch TV when I get home.   She **doesn't** have breakfast.*
> 1 We use **does / doesn't** with she / he / it, and we use **doesn't / don't** with all other pronouns.
> 2 *Don't* or *doesn't* goes **before / after** the verb.
>
> **c** Make the sentences in **a** negative.
>
> ➡ **Grammar 2A** p. 140

⏰ **Common mistakes**

~~wakes~~
She / He ~~wake~~ up at 6:00 a.m.
~~doesn't~~
She ~~don't~~ wake up before 9:00 a.m.
~~has~~
He ~~have~~ breakfast alone.

💬 *I wake up at 7 a.m., but I get up at 7:30. I don't make my bed!*

D ▶2.7 Complete the paragraph about the man's actions. Then listen to check. Is your morning routine similar?

He <u>wakes up</u> (**wake up**) at 8 a.m., but he _____ (**get up**). He sleeps again and then he _____ (**get up**) at 8:50 a.m., but he _____ (**wake up**)! After he wakes up, he _____ (**make his bed**). Then he _____ (**exercise**) and he _____ (**shave**). After that, he _____ (**take a shower**), he _____ (**brush his teeth**), and he _____ (**get dressed**)!

E 🟢 **Make it personal** In groups, play the game.
1 Guess and write four ⊕ and ⊖ sentences about the routines and everyday activities of the people in your group.
2 Take turns checking your guesses. Say one of your sentences and ask the other students to raise their hands if the sentence is true for them.

💬 *I think three people go to the gym on weekends. Is that true?*   💬 *No, it isn't! Only one person goes to the gym on weekends.*

2.3 Who do you live with?

1 Reading and vocabulary Family

A ▶2.8 Who are these characters from an animated TV show? Listen to and read this ad. Then complete their family tree.

Meet the Griffins!

Peter Griffin and his wife, Lois, have three children. Meg is their first child and their only daughter. Chris is their teenage son, and Stewie is his baby brother. He's just one year old. The family is completed by Brian, the talking dog, and Peter's parents, Francis and Thelma. They live in Quahog, Rhode Island, in the U.S.

Watch this show every weeknight at 11:30 p.m. on Channel 44.

Francis and Thelma
____ and Lois
____   Chris   ____

B ▶2.8 Complete the family chart with words from the ad. Then read them aloud to your partner. Listen and check your pronunciation.

Female	Male	Male and female
grandmother	grandfather	grandparent(s)
mother	father	_____(s)
sister	_____	siblings / twin(s)
_____	son	child / children
niece	nephew	
_____	husband	couple
aunt	uncle	
		cousin(s)
girlfriend	boyfriend	partner

⚠ **Common mistakes**

~~parents~~
I have two ~~fathers~~: my mom and dad. The others in my family are my ~~parents~~.
relatives

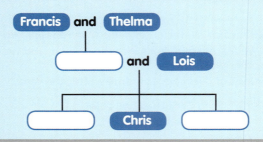

Lois to Peter? | Lois is his wife.

C In pairs, test each other on the relationships in **A**.

D Repeat **C**, this time using the possessive 's.   Who's Francis? | Thelma's husband.

E 👤 **Make it personal** In small groups, draw another famous family tree (from TV, movies, literature) and write a short ad. Answer questions 1–4.
1 What are their names?
2 Who is who? What are their relationships?
3 Where do they live?
4 What is different or interesting about them?

F Exchange ads with another group. Do you know the family? Who has the best ad?

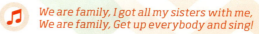

② Grammar Simple present

A Do you know your partner? Guess her / his answers to questions 1–4. Then check.
1 Who does X live with?
   a a friend / relative
   b no one
2 Does X study another language?
   a No, just English.
   b Yes, X studies _____ (language).
3 Which soccer team does X support?
   a _____ (soccer team)
   b X doesn't like soccer / have a team.
4 Does X prefer …
   a tea / coffee?
   b juice / water?

I think you live alone.
No, that's wrong. I live with my parents.

B Complete the grammar box. Are the questions in **A** ASI or QASI?

> There are two different types of questions. Match the word order to each type.
> 1 A question that asks for **information**. *Where does she live?*
> 2 A question to which the **answer** is *Yes* or *No*. *Does he play soccer?*
>
> ☐ **A**uxiliary verb + **s**ubject + **i**nfinitive verb? (ASI)
> ☐ **Q**uestion word + **a**uxiliary verb + **s**ubject + **i**nfinitive verb? (QASI)
>
> → Grammar 2B p. 140

C Are these *Yes / No* (Y / N) or information (I) questions?
1 ☐ What's your full name?
2 ☐ Are you Spanish?
3 ☐ Where do you live?
4 ☐ Do you live with your parents?
5 ☐ Where exactly in the U.S. do you plan to travel to?
6 ☐ Do you know anyone in Alaska?

D ▶ 2.9 Match questions 1–6 in **C** to the answers. Listen to check.
☐ Yes, my sister lives there.
☐ Miguel Hernández.
☐ No, I don't. I live with my girlfriend, Monica.
☐ In Madrid. I work there. It's an amazing city!
☐ Yes, I am. I'm from Valencia.
☐ Alaska.

Common mistakes
does
Where ~~your~~ mother lives?
                                    do
Do you like soccer? Yes, I ~~like~~.

③ Pronunciation: Question intonation and silent e

A ▶ 2.9 Look at AS 2.9 on p. 161. Then listen again and notice how the intonation in each question goes up (↗) or down (↘) at the end. Complete the rules.
1 If it is a *Yes / No* question, the intonation usually goes _____.
2 If it is an information question, the intonation usually goes _____.

B Complete 1–5. Take turns asking and answering the questions. Use the correct intonation.
1 _____ you have a brother?
2 _____ many cousins do you have?
3 _____'s your mother's name?
4 _____'s your father's name?
5 _____ they live near you?

C 🔴 **Make it personal** Write two more *Yes / No* questions and two more information questions. In pairs, take turns asking and answering them. Use the verbs to help you.

| have go like live play (sport) study travel visit |

Do you live in an apartment? *Yes, I do.* *Where exactly do you live?*

23

2.4 When do you check your phone?

1 Listening

A ▶ 2.10 Listen to Miguel talking to a friend about these three photos on his phone. How many questions do you hear? Who are the people?

B 🙂 **Make it personal** In pairs, show photos of your family and say who they are. Ask two questions about your partner's photos.

This is my brother, Carlos. *Where does he live?* *He lives in Canada.*

And who's this woman? *This is Susan, my brother's wife.*

2 Reading

A ▶ 2.11 Read the webposts about cell phone habits and match 1–7 with the correct name. Listen to check.

☐ Ruben   1 checks her phone at breakfast.
☐ Jan   2 doesn't check his phone at dinner.
☐ María's boyfriend   3 doesn't check her phone.
☐ Lucía's friends   4 send messages all day.
☐ Gerry   5 checks his phone at dinner.
☐ Milton's son   6 checks his phone when they go out.
☐ Greg's mom   7 doesn't look at his phone when he eats.

Cell phone habits

I **ne**ver look at my phone when I eat. It's a really bad **ha**bit. Oh, except when I have lunch alone!
Ruben, New York

I **some**times check my phone at breakfast. My dad gets really mad!
Jan, Los Angeles

My boyfriend oc**ca**sionally checks his phone when we go out together. I think that's OK.
María, Mexico City

My mom never checks her phone, so I have to call her!
Greg, London

My friends send me WhatsApp messages all day, so I **al**ways check my phone every five minutes – when I'm not **bu**sy.
Lucía, La Paz

My boss always sends me messages late at night, so I **of**ten need to check my phone at dinner.
Gerry, Boston

My son plays games and uses apps on his phone all the time, so he's always on it. I in**sist** he stops at dinner!
Milton, Rio de Janeiro

B 🙂 **Make it personal** In groups, talk about when you and your family / friends check your / their phones. Who checks it when they eat and why? Who has the best reason?

I check my phone at breakfast because my boss gets up at 5:00 a.m.

My brother checks his phone every two minutes - I think he's addicted to it!

♪ I will never say never! (I will fight) / I will fight till forever! (make it right)   **2.4**

3 Grammar Frequency adverbs

A Complete the grammar box.

1 Put the frequency adverbs in the correct place in the chart.

always   never   occasionally   often   sometimes   usually

○ ◔ ◔ ◐ ◐ ◕ ●

___ ___ ___ ___ ___ ___

2 Number these statements 1–4 from least to most frequent.
   a My sister sometimes goes to the theater. ☐
   b I never go to the gym. ☐
   c My parents always go to work. ☐
   d My friends often go to parties. ☐

3 Does the frequency adverb go before or after the verb?

→ **Grammar 2C** p. 140

Common mistakes

I always
~~Always I~~ go to the movies on the weekend.

B 👤 **Make it personal** Do a class survey.
1 Read the questions and put a ✓ in column 1 for you.
2 In pairs, ask and answer. Put your partner's answers in column 2.
3 Report your answers to the class. Which are good / bad habits? Who has the best habits?

Do you …	never		occasionally		sometimes		often		usually		always	
	1	2	1	2	1	2	1	2	1	2	1	2
take selfies every day?												
check your phone every five minutes?												
text during a conversation?												
make voice calls?												
leave voicemail?												
use earphones (to listen to music)?												
use your phone in the bathroom?												
turn off your phone at night?												

Carla always texts during a conversation — even with her teacher!

Eduardo never uses earphones to listen to music. He listens on the bus. That's a bad habit!

25

2.5 How old are you?

ID Skills Reading Asking for personal information

A Read the interview with Ginny Lomond and complete questions 1–9 with the correct verb.

fresh faces.com

Pop singer Ginny Lomond answers your questions about her life.

1 What _____ your full name?
2 Interesting! And how old _____ you?
3 Don't worry! Do you _____ a pet?
4 Where _____ you live?
5 And where _____ your family live?
6 Great! Do you _____ any brothers or sisters?
7 I see. And what _____ you do on the weekend?
8 OK, and what time do you _____ to bed on weekdays?
9 And our final question! _____ you exercise regularly?

☐ No, I don't exercise. Well, only occasionally (when I walk Boston). I'm a little lazy!
☐ Well, my mom lives in Paris, and my dad lives in L.A.
☐ I sleep a lot and occasionally go for a walk. And I never work on Mondays, so I often go to bed late on Sundays.
☐ I usually go to bed at 11 p.m. from Monday to Thursday, but I sometimes go to parties!
☐ Yes, I do. I have a dog called Boston. I love him!
☐ I live in Paris.
☐ Virginia Marie Lomond.
☐ No. I'm an only child.
☐ Umm … OK, I'm 23.

B ▶2.12 Match the questions to the answers in the interview. Listen to check.

C Find and underline five examples of frequency adverbs in the interview.

D In pairs, ask and answer *How often ...?* questions with the *go* activities in 1A on p. 18.

How often do you go to the gym?   I never go to the gym!

E **Make it personal** In pairs, role-play the interview.
A: Ask the nine questions.
B: Give your own true answers.
Then change roles.

Common mistakes

How often
~~With what frequency~~ do you ...?

2.5 How do you celebrate your birthday?

Music's got me feeling so free, We're gonna celebrate.

ID in Action Celebrating

A Match the phrases with photos 1–6.

- ☐ Congratulations!
- ☐ Enjoy your meal!
- ☐ Happy birthday!
- ☐ Happy New Year!
- ☐ Have a good trip!
- ☐ Merry Christmas!

B ▶ 2.13 Listen to check. Try to remember the answers.

C What do you say on occasions 1–6? Practice saying the phrases with a partner.

1. before dinner
2. at a wedding
3. on your mom's birthday
4. before a friend goes on vacation
5. on December 25th
6. on January 1st

D 🔴 **Make it personal** Write how often you / other people do the activities in the chart on each special occasion.

| always | never | occasionally | often | sometimes | usually |

	On your birthday	At Christmas	On New Year's Eve	On the Day of the Dead	At Carnival	Another celebration?
have a special meal at home						
go to a restaurant						
drink and eat special food						
have a party						
give and receive gifts						
wear special clothes						
go to bed late						
spend a lot of money						
dance and sing						
go to the cemetery						

⚠ Common mistakes

~~On~~ At Christmas Day = a specific day or date.

At / For ~~On~~ Christmas = a festive period.

E In small groups, compare answers. Find one thing you do differently.

I always have a special meal at home on my birthday.

I never eat at home on my birthday. We usually go to a restaurant.

Writing 2   A personal email

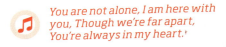

You are not alone, I am here with you, Though we're far apart, You're always in my heart.

A Read the email and number the things that Matt does in order.

- [ ] have breakfast
- [ ] do homework
- [ ] take a shower
- [ ] have dinner
- [ ] go to a café
- [ ] leave home
- [ ] go for a run
- [ ] wake up
- [ ] get up
- [ ] get dressed

To: **James**
Subject: My typical week
Today at 13:23
All Mail

Hi there,

I live in Hamilton, New Zealand, with my parents and sister. A typical weekday for me starts early. I get up at 6:00 a.m., but I **usually** wake up before that. I **often** go for a run first thing. After my run, I **always** take a shower and have breakfast, then I get dressed and get ready for school. I leave home at 8:00 a.m.

After school, I don't **usually** go straight home. I **sometimes** go to a café to meet my friends, to the park to play football, or I **occasionally** go to the gym. We have dinner at 6:00 p.m., but my dad **doesn't always** get home in time to eat with us. I **usually** do my homework after dinner, between 6:30 p.m. and 8:30 p.m. Then I watch TV, play video games, or message my friends. I **never** go to bed before 10:00 p.m.

On the weekend, I get up late and then go out with my friends. We **usually** go to the beach, or to a party. And we **sometimes** visit my cousins in Auckland. Sunday evenings are normally very quiet.

That's a typical week for me. What about you?

Matthew James McCarthy (Matt)

B Imagine you are Matt. Answer the questions.
1. What's your full name?
2. Where does your family live?
3. Do you have any brothers or sisters?
4. When do you get up?
5. Do you exercise regularly?
6. What do you do after school?
7. When do you do your homework?
8. What do you usually do on the weekend?

✓ **Write it right!**

In positive sentences and most questions, put the frequency adverb before the verb. In negatives, put *always*, *usually*, or *often* after the auxiliary (*don't* or *doesn't*).

C Read **Write it right!** Decide where you would put the adverb in the following sentences and questions.
1. Jack goes to the gym on the weekend. (**often**)
2. My brother doesn't remember my birthday. (**always**)
3. Serena checks her phone in class. (**never**)
4. Where do you spend your summer vacation? (**sometimes**)
5. Veronica's friends don't go out on weekday evenings. (**usually**)
6. Do you play games when you should be studying? (**occasionally**)

D Note your own answers to the questions in **B**.

E 🎧 **Make it personal** Write a similar email about your typical week (about 150–180 words).

Before	Use your notes in **D**. Think of some extra information, too.
While	Use frequency adverbs in the correct position.
After	Exchange emails with a partner and give feedback.

2 The critic

Café

1 Before watching

A Complete 1–6 with a word from the box.

| critic | guitar | show |
| record | reviews | voice |

1 Genevieve plays the _____ and writes songs.
2 The _____ listens to music and writes about it.
3 The _____ are great.
4 She's a good singer and has a very beautiful _____.
5 Rory has a video camera to _____ the show.
6 Andrea and August are at the café to watch Genevieve's _____.

B Guess and circle the correct answer. Compare in pairs, then watch to check.

1 **Rory uses / The critic uses / Both of them use** a video camera.
2 **Rory wears / The critic wears / Both of them wear** glasses.
3 **Rory listens / The critic listens / Both of them listen** to the music.
4 **Rory sits / The critic sits / Both of them sit** at a table in the café every day.
5 **Rory drinks / The critic drinks / Both of them drink** a cup of coffee.
6 **Rory writes / The critic writes / Both of them write** at a table.

> Who do you think uses a camera?
>
> > I guess they both use a camera. Do you agree?

2 While watching

A Watch again. Order the sentences 1–10 as you hear them, then complete them. Who says each one?

☐ She plays Monday and Saturday _____ 8 and 9:30.
☐ Excuse me. Do you _____?
☐ Except he needs _____ give me a good review.
☐ Rory _____ you're a great singer anyway.
☐ She's not the _____ one that thinks so.
☐ She's the _____ there is, for sure.
☐ That was _____, cuz. Good job!
☐ This is _____ life!
☐ You are crazy. He _____ do that.
☐ You have _____ amazing voice.

B Order Rory's routine 1–5.

☐ He sits down.
☐ Rory comes to the café.
☐ He orders coffee.
☐ He waits for Genevieve to take his order.
☐ He drinks his coffee and dreams.

C What's Genevieve's schedule? Check (✓) (M) in the morning, (A) in the afternoon, or (N) at night.

Genevieve ...	M	A	N
practices the guitar for two hours.			
takes a class.			
goes to work.			
gets up.			
writes a song.			
sings at the café.			

3 After watching

A How do they feel? Complete 1–4 with the adjectives.

| annoyed | excited | nervous | upset |

1 Genevieve feels _____ about the show.
2 The critic's very _____ at Rory.
3 Andrea's _____ to hear Genevieve's music.
4 Rory's _____ and leaves the café.

B How many hits does Genevieve's video get online?

☐ 9   ☐ 19   ☐ 95   ☐ 99

C 🎤 **Make it personal** Check (✓) the kinds of reviews and reports you read. In pairs, ask and answer about them.

☐ books / art / museums   ☐ news / weather
☐ movies / TV shows / theater   ☐ sports / local events
☐ products / online services   ☐ hotels / vacations
☐ fashion / music / dance

> Do you ever read book reviews?
>
> > Sometimes, but only online. Never in newspapers.

R1 Grammar and vocabulary

A **Picture dictionary.** Cover the words on these pages and use the pictures to remember:

page	
6	8 countries and nationalities
11	11 personal objects
13	10 colors
15	5 short dialogues for photos 1–5
18	8 *go* activities
20	10 morning routine verbs
22	25 family members
27	6 phrases for special occasions
158	16 picture words for vowels

B **Make it personal** In pairs. A: Spell sentences 1–3. B: Write the sentences. Change roles for 4–6. Are the sentences true for you?

1 MY CITY IS INTERESTING.
2 I REALLY LIKE JAZZ.
3 I AM FROM NEW YORK CITY.
4 MY FAVORITE COLOR IS GREEN.
5 MY FAMILY IS LARGE.
6 I OFTEN READ NEWSPAPERS.

C ▶R1.1 Complete with verb *be*. Use contractions where possible. Listen to check. Then role-play in pairs.

Receptionist: What _____ your name?
Sandy: Sandy Clark.
Receptionist: _____ you American?
Sandy: No, I _____ Canadian.
Receptionist: Where in Canada _____ you from?
Sandy: Vancouver.
Receptionist: That _____ a nice place. What _____ your address?
Sandy: 76, Burton Road.
Receptionist: And what _____ your email address?
Sandy: saclark@hotmail.com
Receptionist: Thank you. Here _____ your key. Room 89.

Good afternoon. Can I help you?

Hi! Yes, please. I have a reservation.

D Play *Draw it, name it!* A: Go to p. 8 Exercise D and draw six objects for B to name. Change roles. B: Go to p. 11 Exercise A and draw six objects for A to name.

How do you say this in English? *Sorry, I don't remember.*

It starts with "u".

E **Make it personal** Complete the questions with *do* or *does*. In pairs, ask and answer.

1 What _____ you do on your birthday?
2 _____ you give gifts to your family at Christmas?
3 _____ you eat a special meal on Christmas Eve?
4 _____ your mother usually have a party on her birthday?
5 What _____ you do at weddings in your culture?
6 What _____ your brother (or sister) do on New Year's Eve?

F Match responses a–h to phrases 1–8. Then practice in pairs. Say a phrase for your partner to respond.

1 Thank you.   a Good, thanks.
2 Who's this?   b Not much.
3 What's new?   c It's Jackie.
4 Congratulations!   d Thanks!
5 How're you?   e You're welcome.
6 See you later.   f Purple and white.
7 How old are you?   g Bye for now.
8 What color is your house? h 17.

G Correct the mistakes. Check your answers in units 1 and 2.

1 Are you colombian? Yes, I'm. (2 mistakes)
2 That is a umbrella ridiculous. (1 mistake)
3 David loves her girlfriend. (1 mistake)
4 John go to home after school. (2 mistakes)
5 My girlfriend has 20 close parents. (1 mistake)
6 At what time you go to school? (2 mistakes)
7 My father work in the city. (1 mistake)
8 At Saturday, my mom don't study usually. (3 mistakes)
9 My brother has 25. (1 mistake)
10 When he works? (2 mistakes)

Skills practice

🎵 *But just because it burns, doesn't mean you're gonna die, You gotta get up and try.*

R1

A Match the phone phrases. Read the text to check.
1 send — online
2 make — a meeting
3 take — the dictionary
4 go — a (text) message
5 use — a photo
6 organize — a call

> Everyone has a phone, but people have different attitudes to their phones. Let's take a look at when people check their phones.
>
> 1 "I check it all day all the time. I _____ send messages and post things when I'm at school."
>
> 2 "I don't have a cell phone. I think they ruin conversation! I _____ use my friend's phone to make calls."
>
> 3 "I _____ check my phone for news updates. I _____ read on my phone when I have free time. My parents _____ get annoyed when I look at my phone or go online during meals."
>
> 4 "I _____ check my phone for work. I _____ make calls from the car to talk with clients or organize meetings for the day."
>
> 5 "I _____ use my phone to take photos and to post them on social media all day long! All my friends do the same. I don't want to be different."

B 🔴 **Make it personal** Complete the sentences with the best frequency adverb: *always, usually, often, sometimes, occasionally,* or *never.* Are you similar to any of the people in **A**?

> *I'm similar to 5. I don't want to be different from my friends.*

C ▶R1.2 Listen to a student. Circle the correct number.
1 She's **17** / **70** years old.
2 Her town is **13** / **30** km from Barcelona.
3 She has **6** / **9** brothers and sisters.
4 She gets up at **6** / **8** a.m.
5 It takes **15** / **50** minutes to get to school.

D ▶R1.2 Listen again and answer 1–5.
1 What's her name?
2 Where does she live?
3 Where does she study?
4 When does she go to the movies?
5 Who are her favorite actors?

E In pairs. **A:** Describe family 1. **B:** Describe family 2.

1

2

F 🔴 **Make it personal** Complete the chart by checking (✓) the activities you do. Compare with a partner. Any big differences?

How do you spend your weekends?			
	Friday	Saturday	Sunday
get up early			
go shopping			
go to bed late			
meet friends			
play sports			
watch TV			

G 🔴 **Make it personal** Complete 1–6 and compare your answers in pairs. Any unusual choices?
1 _____ is a rich young person.
2 _____ is a great American actor.
3 _____ is an excellent song.
4 _____ is an interesting new movie.
5 _____ is a cool small piece of technology.
6 _____ is a fantastic big city.

H In pairs, role-play this situation.
A: You're a guest at a hotel. You want to leave your bag in their security box. Pay by credit card.
B: You're the receptionist. Ask A for this information: name; ID card number; room number; description of bag; contents of bag; credit card number.

I 🔴 **Make it personal** **Question time**.
In pairs, practice asking and answering the 12 lesson titles in units 1 and 2. Use the book map on p. 2–3. Where possible, ask follow-up questions, too. Can you comfortably ask and answer all the questions?

> *Are you Canadian?* No, I'm Peruvian.
>
> *Ah, I see. Are you from Lima?*

31

3

3.1 What's the weather like?

1 Vocabulary Weather

A ▶3.1 Listen to a meteorologist and complete the weather chart.

	the sun	a cloud	wind	fog	rain	snow
noun						
adjective	sunny					
verb					to rain	to snow

Common mistakes

~~raining~~
It's ~~rain~~ in this photo.
It's usually rainy /
It usually rains
It's usually ~~rain~~ in January.

B Study the chart and complete the rules.
1 To form adjectives from weather nouns, add _____.
2 For consonant-vowel-consonant words, double the final _____ and add _____.

C Match the temperature words to the correct thermometer position, a–d.
☐ cold ☐ cool ☐ hot [c] warm

D In pairs, use the photos and thermometer to remember the 10 adjectives.

E ▶3.2 Listen and identify the two photos the students are talking about.

F 🅕 Make it personal In pairs, do the same. Take turns describing the photos and guessing the place. Use *it's* + adjective.

In photo 7, it's really snowy. I think it's somewhere in the mountains in the U.S.

I disagree. The houses aren't American. Maybe it's Europe.

♪ *I want to know, Have you ever seen the rain, Comin' down on a sunny day?* **3.1**

2 Listening

A ▶ 3.3 Listen to the TV show and number the places in the order you hear them, 1–5. Why do they say the weather is unusual?

	Usually	Now
☐ the Alps		
☐ the Amazon rainforest		
☐ the Atacama Desert		
☐ Cancún		
☐ Chicago		

Common mistakes

How's the weather ~~like~~?
~~It's~~
~~Is~~ really hot.
            windy
It's ~~winding~~.

B ▶ 3.3 Listen again and complete the chart in **A** with adjectives / words for each place.

C Complete the three questions from the show.
1 And _____'s the weather in Chicago?
2 _____'s the weather usually like there?
3 What's it _____ this year?

D 🗣 **Make it personal** In pairs, ask and answer about the weather in the photos, and in your city / country. Use the model and point to the photos as you ask.

What's the weather usually like in the Amazon rainforest?   It's rainy.

And how is it now?   It's very dry.

33

3.2 Are you busy at the moment?

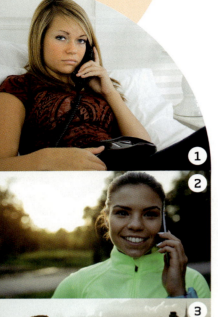

1 Vocabulary Everyday actions

A ▶3.4 Match photos 1–6 to the actions. Then listen to Maddie make five phone calls. Which action don't you hear?

- [ ] buying groceries
- [ ] doing homework
- [ ] running in the park
- [ ] cooking dinner
- [ ] riding a bike
- [ ] talking on a landline

B ▶3.4 Listen again and match the person to the activity that they are doing.

Maddie _____   Susan _____   Rita _____
Eli _____   Michael _____

C 🔴 **Make it personal** In pairs, say which of the activities you do and which you don't do. When do you do them? Can you name other activities that you do?

> Riding a bike?   Yes, I do this on Saturdays when it's warm and when it's not raining.

2 Grammar Present continuous (1)

A ▶3.5 Listen to Maddie's last phone call. Answer the questions.

1 Why is she looking for company?
- [ ] To have dinner.
- [ ] To go to a sports event.
- [ ] She's feeling lonely.

2 How does the story end?
- [ ] She gets depressed and cries.
- [ ] She finally finds a friend who is free.
- [ ] She does her homework.

> ⚠️ **Common mistakes**
> ~~What you do now?~~ *are doing*
> ~~You are studying English?~~ *Are you*
> Yes, ~~I do.~~ *am*

B Complete the grammar box.

> 1 Complete the examples with the verb *be*.
> (+) She _____ talking on the phone. → Subject + *be* + **verb** -*ing*
> (−) I _____ _____ running. → Subject + *be* + not + **verb** -*ing*
> (?) What _____ they doing? → Question word + *be* + subject + **verb** -*ing*
>
> 2 Delete the incorrect options.
> Use the present continuous for actions that happen **every day / at the moment / sometimes**.
> Don't pronounce the /g/ in the -*ing* ending. It's /ɪn/ or /ɪŋ/ (like *king* and *ring*).
>
> ➡ Grammar 3A p. 142

C ▶3.6 In pairs, listen to the sound effects. What are the people doing?

1 They're cooking.   3 _____   5 _____
2 She _____   4 _____   6 _____

D Look back at p. 20. Take turns testing a partner about Jake's morning routine.

> What's Jake doing in "e"?   He's taking a shower.

E 🔴 **Make it personal** Role-play a conversation like Maddie's. **A:** You're calling five friends to do something. **B:** You're A's friends. Make different excuses. Change roles.

> Hi, this is Marcia. Are you busy?   Yes, I'm cooking dinner!   OK, call you later!   Bye!

⚠️ **Common mistakes**
~~I'm~~ working on a new project.

34

Winter, spring, summer or fall, All you've got to do is call and I'll be there, yeah, yeah, yeah, You've got a friend.

3.2

3 Reading

A ▶3.7 Study the months. Is the stressed syllable the same (S) or different (D) in your language? Listen to check. Then say your birthday month.

| January ☐ | February ☐ | March ☐ | April ☐ | May ☐ | June ☐ | July ☐ |
| August ☐ | September ☐ | October ☐ | November ☐ | December ☐ | | |

Common mistakes

in March
My birthday's ~~on march~~.

B Read the extract from an encyclopedia and:
1 write the seven missing months.
2 circle the names of three more seasons in paragraph 1.
3 find two more seasons in paragraph 2.
4 find the names of one continent and two countries.
5 find the words to complete the compass.

N ____
W ____ EAST
S ____

Four seasons or two?

Countries with a temperate climate, like the ones in Europe and North America, have four defined seasons: hot summers in June, _____, and August; cold winters in December, January, and _____, with heavy snow in some countries; cool, windy falls in September, _____, and November, and warm springs in _____, April, and _____.

In contrast, tropical regions, especially around the equator, have only two seasons: the dry season and the rainy season. So, in places like India, West Africa, Central America, the north of South America, and the north coast of Australia, the rainy season is in their winter (_____, July, and _____), and it's accompanied by very high temperatures.

C ▶3.8 Listen to and read the encyclopedia extract. Any pronunciation surprises?

D In pairs, answer the questions.
1 Which months correspond to which seasons in your country?
2 What's your favorite season? What's the weather like in your favorite season?
3 Say three things you usually do in your favorite season, and three you don't.

I don't usually go out a lot in the rainy season. I watch a lot of TV!

E **Make it personal** In groups. Think of a month and season. Mime an activity that you usually do in that season. Your group guesses what you are doing, the month, and the season.

Are you swimming?   Yes, I am.   Is it summer?   Yes.

Is it December?   Yes, it is.

35

3.3 What are you doing these days?

1 Listening

A ▶3.9 Listen and identify the people in the pictures.
1 Marisa 2 Jennifer 3 Kevin 4 Steve

B ▶3.9 Listen again. True (T) or False (F)? Correct the false statements.
1 Marisa is working at the moment. _____
2 She's studying art. _____
3 She's living with her parents. _____
4 She's dating Kevin. _____

2 Grammar Present continuous (2)

A Complete the grammar box.

1 Put the questions in the correct column.
   What are you doing these days?   Are you studying art?
   Are you dating Kevin?   Where are you living?

Wh-?	Yes / No?

2 Which question type (*Wh-* or *Yes / No*) uses which structure?
   a verb *be* + subject + verb *-ing* _____
   b question word + verb *be* + subject + verb *-ing* _____

3 Delete the incorrect option.
   We use the present continuous to talk about things happening:
   a right now.   b in the past.   c around now.

→ Grammar 3B p. 142

B Put the words in order to make questions. Ask and answer with a partner. Talk about other people, too.
1 you / are / doing / what / ?
2 working / where / you / are / ?
3 are / what / studying / you / ?
4 at home / living / you / are / ?
5 dating / are / you / ?

What are you doing at the moment?   *Nothing special. I'm working a lot during the week.*

Oh, really! Where are you working?   *I have a new job now! At the aquarium. I feed the fish!*

C 🗣 **Make it personal** Invent a new personality! Ask and answer questions. Use the ideas below. Who has the most interesting life?

do a lot of exercise   go out a lot   listen to music   read   sleep well
speak more English   spend a lot of money   watch (a show on) TV

⚠ Common mistakes

Are you coming
D̶o̶ ̶y̶o̶u̶ ̶c̶o̶m̶e̶ for coffee?

are you going
Hi! Where d̶o̶ ̶y̶o̶u̶ ̶g̶o̶?

'm going
I g̶o̶ home.

3 Reading

🎵 *Don't stop me now, I'm having such a good time, I'm having a ball.*

3.3

A Match the technology problems 1–5 to photos a–e.
1 identity theft
2 addiction
3 consumerism
4 isolation
5 violence

B Read the online debate and match the person to the problem in **A** they write about.

Sammy
What do you think of technology?

Marsha
It's dangerous. Social media companies are changing the way we see privacy. Everyone is getting access to our personal information.

Lucinda
I don't like a lot of the new video games. They're getting more violent and it makes people act more violently.

KoolKat
People are going out less and spending more time alone with technology. We don't know our neighbors.

Dadofthree
People today are becoming obsessed with things! They want new clothes, new cars, new electronic devices, and they can buy it all online.

BBBaxter
My kids are spending more and more time on their devices and online, especially on social media. I don't know what to do. They panic when they don't have their phone with them. They just want to look at their phones.

C ▶ 3.10 Now listen and check your answers. Who do you most agree with? Practice saying what they say.

D 🗣 **Make it personal** What do you think the problems with technology are? List the problems in **A** in order of importance. Say why. Who agrees with you?

> What's your most important problem?

> Isolation. People are spending too much time on their phones.

> I agree. Communities are changing. I don't know my neighbors.

37

3.4 What do you do after school / work?

1 Grammar   Simple present vs. present continuous

A In pairs, can you recognize the celebrities in the photos? What do they do?

Who's this?   *I think this is Naomi Watts.*   *What does she do?*   *I think she's a movie star.*

B Match photos 1–6 to these actions. What are the people doing? In pairs, take turns asking and answering.

☐ walk the dog   ☐ watch a game   ☐ shop
☐ listen to music   ☐ watch a show   ☐ drive a car

What's Steph Curry doing?   *He's listening to music.*

C Complete the grammar box.

1 Read the paragraph and for sentences a–d write SP (simple present) or PC (present continuous).

Jack Morley is a celebrity journalist. ᵃ He usually works from 8 a.m. to 5 p.m. in his office ☐, and ᵇ he talks to his editor every morning ☐. ᶜ This week, Jack's doing a lot of different things ☐. ᵈ Right now he's interviewing a famous actor ☐.

2 Match the rules.

a Use the present continuous to   1 talk about routines.
b Use the simple present to   2 talk about something happening around now.
                                        3 describe actions in progress now.
                                        4 describe habits.

→ Grammar 3C p.142

⚠ **Common mistakes**

I'm living
~~I'm live~~ at home at the moment.
I like
~~I'm liking~~ this movie.

38

🎵 *I'm giving it my all, but I'm not the girl you're taking home, oh, I keep dancing on my own.*

3.4

D For each of the people in **A**, imagine what they usually do at these times and what they are probably doing right now or, more generally, around now.

	1	2	3	4	5	6
8:00 a.m.						
12:30 p.m.						
7:30 p.m.						

I think Steph Curry usually gets up before 8:00 a.m. Right now, I guess he's training. More generally, he's probably working on a new charity project.

E 🔵 **Make it personal** Make a timeline of what you usually do during a regular day. Are there any things that you are doing around now that you don't usually do?

I go to college on weekdays. But, I'm training for a marathon, so now I'm running every morning.

At the moment, I'm taking an English class at a language school.

✏️ **Common mistakes**

I'm running ~~all the mornings~~ *every morning* at the moment.

2 Listening

A In pairs, share what you know about these celebrities.

That's George Clooney. He's married to a Lebanese-British lawyer.

B ▶ 3.11 Listen to Jack Morley talk about celebrities. Does he think celebrity activists are a good thing or a bad thing?

C ▶ 3.11 Listen again and check (✓) which causes are mentioned.
- ☐ cyberbullying
- ☐ clean water
- ☐ corruption
- ☐ peace
- ☐ climate change
- ☐ animal rights
- ☐ education for girls
- ☐ women's rights
- ☐ racism

D ▶ 3.11 In pairs, complete these sentences. Then listen to check.
Celebrities _____ _____ a lot of publicity to these causes and people _____ _____ more money on the causes. But what do celebrities know about these _____?

E 🔵 **Make it personal** What do you think of celebrity activists? Give a reason.

I think Emma Watson is a good person and she helps people.

Yes, but she is an actor, not a politician.

But she's smart!

3.5 Why are you learning English?

ⓘD Skills Analyzing your English

A Read the introduction to the questionnaire. Are questions 1–2 True (T) or False (F)?
1 We know exactly how many people speak English in the world.
2 The questionnaire is for the authors of this book.

Approximately 25% of the world speaks or is now learning to speak English, and this number is rapidly increasing. Please help the ⓘD team to learn more about our users' motivation and experiences. Complete our questionnaire, checking (✓) all relevant answers, and let us know.

1 Why are you learning English?
   a ○ for my current or future job   ○ for school   ○ for college
   b ○ for pleasure   ○ I love learning languages
   c to communicate: ○ online   ○ in writing   ○ speaking
   d ○ to communicate with other people face-to-face
   e ○ to pass an exam
   f ○ to travel
   g ○ to emigrate
   h other (what?) _____

2 Which are the three most important for you? Number them 1 to 3.
   a ○ grammar   d ○ listening   g ○ writing
   b ○ vocabulary   e ○ speaking   h ○ all equally
   c ○ pronunciation   f ○ reading   important

3 Which items in **2** do you find the most difficult?
   _____

4 How often do you do these things in English outside class? Mark them:
   E=Every day   V=Very often   S=Sometimes   O=Occasionally   N=Never
   a ○ read   e ○ watch TV / movies
   b ○ study   f ○ speak to people face-to-face
   c ○ write / send messages   g ○ communicate online
   d ○ listen to music / the radio   h ○ other (what?) _____

5 What do you like about your ⓘD classes?
   a ○ the coursebook
   b ○ the workbook
   c ○ the ID student's learning platform
   d ○ my classmates
   e ○ other? _____

ⓘ Common mistakes

I need ~~learn~~ English ~~for~~ pass my course. *(to, to)*
I have ~~learn~~ English ~~to~~ my job. *(to, for)*
I'm ~~needing~~ to get a new ~~work~~. *(job)*

B Answer the questionnaire. In pairs, compare your answers.

C 🅜 **Make it personal** In groups, explain your answers to the questionnaire.

> I'm learning English for many reasons. I need it in school. I'm taking some exams in English.

> I'm working at an international company at the moment. I need to talk to people from many different countries in English.

40

3.5 Are you thirsty?

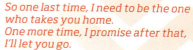

*So one last time, I need to be the one who takes you home.
One more time, I promise after that, I'll let you go.*

ID in Action Making offers

A ▶ 3.12 Listen to two friends and answer 1–5.
1. What time is it?
2. What's Linda working on?
3. When does she have to finish it?
4. How many more pages does she have to write?
5. Is she tired?

B ▶ 3.12 Listen again and write Mark's three questions. Guess what happens next.

Maybe Linda decides to go home.   *Yeah. Perhaps. Or maybe she doesn't …*

C ▶ 3.13 Listen to the next part of the conversation to check. What does Linda want?

D ▶ 3.12 and 3.13 Listen again and match the formal and informal expressions.

Grammatical English	Informal English
1 Are you tired?	a Yep. / Yeah.
2 Do you want to go home?	b Cookie?
3 Yes.	c You tired?
4 Would you like a cookie?	d Wanna go home?

E ▶ 3.12 and 3.13 Listen again. In pairs, role-play the dialogue using the picture clues.

Mark		Linda
☕	→	U/1?
✓	→	✓ ● no 🥄
🍔 too?	→	✗
🍪 ?	→	✗
☕ ↑	→	U R GREAT !

Common mistakes

~~I don't have~~ 'm not hungry, but I'm ~~with thirst.~~ y
~~Would~~ Do you like a drink?

F ▶ 3.14 Match the questions and offers. Listen, check, and practice the different responses.

Questions	Offers	Responses
Are you bored?	Do you want a sweater / to use my jacket?	Yes, please. Great!
Are you cold?	Do you want a sandwich? / Wanna cookie?	Sure. Why not?
Are you hot?	Would you like a coffee / to go home?	Yep / Yeah!
Are you hungry?	Would you like a drink?	Uh-huh, just …
Are you thirsty?	Do you want a cold drink / some ice cream?	No, thanks.
Are you tired?	Maybe you need a vacation / a new job?	No, really, I'm fine.
Are you stressed?	Wanna go out for a coffee / a walk?	That sounds great!

G 🔴 **Make it personal** In pairs. **A:** Mime an adjective from the chart in **F**. **B:** Ask a question and make an offer from the chart or one of your own. **A:** Respond.

Are you bored? Wanna read my newspaper?

Writing 3   A language profile

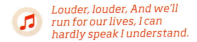
Louder, louder, And we'll run for our lives, I can hardly speak I understand.

A Read two student profiles and label the diagrams.

Personal details

My name's Marta and I'm 20.

Why are you learning English?
I often travel _____ other countries, so English is very important. I want _____ go _____ Los Angeles and India.

Which aspect of language is the most important for you?
_____ me, the most important thing is speaking. I need _____ communicate _____ people when I go on vacation.

What aspects of language are you good / bad at?
I'm not good _____ writing. I know how to say English words, but they are difficult _____ spell! I enjoy speaking _____ people and exchanging opinions. I'm good _____ talking – in fact, I never stop!

How do you practice English outside your classroom?
I use the Internet all the time, so I read the news _____ English and talk _____ my cousins in Canada online.

Personal details

My name's Mateo and I'm 24 years old.

Why are you learning English?
English is important for my career. I often have to read documents in English and I hope to get a promotion soon. Also, I'm going to New York next month!

Which aspect of language is the most important for you?
For me, the most important thing is pronunciation. It's often difficult to communicate with people because they don't understand me – and I don't understand them. It's very frustrating!

What aspects of language are you good / bad at?
I'm terrible at speaking! I want to speak to other people, but it isn't easy. When I'm reading, I go slowly and use a dictionary. I think I'm good at vocabulary, especially because many English words are similar to Italian words!

How do you practice English outside your classroom?
I don't have much time to practice at home because I work a lot. I occasionally watch American movies and read the subtitles. I need to practice more!

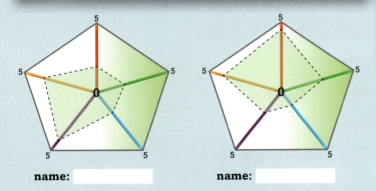

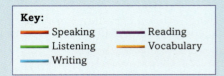

Key:
— Speaking   — Reading
— Listening   — Vocabulary
— Writing

B Read **Write it right!** In Mateo's profile, circle five more words / phrases followed by *to* + infinitive.

> ✓ **Write it right!**
>
> *To* + infinitive and prepositions are often difficult to remember. When you read, try to notice phrases, and then use them when you write and speak.

C Notice the underlined preposition phrases in Mateo's profile. Complete Marta's profile with *to, for, with, at,* and *in*.

D Complete the diagram in **A** for you. Rate each aspect of language 0–5.

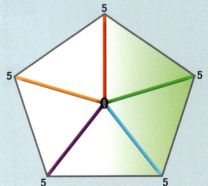

E 🎧 **Make it personal** Write your language profile in 80–120 words.

Before	Use the diagram in **D** and the questionnaire on p. 40.
While	Use prepositions carefully.
After	Read a partner's profile and draw their diagram.

3 Storm tracker

Café

B In pairs, take turns asking and answering about 1–8 in A.

Is Daniel filming the storm?

No, he's not. August is filming the storm.

3 After watching

1 Before watching

A What are they doing? Look at the photo and check (✓).

August	Daniel	
		is looking in a bag.
		is sitting on a sofa.
		is standing behind the sofa.
		is using a computer.
		is checking a list.
		is holding a smartphone.

B Cover the chart. In pairs, take turns describing the scene.

The two guys are at home. August is …

C Put the words in the correct column. Watch and number them 1–10 in the order you hear them.

clouds	fast	heavy	lightning	storm
steady	filmmaker	video disc	shaky	
zoom lens				

Weather	Equipment	Adjectives	Job

2 While watching

A What's Daniel doing? Write Yes (Y) or No (N).

Daniel's …
1. carrying the equipment.
2. reading the list.
3. carrying the keys.
4. driving the car.
5. keeping the camera steady.
6. applying for an internship.
7. filming the storm.
8. introducing his storm tracker.

A Write True (T) or False (F). Correct what's false.
1. August uses the tripod.
2. Daniel's talking slowly into the microphone.
3. The storm's coming at 3:33.
4. The clouds behind Daniel aren't moving fast.
5. There's no lightning in the sky.
6. It's raining while August is filming.
7. They're making the video before the rain comes.
8. Daniel drops the microphone.
9. August keeps the camera steady.
10. Daniel is disappointed with the video footage.

B Order the story 1–9. In pairs, take turns saying a line of the story at a time.

- ☐ Daniel and August get wet and go home.
- ☐ Daniel and August are checking their list and Daniel asks about the tripod.
- ☐ Daniel invents a storm tracker app.
- ☐ Daniel checks if August can hear him.
- ☐ August doesn't bring the tripod.
- ☐ Daniel gets annoyed with August about the video footage quality.
- ☐ August and Daniel drive to the field.
- ☐ August films Daniel while the storm's passing over them.
- ☐ There's lightning just before they make the video.

C 🔴 **Make it personal** In groups, talk about photography. Who uses their camera the most?
1. In an average week, how many photos and videos do you take?
2. What do you usually take photos and videos of?
3. Do you ever use a tripod or selfie stick?
4. What's your best recent photo or video?
5. How often do you share or upload photos?

It depends. I like to take photos of nature.

I don't normally take videos, except when I'm out with friends.

43

4.1 Do you like tennis?

🎵 *No time for losers, 'cause we are the champions of the world.*

1 Vocabulary Sports   4.1

A ▶4.1 Match the sports with photos 1–7. Try to pronounce them. Then listen to part of a sports show to check. Find two reasons why they are in two groups.

- [1] ba**s**ketball ✓
- [ ] vo**ll**eyball
- [ ] te**nn**is
- [ ] **s**occer
- [ ] **c**y**c**ling (bike riding)
- [ ] **sw**i**mm**ing
- [ ] **r**u**nn**ing

Maybe it's because the first four we play …

B Listen to and repeat what your teacher says only if it's true for you. In groups, do the same.

Teacher: I like tennis.   *Some students: I like tennis.*

C ▶4.2 Listen to more of the sports show and check (✓) in **A** the five sports Mac mentions. Can you remember the six countries, too?

D ▶4.2 Listen again and match the times to the places.
1 9:00   [ ] the Igloo
2 9:30   [ ] North Park
3 10:00   [ ] the O**l**y**m**pic **Ar**ena
4 10:30   [ ] the Olympic **St**adium
5 11:00   [ ] the Central Courts

E ▶4.2 Say the places in **D**. What's the difference in the pronunciation of *the*? Complete the rules with *th*/ə/ ("the") or *th*/iː/ ("thee"). Listen to check.
1 Before a vowel sound, pronounce *the* _____.
2 Before a consonant sound, pronounce *the* _____.

F ▶4.3 Listen and repeat the noun with *th*/ə/ or *th*/iː/ before you hear the beep.
Airport: *The airport.*

> **⏱ Common mistakes**
> I love ~~the~~ games.
> I don't like ~~the~~ fruit.
> I hate ~~the~~ soccer.
> **Don't use *the* with plural nouns or uncountable nouns or to talk about things in general.**

G ▶4.4 Listen to four interviews and order the sports you hear, 1–6. Which sports don't you hear?
- [ ] ba**s**eball
- [ ] **f**oo**t**ball
- [ ] golf
- [ ] ho**c**key
- [ ] rug**b**y
- [ ] **s**ka**t**eboarding
- [ ] **sk**iing
- [ ] **s**occer
- [ ] **s**ur**f**ing
- [ ] **t**a**b**le tennis

H 👤 **Make it personal** Answer in pairs. Which sports in this lesson …
1 need a ball?
2 need a net?
3 can you practice in the ocean?
4 are your favorite to watch / practice?
5 are your country usually good at in the Olympics?
6 are the most and the least dangerous?

Our country is usually good at …   *For me, the most dangerous is …*

In my opinion, the least dangerous sport is …

45

4.2 Can you drive a tractor?

1 Grammar Can: Yes / No

A ▶4.5 It's Mark's first day at the gym. Listen and complete the form.

B ▶4.5 Listen again and complete the grammar box. Notice the weak pronunciation of *can* in the questions.

	Yes / No ? with can	Short answers
1	_____ you run two kilometers?	No, I _____.
2	_____ you swim?	Yes, I _____.

→ Grammar 4B p. 144

Common mistakes

Can you play soccer well?
~~You can play well the soccer?~~

C Ask two friends the same questions and complete this form with ✗ or ✓. Now ask about four other sports. How many *Yes* answers can you get?

Name						

D 🟢 **Make it personal** Match the verbs to the noun groups. Ask your classmates about these abilities using *Can ...?* Find someone who can do each one well.

play   drive   sing
speak   cook

Can you cook Chinese food?
No, I can't. Not at all! Can you?
Yes, I think so. But not very well.

_____	_____	_____	_____	_____
the piano	English	in harmony	a tractor	Chinese food
the guitar	French	karaoke well	a truck	Mexican food
the saxophone	Chinese	a song in a third language		French food
the drums	German			Japanese food
the violin				

② Listening

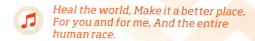

Heal the world, Make it a better place, For you and for me, And the entire human race.

4.2

A What do you know about Malala Yousafzi? In pairs, say what you know about her, or make guesses. Read the article to check.

Malala Yousafzi

is probably the world's most famous Pakistani. Her 2009 blog about life under the Taliban for the BBC, and her activism made her many enemies. She was shot in the head when she was only 15 years old. But she survived, and in 2012 won the Nobel Peace Prize. She lives in the UK now and campaigns for education for girls across the world.

B ▶ ◉4.6 Watch / Listen and order the words as you hear them, 1–8. Which items are in the photos?

- [ ] book
- [ ] child
- [ ] education
- [ ] pen
- [ ] powerful
- [ ] solution
- [ ] teacher
- [ ] weapons

C ▶ ◉4.6 Watch / Listen again and write Malala's speech. In pairs, compare. Check your answer in AS 4.6 on p. 162.

D ◉4.7 58% of English comes from Latin, so you can guess many English words, like words with the suffixes *-tion* and *-sion*. Do you recognize the words below? Read the pronunciation rule. Then try to pronounce the words correctly. Listen to check.

With suffixes *-tion* and *-sion*, always stress the syllable before the suffix.

action	corruption	motivation
combination	expression	opinion
conversation	information	organization
cooperation	isolation	question

E 🔘 **Make it personal** Which of the items in the photos in B can best change the world? In pairs, order them 1 to 4 from the most to the least powerful. Then compare with another pair. Do you agree?

Number 1?   *We think it's a teacher.*

We believe a book can be more powerful.   *For us, that's number 2.*

4.3 What languages can you speak?

1 Grammar *Can* : ➕➖ and *Wh-* ❓

A ▶4.8 Listen to the interviews. Complete sentences 1–6 with *can* or *can't*. Listen again to check.

1 I _____ dance very well, but my wife _____. She's a very good dancer.
2 My father _____ cook really well. His food is delicious.
3 My best friend _____ play baseball or volleyball. He doesn't like team sports.
4 I _____ skate, but I _____ ski at all. Skiing is too difficult!
5 My friends _____ play soccer very well. They play every weekend.
6 _____ you do any martial arts? Yes, I _____. What _____ you do? Tae Kwondo.

B Complete the grammar box.

> 1 We use *can* to talk about ability. Study the examples in **A** and circle the correct option.
>   a *Can* goes **before / after** the main verb in a sentence.
>   b *Can* **changes / doesn't change** form in the 3rd person.
>
> 2 Complete rules c and d with the words.
>
> | can | *Wh-* question word | person | verb |
> |---|---|---|---|
>
> c To form a *Yes / No* question with *can* use: _____ + _____ + _____.
> d To form a *Wh-* question with *can* use: ____ + _____ + _____ + _____.
>
> ➡ **Grammar 4B** p. 144

C ▶4.8 Listen again and notice the pronunciation of *can* and *can't*. In pairs, practice pronouncing the sentences in **A** correctly.

D 🧑 **Make it personal** Write three true and three false sentences about you and people you know and their abilities. In pairs, decide which are true and which are false.

> Anna can play the guitar well.   I think that's false. Anna can't play the guitar at all!

E 🧑 **Make it personal** *Can* is also used for requests. Read and choose the three most useful phrases for 1) everyday life and 2) English classes. Compare with a partner. Any similarities?

Can you help me?   Can I say it in (my language)?
Can you trans late this?   Can I open the window?
Can you speak loud er?   Can I park here?
Can you spell it, please?   Can I have a little more (coffee)?
Can you close the door?   Can I go home now?
Can I go to the bathroom?

48

♪ *Filled with all the strength I found, There's nothing I can't do! I need to know now, Can you love me again?*

4.3

2 Reading

A ▶ 4.9 Listen, read, and match photos a–f to six of the abilities.

Ten Keys to 21st Century Success

To fly high in the modern world, certain abilities are essential. Here are our top 10 in no particular order:

1 to Google efficiently
2 to understand directions quickly
3 to cook the basics
4 to remember names
5 to use simple tools
6 to speak two common languages
7 to dress appropriately
8 to bargain well
9 to make friends easily
10 to make a good first impression

a

b

c

d

e

f

B Many adverbs are formed adjective + -ly, e.g., *probably, finally, especially, certainly, exactly*. Underline four examples in **A**. Can you find an irregular one, too?

C Use these symbols to mark the list in **A** according to your ability. Then interview a partner about their abilities. What can they do well?

XX = I can't at all.   *X* = I can't very well.   ✓ = I can.   ✓✓ = I can very well.

> Can you use simple tools?   No, I can't! I always ask my mom to help me.

Common mistakes

I can type ~~quick~~ *quickly*.
I can't cook ~~good~~ *well*.

D 🙂 **Make it personal** Choose the five most important abilities for you.

> I'm at school and I don't have a job, so my most important are …

3 Listening

A ▶ 4.10 Listen to a job interview. Circle the job that Maddie wants.

a babysitter   a journalist   a secretary   a teacher

B ▶ 4.10 Listen again and complete with *can* or *can't*.
1 Maddie _____ speak Spanish very well.
2 She _____ play volleyball and tennis but not very well.
3 She _____ text fast.

C 🙂 **Make it personal** In pairs, think of a job. Write a list of questions to ask about abilities for that job. You can use AS 4.10 on p. 163 to help you. Now interview another pair. Do you give them the job?

> Can you speak Portuguese fluently?   No, I can't.   Sorry. We're looking for a Portuguese teacher!

4.4 Are you an organized person?

1 Vocabulary Clothes

A ▶4.11 Listen to the fashion show. Who's JKK? Do you like the designs?

B ▶4.11 Match 1–16 to the clothes items.

- [ ] a silver belt
- [ ] a brown blouse
- [ ] blue boots
- [ ] a gold jacket
- [ ] a yellow dress
- [ ] black sandals
- [ ] a purple shirt
- [ ] orange shorts
- [ ] a pink skirt
- [ ] beige socks
- [ ] a blue suit jacket
- [ ] blue shoes
- [ ] a green T-shirt
- [ ] a white tie
- [ ] gray sneakers
- [ ] blue suit pants

C Cover the words in **B**. In pairs, describe the four models.

D 👤 **Make it personal** Look at what your classmates are wearing for a minute. In pairs, take turns describing without looking and guessing. Now do the same with photos of people on your phone.

> She's wearing a red sweater. Is it Carmen?

⚠️ Common mistakes

She always wears a green shirt and ~~a~~ gray pants to school.

He's ~~using~~ *wearing* a suit.

She has two ~~jeans~~ *pairs of jeans*.

> I have about twenty pairs of jeans.
> Twenty? I only have three pairs.

2 Reading

A Do you have a lot of clothes? Describe your closet to your partner.

B Answer the title question from the forum. Then read the three posts and match them to pictures 1–3.
Victoria: _____   Kyle: _____   Tanya: _____

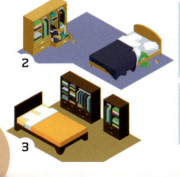

Can organized and messy people live together?

It's not impossible, but it's difficult. At home, it's only me and my husband. My clothes and shoes are always organized, but his are not! Sometimes I get angry because he is messy and I'm neat, but usually it's OK. **Posted by Victoria**

I confess: I don't like to share – it's too difficult! So my wife and I have separate closets. I have more things than she does, so my closet is enormous and hers is not. We are both clean and organized, but the problem is our kids! We clean our room, but we never look in theirs! Their rooms are messy and full of dirty sports equipment – balls, rackets, skis, etc. Horrible! It's hard for people who are very different to live together, but if you're family you can do it! **Posted by Kyle**

In my house, we don't say "mine" or "yours". Everything is ours. Our house is small, and a little disorganized, but we like it like that. We share space and clothes. We occasionally have a conversation like this: "Whose sweater is this?" "It's yours!" "No, it's yours!" That's a big advantage of living with your twin sister! We are very similar. I can't live with people who are different from me. **Posted by Tanya**

♪ Oh, oh, oh, Sweet child o' mine,
Sweet love o' mine.

4.4

C Complete the sentences with the names from the forum and *her* or *his*.
1 _____ lives with _____ sister.
2 _____ lives with _____ husband.
3 _____ lives with _____ wife and children.
4 _____ is different from _____ children.
5 _____ can share easily.
6 _____ can't share at all.

D ▶ 4.12 Match the four underlined words in **B** with their opposites below. In pairs, try to pronounce all the words in **B** with pink syllables. Listen to check. Any surprises?

| calm   clean   disad**van**tage   **sep**arately |

E 🔵 **Make it personal** Who are you more similar to: Victoria, Kyle, or Tanya? Find one person in the class who is like you and one person who is different.

I share a room with my sister, but I'm organized and she isn't. I think I'm similar to Victoria.

③ Grammar — Possessive pronouns

A ▶ 4.13 Look at the highlighted phrases in **2B**. Complete the grammar chart. Listen to check. Then answer questions 1–3.

	Possessive adjectives	Possessive pronouns
This is	my closet	mine
	your closet	
	her	
	his	
	our	
	their	

1 How many possessive pronouns end in *s*?
2 Is the final *s* pronounced /s/ or /z/?
3 Read the rules and complete the dialogue with *hers, mine,* or *whose*.
   Use *Whose?* to ask about possession.
   Use a possessive pronoun to replace a possessive adjective + noun.
   A: _____ phone is that?
   B: I think it's _____. (not "her phone")
   C: No, it isn't. It's _____. (not "my phone")
4 Rewrite the dialogue above using *phones* instead of *phone*.

➡ Grammar 4C p. 144

🔴 **Common mistakes**
These glasses are ~~the~~ mines.
Whose pen is this?
Of who is this pen?
                  's
It's ~~of~~ Maria.

B In groups, take turns describing one item of clothing in the classroom to the rest of the group. Then point and say whose it is.

It's a green and white T-shirt. Whose is it?   *It's hers!*   *No!*   *It's his!*   *Yes.*

C 🔵 **Make it personal** Write your own post for the forum. Use the prompts to help you. Compare in pairs. How are you similar and how are you different?
I live with …
My room is …
I (don't) share my room …
I am (an organized / a messy …) person.
I (can / can't share) things (easily).
I think people who are different (can / can't) live together.

I share a room with my brother. We have a lot of things, and our room is very messy!

4.5 Do you like spas?

ID Skills Reading for details

A Quickly look at the text and answer the questions.
1 Where do you think it's from? ☐ the Internet ☐ a book ☐ a magazine
2 What is it? ☐ a poster ☐ an ad ☐ a blog

{ALL YOURS}

Do you like *healthy* food and healthy living?

All Yours is the perfect place for you. There, in the same ultra-modern center, you can find:

† **Super Salon** with unisex hair stylists, manicurists, and pedicurists available from 8 a.m. to 10 p.m., seven days a week.

† **Natural Foods** restaurant that serves high-quality, healthy foods, specially prepared by our expert chefs and nutritionists. Open from 7 a.m. to midnight daily.

† **World Boutique** with unique fashion designs from around the world for everybody, young or old.

† **Marvelous Me** massage suite. Our fantastic therapists can eliminate all your stress.

† **Giant Gym.** A great place to stay in shape and keep your heart and muscles healthy.

B Read the text. True (T) or False (F)?
1 All Yours is a shopping mall.
2 The hair stylists work on Sundays.
3 It's possible to eat, buy clothes, de-stress, and exercise there.
4 It's for women and men.
5 Five different professions are mentioned.

C Find the words in the text that mean:
1 the opposite of different =
2 in good health =
3 take away =
4 continue to be =

Yes, the suffix -ist isn't stressed in English.

D ▶ 4.14 In pairs, pronounce the words with pink syllables. Listen to check. Any surprises?

E 🎧 **Make it personal** In pairs, plan the perfect day at All Yours. Tell another pair about your day. Who has the best day?

We arrive at 7 a.m. and go for breakfast at Natural Foods.   *We go to the gym first at 7 a.m.*

4.5 What shoe size are you?

You can't always get what you want. But if you try sometimes, yeah, you might find you get what you need.

ID in Action Shopping for clothes

A ▶ 4.15 Listen to the dialogue and complete 1–4. Predict how it ends.
1 The man's at a …
2 He wants …
3 The color he wants is …
4 The size he wants is …

B ▶ 4.16 Listen to part two of the dialogue and answer the questions.
1 Who's the sweater for?
2 Why does he want it in blue?
3 Do you think the salesclerk is good at his job?

C Listen to ▶ 4.15 and ▶ 4.16 again and find:
1 the preposition we use before colors.
2 the verb that means "to test clothes on your body".
3 the name of the room where we go to do this.

D ▶ 4.17 Listen to and complete a short version of the dialogue. What three changes do you need to make if he asks for jeans?

Salesclerk: Can I _____ you?
Jason: Yes, please. Can I _____ the _____ in the window?
Salesclerk: Sure! What _____? We have it in _____, blue or _____.
Jason: _____, please.
Salesclerk: All right. What _____?
Jason: Extra _____.
Salesclerk: _____ small in blue? OK, just a _____, please. Here you _____.
Jason: Thanks. Can I _____ it on?
Salesclerk: Sure. The fitting _____ are over _____.

Common mistakes

~~these pants~~ / them
Do you like ~~this pants~~?
~~do~~ / like them
Yes, I ~~like~~.

E In pairs, practice the dialogue in **D**. Use other clothes items from this unit. Be careful with singular and plural forms.

F ▶ 4.18 Punctuate the rest of the dialogue. Listen to check. Then cover and practice from the photos.

Jason: nothanksjustthesweaterhowmuchisit
Salesclerk: fortynineninetynine
Jason: greatheresmycreditcard
Salesclerk: thankyoupleaseenteryourpinnumber
Jason: hereyougo
Salesclerk: heresyourreceipthaveanicedaybyejackson

G Make it personal Go shopping!
1 In groups, discuss the questions.
What do you wear …
  a to school / work?
  b to go to a party?
  c on the weekend?
  d to a job interview?
2 In pairs, go shopping for clothes for one of the situations in 1.
  A: You're the customer. **B:** You're the salesclerk.

Hi! I like these black shorts. How much are they?

Writing 4   A job application

Sweet home Alabama,
Where the skies are so blue
Sweet home Alabama,
Lord, I'm coming home to you.

A Read the job ad and find the names of
1   the company advertising the job.
2   the job the ad is for.
3   the person you have to write to.

Make this your best ever summer – at 50 States Summer Camp!

Would you like to: ○ have the chance to visit the U.S.?   ○ spend the summer working with young people?   ○ teach a sport or a skill that you are passionate about?   ○ make amazing new friends and have a fantastic time?

If so, send an email to: **rebecca@50states.com**. Tell us about you, your skills, your likes and dislikes, and why you want to be a counselor at 50 States Summer Camp. Include any questions you'd like us to answer. One of our team will contact you for a phone interview.

To: Rebecca
Subject: 50 States Summer Camp Counselor
Today at 16:03
All Mail

Dear Rebecca,

I am an 18-year-old high school graduate from Granada in the south of Spain. Right now, I'm working in a local restaurant. I <u>really</u> enjoy it, but I'm planning to go to college in the fall to study sports science.

I can play most sports. I play soccer very well, and I'm a good swimmer, so I'm sure I can teach those. I'm teaching my younger brother to play guitar at the moment – I play the guitar quite well, but I can't sing at all, unfortunately. I'm good at languages – in addition to Spanish, I speak English and French.

As a person, I'm quite organized and tidy, and I'm not good at living with other people if they are messy. I like music and reading, but I really love being outside and spending time with my friends. I also love food. I can cook, but not very well. I hate shopping.

This summer, I want to do something that is connected to my future studies and also uses my skills. I like helping other people, and I love to see them enjoying the same things I do. And, of course, I'd love to visit the U.S.!

I look forward to hearing from you.

Sincerely,
Ana Sofía Reynoso

B Read Ana's email and <u>underline</u>.
1   her job and current plans.
2   five things she's good at and one she's not.
3   the languages she speaks.
4   two positive adjectives to describe her.
5   five things she does well and one she doesn't.
6   five reasons she wants the job.

○ **Write it right!**

Use a variety of intensifying adverbs with adjectives, adverbs, or verbs – *not … at all, not very, quite, really, very*.

C Imagine you want to apply for the job in **A**. Note your answers to 1–6 in **B**.

D 🎧 **Make it personal**   Write a similar email applying to 50 States Summer Camp (about 180–200 words).

Before	Use your notes in **C**. Add any information you think is important.
While	Use intensifying adverbs to describe your skills and likes.
After	Exchange emails with a partner. Decide who is the best candidate.

54

4 Whose action hero?

1 Before watching

A Look at the photo. Where are Andrea and Lucy?
☐ at a tennis court   ☐ at a gym   ☐ at a stadium

B 🎧 **Make it personal** Check (✓) which are true for you and correct the others.
1 I can sing.
2 I can do acro**ba**tics.
3 I can do martial arts.
4 I can box, but I can't do **kick**boxing.
5 I can dance, but I can't sing.

C 🎧 **Make it personal** In pairs, take turns asking and answering *can / can't* questions about the activities in B.

Can you sing?   *No, I can't. What about you?*

2 While watching

A Check (✓) the correct columns according to what Lucy, Andrea, and Paolo say.

	Andrea		Lucy		Paolo	
	can	can't	can	can't	can	can't
talk to Paolo						
still join the class						
dance						
do gym**nas**tics						
be in Lucy's film						
text their number						
help someone catch up						

B Write True (T) or False (F). Correct the false sentences.
1 Lucy and Andrea can't take Paolo's kickboxing class.
2 Andrea's film pro**ject** is due next week.
3 Andrea can't do gymnastics.
4 Martial arts is Andrea's taste.
5 Andrea is **flex**ible but not so strong.
6 Lucy says that Andrea can't be in her film.
7 Paolo offers to help Lucy catch up before the class starts.

3 After watching

A Complete this extract.
Lucy: Hey, what's up?
Andrea: I want to take an exercise class. Summer _____ coming.
Lucy: Summer? I _____ only think about _____ action film. It's due next week.
Andrea: _____ class should I take? Jim _____? Marie _____? Whose class _____ best?
Lucy: You see that guy over there? Whatever _____ taking.
Andrea: Martial arts? That's _____ taste, not mine.
Lucy: I think I just found _____ new action hero. Let's go.

B Complete with *his / her / their* or noun + possessive *'s*.
1 Lucy's going home to work on _____ script.
2 Paolo's taking Andrea to _____ class.
3 Lucy can text Paolo _____ number.
4 Andrea can also be in _____ film.
5 Lucy and Paolo are sharing _____ cell phone numbers.

C 🎧 **Make it personal** In groups of three, design your ideal superhero. What can she / he do? Present her / him to the class.

This is our superbot, Queen Fantastic! She can do many things ...

55

R2 Grammar and vocabulary

A **Picture dictionary.** Cover the words on these pages and use the pictures to remember:

page	
32–33	10 weather adjectives
34	6 everyday actions
35	4 seasons
37	5 technology problems
38	6 activities
45	7 sports
46	5 abilities
48	6 talents
50	16 clothes items
53	the clothes store dialogue
158	10 picture words for diphthongs

B Complete with weather adjectives and the month (January = 1, December = 12).
1 In <u>December</u> (12), New York is usually very c <u>o l d</u>.
2 Lima is a very c _ _ _ _ y city in _____ (7).
3 London is a r _ _ _ y place in _____ (10).
4 The coast of Canada is very f _ _ _ y, especially in _____ (1).
5 It is s _ _ _ y in Bariloche. Winter there starts in _____ (5).
6 Sydney's very s _ _ _ y, especially in _____ (2).
7 La Mancha's very w _ _ _ y in _____ (8).

C 🎧 **Make it personal** Match questions 1–3 to answers a–c. Complete a–c so they're true for you.
1 What's the weather usually like in your city in July?
2 Is it raining at the moment?
3 Does it usually rain a lot in your city?
  a _____, _____ does / doesn't.
  b It _____ and _____.
  c _____, _____ is / isn't.

D ▶R2.1 Circle the correct alternatives. Listen to check. In pairs, role-play the dialogue.
Tyler: Hello?
Shannon: Hi, Tyler. This is Shannon. What **are you doing / do you do**?
Tyler: Oh, hi, Shannon. I **'m watching / watch** the football game.
Shannon: Oh? Who **'s playing / plays**?
Tyler: You **'re kidding / kid**, right?
Shannon: Tyler, you **'re knowing / know** that I **'m not liking / don't like** sports.
Tyler: OK, OK ... the Cowboys and the Giants **'re playing / play** right now.
Shannon: And who **'s winning / wins**?
Tyler: The Giants, 31–14. They **'re always winning / always win**.
Shannon: Sorry to hear that! Um ... **do you want / are you wanting** to go out later?

E Cross out the incorrect response.
1 When are you leaving?
  a Every day at 6:30 a.m.
  b Tomorrow morning.
  c In two weeks.
2 Can I see the sweater in the window?
  a Sure. What size are you?
  b Sure. How much is it?
  c Sure. What color do you prefer?
3 Here are the boots.
  a I like them very much.
  b How much are they?
  c Can I try it on?
4 Are you busy on the weekend?
  a No problem.
  b Yes, I'm working both days.
  c Not really. What are you doing?
5 Can you sing?
  a I can, but not very well.
  b Not at all.
  c Yes, I am.
6 What sports can you play?
  a No, I can't.
  b I can play volleyball and tennis.
  c I can't play any sports.

F 🎧 **Make it personal** In pairs, ask and answer 4–6 in **E**. Make more questions by changing the verbs.

G 🎧 **Make it personal** Play *Last-to-first Race!* In pairs, take turns saying these in reverse order.
1 The months: December, ...
2 The days of the week: Sunday, ...
3 Numbers 1 to 20: Twenty, ...
4 Your daily routine: I go to bed, ...
5 Your phone number: ...

H Correct the mistakes. Check your answers in units 3 and 4.
1 How's the weather like in June? (1 mistake)
2 Is raining in Patagonia at the moment. (1 mistake)
3 Do you hungry? You would like a sandwich? (2 mistakes)
4 Is usually cold in december in Canada. (2 mistakes)
5 My daughter studying at the moment. (1 mistake)
6 What your best friend is doing now? (2 mistakes)
7 He go to Europe the next month. (2 mistakes)
8 Patty can to play very well the tennis. (3 mistakes)
9 Gloria is using a blue jeans. (2 mistakes)
10 Of who are these shoes? They're of Jane. (3 mistakes)

Skills practice

🎵 *California girls, we're undeniable, Fine, fresh, fierce, we got it on lock, West Coast represent, now put your hands up.*

R2

A ▶R2.2 Listen to an interview with Paralympic swimmer Ricky Pietersen and number the questions in the order you hear them, 1–4.
- ☐ What else do you like doing when you're not swimming or watching your team?
- ☐ Do you like soccer?
- ☐ What is your next big challenge?
- ☐ So, Ricky, what's your favorite sport?

E ▶R2.3 Read the blog page. Can you guess the missing words? Listen to check your answers.

My name is Cristina Valenzuela and I [1]_____ twenty-three years [2]_____. I live in Santa Monica, California. My parents are originally [3]_____ Chile, so I [4]_____ speak Spanish very well. I love sports. I go to the beach every day, and I surf and swim when the [5]_____ is good. It's usually very [6]_____ and sunny here! I love it!

I'm [7]_____ very casual person. I usually [8]_____ shorts and a T-shirt during the day and jeans at night. When it's cold, I sometimes wear [9]_____ sweater, but I don't like it very [10]_____. I prefer to wear summer [11]_____. Write me an email! Maybe we [12]_____ go to the beach together next summer.

B ▶R2.2 Listen again and correct 1–5.
1. Well, I love singing, of course.
2. Yes, I love to watch my team win.
3. I like to read to young kids with disabilities.
4. I'm working hard to prepare for the next Panamerican Games.
5. I have to beat my own result.

C Match words 1–3 from the interview to their meanings a–c.
1. Paralympics
2. disability
3. beat the record

a. a physical or mental condition that limits a person's activities
b. to do better than the last person to hold the record
c. the Olympic Games for athletes with disabilities

D In pairs, use the information in A and B to role-play the interview. Then change roles.

> So, here I am with today's guest, Paralympic swimmer, Ricky Pietersen. Hi, Ricky!

F Answer questions 1–4 about her blog page.
1. Why can Cristina speak Spanish well?
2. What sports does Cristina usually practice?
3. What's the weather usually like in Santa Monica?
4. What does she like to wear?

G 🔴 **Make it personal** **Question time**.
In pairs, practice asking and answering the 12 lesson titles in units 3 and 4. Use the book map on p. 2–3. Where possible, ask follow-up questions, too. Can you comfortably ask and answer all the questions?

> What's the weather like?   It's very hot again!
>
> Is it windy, too?   No, it's not. No wind, no rain, only sun!

5

5.1 Is there a mall in your area?

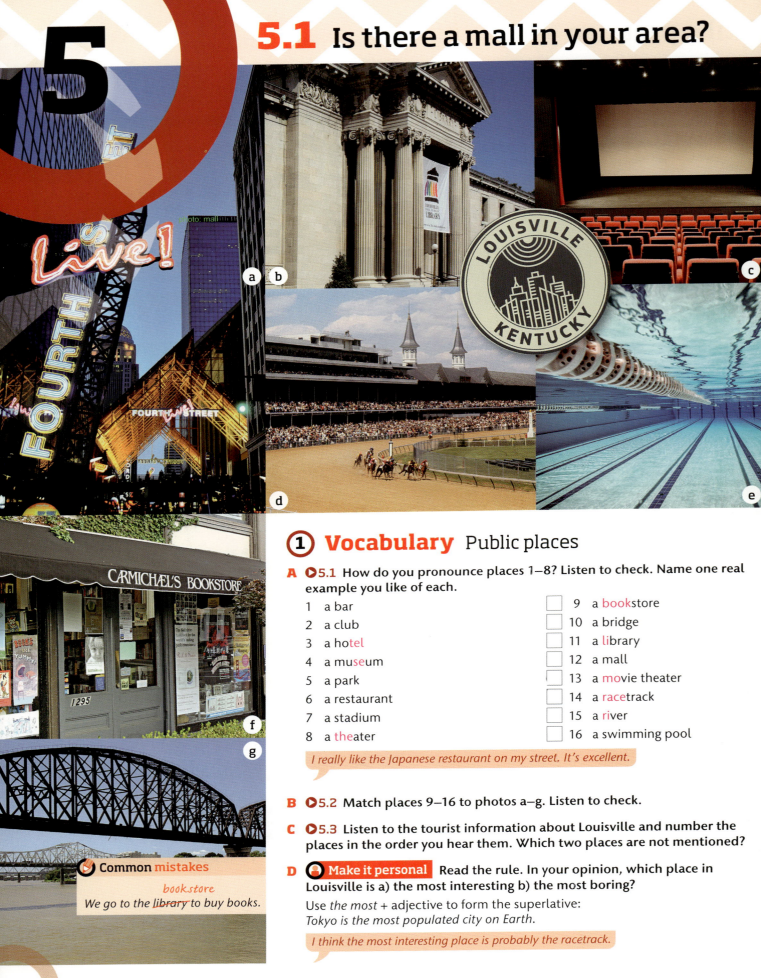

1 Vocabulary Public places

A ▶5.1 How do you pronounce places 1–8? Listen to check. Name one real example you like of each.

1 a bar
2 a club
3 a ho**tel**
4 a mu**se**um
5 a park
6 a restaurant
7 a stadium
8 a **the**ater

☐ 9 a **book**store
☐ 10 a bridge
☐ 11 a **li**brary
☐ 12 a mall
☐ 13 a **mo**vie theater
☐ 14 a **race**track
☐ 15 a **ri**ver
☐ 16 a swimming pool

I really like the Japanese restaurant on my street. It's excellent.

B ▶5.2 Match places 9–16 to photos a–g. Listen to check.

C ▶5.3 Listen to the tourist information about Louisville and number the places in the order you hear them. Which two places are not mentioned?

D 🔴 **Make it personal** Read the rule. In your opinion, which place in Louisville is a) the most interesting b) the most boring?

Use *the most* + adjective to form the superlative:
Tokyo is the most populated city on Earth.

I think the most interesting place is probably the racetrack.

Common mistakes
bookstore
We go to the ~~library~~ to buy books.

58

2 Grammar *There is / are* ➕➖❓

🎵 *There's nothing you can't do,*
Now you're in New York.
These streets will make you feel brand new
Big lights will inspire you.

5.1

A ▶ 5.4 Complete 1–4 in the grammar box with *a*, *any*, *are*, or *no*. Listen to check.

	➕	➖	❓
Singular	There is a …	There is no …	Is there a …?
Plural	There are …	There are no … There aren't any …	Are there any …?

1 There _____ seven museums downtown.
2 There's _____ famous racetrack at Churchill Downs.
3 There aren't _____ swimming pools in downtown Louisville.
4 There are _____ unfriendly people.

➡ **Grammar 5A** p. 146

🔔 **Common mistakes**

There's a
~~Have one~~ famous baseball stadium in Louisville.

There are no
~~No have~~ swimming pools in downtown Louisville.

B In pairs, each ask four *Can you …?* questions about Louisville using these verb phrases.

eat out   go to the beach / the movies / the theater
go shopping / skiing / swimming   stay in a nice hotel   watch horse racing

Can you go skiing?

No, you can't. There aren't any mountains.

C 👤 **Make it personal** Compare your hometown to Louisville. Find at least five differences.

In Louisville there's a baseball stadium, but there's no baseball stadium in my hometown.

3 Reading

A ▶ 5.5 Read and complete the brochure with *a*, *an*, *is*, *are*, or *no*. Listen to check.

Come to **Markville!**

It's *a* great place to live. There _____ two museums and _____ great public library. There _____ also a movie theater, so you can see _____ movie if you want. There's _____ mall, but there _____ lots of cool shops and _____ historical bank. Markville has two hotels: there's _____ old traditional hotel and there _____ a new modern one, so you can choose where you stay. There are _____ clubs, but there _____ a bar inside one of the hotels. For food lovers, there _____ two delicious restaurants, one French, the other Mexican, and _____ interesting café, too. Downtown is for pedestrians, so there are _____ cars to ruin the peace. People are warm, the weather is, too. The food is great, so see you soon!

B Which picture is Markville, 1 or 2? Explain.

C Work in pairs. **A**: Look at the pictures and answer.
B: Don't look! Ask **A** questions to find four differences between the two pictures.

Is there a …?   *Are there any …?*

D 👤 **Make it personal** In groups, describe a town or neighborhood you know. Is it a great place to live?

_____ is a nice place to live. There is a big mall downtown and so many things to do.

59

5.2 What are your likes and dislikes?

1 Vocabulary Free-time activities

A ▶5.6 Listen to Sandy and complete her blog post with the words.

cleaning   cooking   eating   going   playing   shopping   watching

Home | About me | Archive   Contact me

Sandy's blog

Here are the 10 things I do most every week in order of how much I like them. ☺

1. _____ video games ☐
2. going out with friends ☐
3. _____ ☐
4. _____ out ☐
5. blogging ☐
6. _____ to work ☐
7. _____ with a friend ☐
8. working out / exercising ☐
9. _____ TV ☐
10. _____ the house ☐

What about you? Are you like me? ☺

B ▶5.7 Match her blog activities to photos a–j. Listen and write the number of the activity in the chart.

😍 love	😀 like	😐 don't mind	😣 don't like	🤢 hate
1				

C 👤 **Make it personal** Make a chart like the one in B and write 10 activities. Compare in pairs. Find two things you have in common.

I hate going to the dentist, and I don't like exercising.   *We both love dancing salsa.*

2 Grammar like / love / hate / not mind + verb -ing

A Match the statements that have similar meanings.

1 I like to clean the house.
2 She hates swimming.
3 He doesn't like to clean the house.
4 I don't mind swimming.

a Swimming is OK with me.
b He hates cleaning the house.
c She doesn't like swimming.
d I like cleaning the house.

🎵 *I don't mind spending every day,*
Out on your corner in the pouring rain,
Look for the girl with the broken smile.

5.2

B Use the statements in **A** to help you complete the grammar box.

> Choose the correct answer.
> a With *love, like, hate*, use:
>   1 to + verb   2 verb -ing   3 both are possible
> b With *not mind*, use:
>   1 to + verb   2 verb -ing   3 both are possible
>
> → Grammar 5B p. 146

> ⚠ **Common mistakes**
> *driving*
> I hate ~~drive~~ in traffic.
> *driving*
> I don't mind ~~to drive~~ at night.

C Order the words to make sentences.
1 like / soccer / on / don't / I / watching / games / TV / .
2 friend / loves / go / to / movies / my / best / the / to / .
3 mind / in / don't / shopping / I / malls / .
4 my / hate / out / work / sisters / to / .

D 👤 **Make it personal** Change the sentences in **C** so they are true for you. Find someone who has the same sentences as you.

> *I don't mind watching soccer on TV.*   *I don't mind either!*

③ Pronunciation

A ▶ 5.8 Listen to the people talking about household chores. Match sentences 1–4 to photos a–d.
1 I don't <u>mind</u> cleaning the <u>bath</u>room.
2 I love <u>ti</u>dying my room.
3 I hate doing the <u>laun</u>dry.
4 I like <u>wash</u>ing the dishes.

B ▶ 5.8 Listen again. <u>Underline</u> the stressed words in sentences 2–4. Are pronouns, articles, and possessive adjectives normally stressed or unstressed?

> *I don't mind washing the dishes, but I hate doing the laundry.*

C 👤 **Make it personal** Change the sentences in **A**, 1–4, so they are true for you. Compare with a partner. Do you agree?

④ Listening

A Read the ad for the show. Guess the answers to questions 1–3.
1 How old is she?
2 What does she love to do?
3 Who does she want to be like?

B ▶ 5.9 ▶ Watch the video and check your guesses. Do you think she has talent?

C 👤 **Make it personal** Imagine you're on a talent show. Introduce yourself and say what you love doing and who you want to be like.

> *Good evening, everybody, I'm Sam, and I love to rap. I want to be like Jay-Z.*

The *Got Talent* franchise is a very popular TV talent show. There are versions of this show in more than 50 countries. Before the contestant shows his or her talent, there is an introduction to the person.

61

5.3 What do you like doing on vacation?

1 Vocabulary Vacation

A ▶5.10 Listen to and repeat 1–7, but say *I like* or *I don't like* before the activities.

Subject		Emily	Josh	You
1	camping			
2	cooking			
3	dancing			
4	hiking			
5	eating out			
6	buying souvenirs			
7	swimming			
8	visiting museums			
9	kayaking			
10	reading novels			
11	sightseeing			
12	snorkeling			
13	sunbathing			
14	taking a class			

B ▶5.11 Match activities 8–14 to the photos. Listen to check.

C ▶5.12 In pairs. Listen to Emily and Josh. **A:** Check (✓) Emily's likes in the chart. **B:** Check (✓) Josh's likes. Check together, and listen again to confirm. Do you think they can go on vacation together?

I think they really can't go on vacation together, because …

Common mistakes

He's similar ~~with~~ *to* you.

D **Make it personal** Check (✓) the activities you like doing on vacation. Are you more similar to Emily or Josh? Why? Tell a partner.

I love to swim, and I don't like camping, so I'm more similar to Emily.

2 Reading

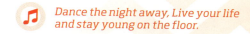 *Dance the night away, Live your life and stay young on the floor.* **5.3**

A ▶5.13 Read the two vacation ads quickly and answer questions 1–3 for each. Listen to check.

1. What country is the ad for?
2. What kind of vacation is it?
3. When can you go?

Tropical Trek

Our backpacker bus tours offer something for everyone who enjoys adventure.

What to do: Swim, snorkel, scuba dive, kayak, visit ancient Mayan pyramids, hike through a fantastic rainforest, search for crocodiles, camp in the jungle.

Don't miss the spectacular sunrises, the howler monkeys, and the flamingos!

Don't forget to lie in a relaxing hammock under a tree and spend some time doing nothing.

When to go: Mexico is a year-round destination and the fun never stops.

YOGA RICA

Discover our yoga retreats offered by local and international yoga professionals.

What to do: take a yoga class, meditate, have a massage, relax and read, walk in the forest, drink herbal tea.

Don't miss our guided tours to an active volcano, wonderful waterfalls, rivers, mountains, and beautiful beaches.

Don't forget to finish your day with a gourmet vegetarian meal in our restaurant.

When to go: we offer retreats all year round in Costa Rica.

B Read the rule, then answer the questions.

Use *more* + adjective to form the comparative.

Which vacation in **A**:

1. is more active?
2. is more relaxing?
3. has more variety?
4. is more healthy?
5. is more dangerous?
6. is more adventurous?

C ▶5.14 Match the highlighted words and phrases in the ads to photos 1–9. Listen, check, and repeat them. Which of the words with pink syllables are similar to your language?

D Which vacation do you prefer? Why?

I prefer the yoga retreat because I love relaxing on vacation, and I don't like hiking!

> **Common mistakes**
>
> *taking*
> I enjoy ~~to take~~ selfies.

E 🙂 **Make it personal** In groups, design the perfect vacation. Decide:

a. what type of vacation?
b. when?
c. where?
d. how long?
e. what activities?

5.4 How often do you leave voice messages?

1 Listening

House sitters
Young, active, professional couple looking to house sit in downtown area before buying. No kids, no pets. We totally understand the importance of loving your home. References provided.

A ▶ 5.15 Read the ad and guess True (T) or False (F). Listen to / Watch the video to check.

A house sitter is someone who:
1 usually pays to stay in a house.
2 lives in a house all the time.
3 cleans and cooks for the owner.
4 often takes care of pets.
5 leaves when the owner comes back.

B **Make it personal** In pairs, think of two advantages and disadvantages of being a house sitter. Would you like 1) to be or 2) to have a house sitter? Why (not)?

One advantage is that you can see if you like the area.

A disadvantage is that you have to leave when the owners return.

2 Vocabulary House sitting

A ▶ 5.16 Match the phrases to a–h in the picture. Listen, check, and repeat. Mime a phrase for a partner to say.

- [d] feed the cats / dog ____
- [ ] give the cats / dog some water ____
- [ ] turn on / off the lights ____
- [ ] walk the dog ____
- [ ] open / close the windows ____
- [ ] pick up / put the mail on the table ____
- [ ] water the plants ____
- [ ] don't let the cats out ____

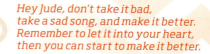

Hey Jude, don't take it bad,
take a sad song, and make it better.
Remember to let it into your heart,
then you can start to make it better.

5.4

B ◯ 5.17 Listen to a phone message for a house sitter. Number the activities in **A** in the order you hear them, 1–8.

C ◯ 5.17 Listen again and complete Lori's notes with these pronouns. What does each pronoun refer to?

him   it   me   them (x 4)   us

1- Open the windows and close _____ again every day.
2- Pick up the mail, and put _____ on the table.
3- Feed the animals in the morning and evening (don't give _____ too much food).
4- The lights and air-conditioning - turn _____ off when you go out.
5- Don't forget to give _____ some water.
6- Walk Chips in the morning and afternoon (don't take _____ near the road).
7- Call _____ if you have any questions.
8- Please tell _____ if Salt, Pepper, or Chips escape.

➡ **Grammar 5C** p. 146

D 🧑 **Make it personal** Which is the most important thing to do when you house sit? Which is the least important? Compare in groups.

I think it's most important to feed the animals.

I think it's more important to give them water.

⏺ **Common mistakes**

Which is the ~~thing most important~~ *most important thing*?
The ~~less~~ *least* important thing is to put it on the table.

③ Grammar Imperatives

A Listen and read Lori's instructions in **2C** again and circle the correct options in the grammar box.

> Imperative verb forms:
> 1 **have / don't have** a subject.
> 2 use **don't / doesn't** for negative forms.
> 3 **are statements of fact / tell you to do something**.
> 4 go **up ↗ / down ↘** at the end.

➡ **Grammar 5D** p. 146

B In pairs, make ten instructions combining the words. Try them out with another pair. Use *please* to sound more polite.

open / close   your book / eyes
pick up / put down   your phone / pen
turn on / off   the lights / the air conditioning
point to   the teacher / the door

Please close the door. Don't open it again!

C 🧑 **Make it personal** Imagine you're going on vacation.
1 Complete this list of instructions for a house sitter. Compare in groups. Who has the most useful instructions?
   1 Don't forget to _____.
   2 Please _____.
   3 Please don't _____.
   4 Remember to _____
   5 _____

Please don't have a party!

2 Leave a phone message for the house sitter. Use AS 5.17 on p. 163 to help you.

65

5.5 What's a staycation?

Skills Understanding instructions

A ▶ 5.18 Listen to the pairs of opposite adjectives and match them to pictures a–d. In pairs, can you think of others?

1 boring – fun / interesting
2 expensive – cheap
3 safe – dangerous
4 neat – messy

How about rude and polite?

B ▶ 5.19 Listen, and read about two alternative types of vacations, 1 and 2. Match them to their best definition. There's one extra.

☐ You take a vacation at home.
☐ You go and stay in another person's home.
☐ You pay to stay in someone's home.

Vacations for less!

1 Couchsurfing helps you stay free in about 200,000 cities around the world. Couchsurfing.org is an international network and there are more than 12 million members. Members offer people a place to stay in their homes. In return, they can stay free at another member's home. Members are students and professionals. You can be a surfer or a host or both!

If you want to couchsurf, here's what to do:
- Find a host who has positive references and a complete profile.
- Look for a host who has similar interests.
- Write a request to your potential host.
- Be a good guest.
- Don't be rude or messy! Help with the household chores.
- Write a reference as soon as possible to help other couchsurfers.

2 A **stay**cation is a vacation that you spend at home! It's a way to have a rest from work and your routine without spending much money. Maybe it sounds boring, but it doesn't have to be.

Here are some tips to make your staycation fun:
- Spend time at home. Invite friends to use your pool or have dinner.
- Visit local parks and museums. There are often really cool things in your hometown.
- Find out about local festivals in your area.
- Change your routine – don't do what you usually do every day. Do something different. Get up late. Change stores. Eat different foods. Take a bus, ride a bike, or walk for a change.
- Relax and don't think about work until your staycation is over.

C Read again and write True (T) or False (F).
1 Couchsurfing only happens in Europe.
2 You don't pay to couchsurf.
3 Couchsurfers write references and requests.
4 Staycations are for boring people.
5 People on staycation don't go out.
6 On a staycation, the idea is to do different things.

D ▶ 5.20 Listen to six sentences from the text and say *staycation* or *couchsurfing* after each.

E 🔵 **Make it personal** In pairs. Write five instructions for:
a) a couchsurfer visiting your town OR
b) a person who wants to staycation in your hometown.

Compare instructions with another pair. Do you agree with theirs?

Our first instruction for a couchsurfer is: Don't make noise.   *That's a good one. That's very important.*

For a staycation in our hometown: Visit the market.

5.5 Do you live near here?

In my place, in my place. Were lines that I couldn't change, And I was lost, oh yeah, I was lost.

ID in Action Giving directions

A ▶5.21 Match the phrases to photos 1–6. Listen, repeat, and mime them.

- [ ] a **cor**ner
- [ ] cross at the **stop**light
- [1] go straight
- [ ] a stop sign
- [ ] turn left
- [ ] turn right

B In pairs, share what you know about San Francisco in one minute.

> I know it's a large city on the west coast of the U.S.

Common mistakes

Do you know where ~~is~~ the stadium? *is*

Turn ~~to~~ left.

C ▶5.22 Listen to and order the tourist's questions, 1–4. How many people does he speak to?

- [ ] Is there a movie theater around here?
- [ ] Are there any bookstores near here?
- [ ] Where's the mall?
- [ ] Do you know where the library is?

D ▶5.22 Listen again and complete 1–4. Do you think he understands the last man?

1 It's _____ front of you _____ Market Street. Cross _____ at the stoplight.
2 Go _____ on Market Street and turn _____ on Fourth Street. Go _____ for one block, and the movie theater's on the _____ of Fourth and Mission Street.
3 Turn _____ on Grove Street.
4 Go straight for about _____ blocks. The bookstore's on your _____.

E In pairs, use the language above to ask for and give directions to places 1–4. Start at Powell Street Station.

1 City Hall
2 the Museum of Modern Art
3 Union Square Park
4 a parking garage

F **Make it personal** In pairs. **A:** Give directions to your home from school. **B:** Follow the directions on a map until you find where **A** lives.

> Leave the school and turn left. Go straight for two blocks. My house is on the left.

Writing 5   A city brochure

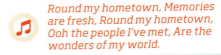
Round my hometown, Memories are fresh, Round my hometown, Ooh the people I've met, Are the wonders of my world.

A What do you know about Vancouver? Say what you see in the photos.

B Read the brochure entry and answer questions 1–8.
1. Where's a good place to start the day?
2. Where's a beautiful place for photos?
3. What's a good place to go when it's rainy?
4. What's a good place to go to buy souvenirs?
5. What are three examples of places to eat lunch?
6. Is there a romantic place in this city?
7. What can tourists do at night?
8. Is this city famous for anything?

C Study the underlined words in **B** and answer 1–3.
1. Do adjectives come before or after a noun?
2. Do adjectives come before or after the verb *be*?
3. Can you make adjectives plural?

D Order the words to make sentences.
1. is / wine / for / France / famous / .
2. the / try / cheese / local / .
3. spectacular / a / there / view / is / .
4. mountains / can / in / beautiful / the / walk / you / .
5. visit / amazing / can / you / museum / the / .

A DAY IN VANCOUVER

- Welcome to Canada's third – but most beautiful – city! First, have breakfast at Purebread Bakery in Gastown. The coffee and chocolate brownies are delicious!
- After eating, rent a bike and ride to Stanley Park. This is an enormous park downtown with lots of monuments, live concerts, street artists, and wildlife. There are beautiful views of the mountains. Before leaving, visit Prospect Point and take some photos of the ocean.
- After that, take the subway to the Museum of Vancouver. Vancouver is famous for its First Nations art, and you can see some amazing old and modern art, and cultural objects.
- When you leave the museum, go back downtown. There are hundreds of restaurants for lunch: Asian noodle restaurants, Canadian seafood cafés with fresh fish, and lots of great American burger bars. Go to Main Street after lunch and shop in the local independent stores, then take a water taxi to the public market at Granville Island.
- Finally, Vancouver has great nightlife, with many clubs and music venues. And you have to visit the Top of Vancouver revolving restaurant for a night-time view of this incredible city – it's very romantic.

E Read **Write it right!** and find eight sequencing words in **B**.

> ✓ **Write it right!**
>
> Use sequencing words to order actions: *before, after, when, first, then, finally,* etc.
> You can take photos in the park. **After that,** go to the museum.
> **After** taking (or **After** you take) photos, go to the museum.
> **Before** going (or **Before** you go) to the museum, take some photos in the park.

F Note your answers to 1–8 in **B** for your town or city.

G 🎧 **Make it personal** Imagine a tourist is coming to your town / city. Plan a day for her / him.

Before	Use your notes for **F**. Give extra information, too, e.g., your opinion.
While	Use adjectives and a variety of sequencing words.
After	Check your writing carefully and / or email it to a partner before giving it to your teacher.

5 Miss GPS

1 Before watching

A Match the nouns with the verb phrases to make sentences.

1 A map — gets you from one place to another.
2 A car — picks up a signal so you can make a call.
3 GPS / sat nav — always shows you where north is.
4 A compass — shows roads and highways.
5 A cell phone — can give you directions by voice.

B Number the items 1–8 in your order of importance for a road trip to a new place.

a car / motorbike ☐   a phone charger ☐
a cell phone ☐   food and drink ☐
a map ☐   good company ☐
extra batteries ☐   music you enjoy ☐

C 🔵 **Make it personal** Compare and explain in pairs. Many differences?

> I hate maps, so for me that's number 8. My number 1 is good company!

> I'm different. I like to travel alone, so my number 1 is music I enjoy.

D In pairs, choose four items from A and B you think the actors use on their trip. Watch to check. Were you right?

2 While watching

A Complete 1–12 with the correct form of the verbs. Who says them?

avoid	hate	have	go	like	love (x 2)
save	take	tell	use	waste	

1 Does anyone _____ a map?
2 Maps? Who _____ maps anymore?
3 I _____ using maps. Especially old maps.
4 Here she is. Miss GPS. You _____?
5 We don't _____ anywhere without GPS, right Auggie?
6 Technology _____ all the fun out of traveling.
7 I disagree. Technology _____ time.
8 And it _____ us where we're going, while we're driving.
9 Come on. Let's not _____ time arguing.
10 And a GPS helps us _____ traffic. A map can't do that.
11 And I _____ hearing the sound of my GPS girl's voice.
12 I _____ hearing that voice. It's so annoying!

B 🔵 **Make it personal** In pairs, talk about technology. Which items do you love? Any you find annoying?

> I love electricity. Without it, I can't do anything!

> I love cell phones, but sometimes ring tones are annoying.

ID Café

3 After watching

A What happens on the trip? Write True (T) or False (F). Correct the false sentences.

1 They get lost.
2 Daniel forgets to plug in the GPS.
3 The GPS battery's dead.
4 August has a strong signal on his cell phone.
5 They stop the car and ask for directions.
6 Andrea uses a map and gives directions.
7 August gets a signal on his cell phone.

B Who says it? Match 1–8 to Andrea (An), August (A), Daniel (D), Lucy (L). Watch again and imitate the actors.

	An	A	D	L
1 GPS! Not always reliable.				
2 Are you kidding me?				
3 Not a car in sight and no signal. We are so lost.				
4 Especially when you forget to plug it in.				
5 I'm gonna get a signal, don't worry.				
6 What are we gonna do? Turn back?				
7 Lucy and I will give directions from now on.				
8 After that, we're back on the main road.				

C 🔵 **Make it personal** Which do you prefer? Compare in pairs. Why?

1 giving the driver directions or driving the car
2 driving or taking a taxi
3 driving in the city or in the country
4 walking or cycling
5 using a GPS with the voice on or off

> I like driving and I'm not good with maps. So, I prefer driving.

69

Mid-term review — Play *Thirty Seconds*.

- 4 to 8 players. Divide into 2 teams.
- From the start, teams go in opposite directions.
- Toss a coin.
  - **Heads** move 1 square.
  - **Tails** move 2 squares.
- Talk about the topic, answer the question, or do the activity on the square. Maximum 30 seconds per person.
- The winning team is the first to complete the full circuit.

6.1 What's in your refrigerator?

1 Vocabulary Food and drink

A ▶6.1 Match the food on the counter 1–8 to these words. Try to pronounce them. The highlighted letters are all pronounced /ə/. Then listen to Jeff making a shopping list to check.

| ☐ ba**na**nas | ☐ **oi**l | ☐ sp**a**ghetti | ☐ t**o**matoes |
| ☐ ch**o**c**o**late | ☐ s**a**lt | ☐ t**ea** | ☐ vi**ne**gar |

72

B ▶ 6.2 Match the food in the refrigerator to these words. Try to pronounce them. Then listen to Jeff completing his list to check.

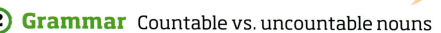

♪ *Your sugar, Yes, please, Won't you come and put it down on me?*

6.1

- ☐ apples /ˈæpəlz/
- ☐ bread /brɛd/
- ☐ butter /ˈbʌtər/
- ☐ carrots /ˈkærəts/
- ☐ cheese /tʃiːz/
- ☐ chicken /ˈtʃɪkən/
- ☐ eggs /ɛgz/
- ☐ fish /fɪʃ/
- ☐ lettuce /ˈlɛtəs/
- ☐ milk /mɪlk/
- ☐ onions /ˈʌnjənz/
- ☐ oranges /ˈɔrəndʒəz/
- ☐ potatoes /pəˈteɪtoʊz/
- ☐ sugar /ˈʃʊgər/

C In pairs, cover the words in **A** and **B**, and name all the items in the photo.

> *Five oranges …*

D ▶ 6.3 In pairs, listen to Sandra and Jeff. What's their problem?

E ▶ 6.3 Listen again and number the items in **B** in the order you hear them. Then …
1. What three items can they put in the freezer?
2. What fruit doesn't Sandra like? What food doesn't she eat?
3. What three items can they can use for dinner?

F 👤 **Make it personal** In pairs, ask and answer. Which items on p. 72–73 do you eat / drink
- (almost) every day?
- more or less every week?
- occasionally?
- never?

> *I eat bananas almost every day. I love them!*

> *Really? I like bananas, too, but I only eat them occasionally.*

2 Grammar Countable vs. uncountable nouns

A Look at the words in exercises **1A** and **1B**. In pairs, answer 1 and 2.
1. Circle the eight plural words. Are the other words usually singular or plural in your language?
2. Which of these foods can you have more than one of?
   a coffee b egg c orange d rice e spaghetti f sugar g juice

B Read the grammar box. Then complete the sentences.

Countable nouns		Uncountable nouns
a carrot	carrots	butter
an egg	eggs	cheese
a mango	mangoes	fish
a melon	melons	ice
a potato	potatoes	juice
		milk
		water

Countable nouns have plural forms that end in _____, and the word *a* or _____ before them in the singular. We use _____ when the word begins with a vowel. Uncountable nouns have only _____ form and do _____ have *a* or *an*.

→ Grammar 6A p. 148

⚠ **Common mistakes**
We have ~~a~~ bread for breakfast.
I don't eat fish~~es~~.

C In pairs, take turns asking and answering about the items in the photo.

> *What's this?*   *It's chocolate.*   *What are these?*   *They're fish.*

D 👤 **Make it personal** Play *Refrigerator Secrets*!
1. Make a list of 10 items you usually have in your refrigerator.
2. In pairs, take turns asking and answering. Who can guess all 10 items first?

> *Do you usually have milk?*   *Yes, I do. And you?*

> *Do you usually have soft drinks?*

> *Yes. I usually have two or three soft drinks in my refrigerator.*

6.2 What do you eat for lunch and dinner?

1 Vocabulary Food portions and containers

A ▶6.4 Match photos 1–13 to the food items. Listen to check. Which item isn't very healthy?

- ☐ a bottle of water
- ☐ a bowl of rice
- ☐ a cup of tea
- ☐ a glass of juice
- ☐ a piece of cake
- ☐ a piece of fruit
- ☐ a slice of bread
- ☐ some carrots or nuts
- ☐ some eggs
- ☐ some meat
- ☐ some fish
- ☐ some salad
- ☐ some vegetables

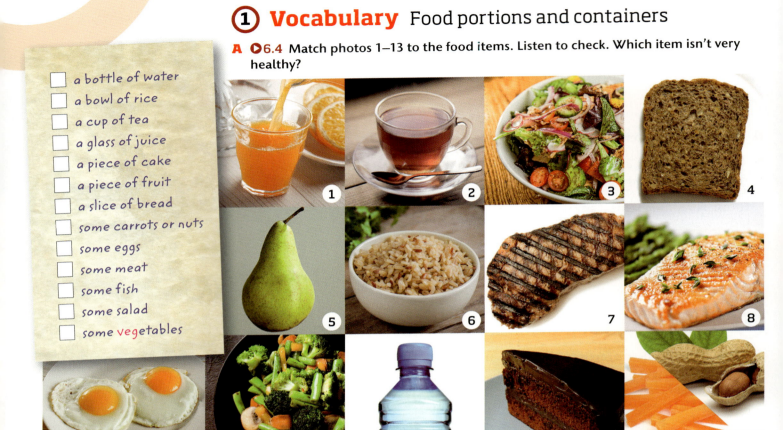

B ▶6.5 Listen to Tony recording Day One of his healthy eating plan. Write Breakfast (B), Lunch (L), Dinner (D), or Snack (S) next to the items in **A** that he eats.

C ▶6.6 Listen to Tony and his friend María. True (T) or False (F)? Correct the false sentences.
1 Tony doesn't like cake.
2 His juice is natural.
3 He thinks potato chips are healthy.
4 He eats a slice of bread only in restaurants.
5 María wants to eat healthy food, too.

⚠ **Common mistakes**
for
I don't like the tea ~~in the~~ breakfast, I prefer ~~the~~ coffee.

D 🔴 **Make it personal** Each day you can eat only five of the items in the photos, and each week you can eat a particular food no more than three times. In pairs, plan your weekly menu.

> How about some salad for lunch on Monday?   OK. And let's have fish on Tuesday.

2 Grammar Quantifiers: *some* and *any*

A ▶6.7 Complete the extracts using *some* or *any*. Listen to check. In pairs, change 1–4 to make them true for you.
1 I usually have _____ brown rice.
2 I don't eat _____ red meat. I'm a vegetarian.
3 I never eat _____ sugar.
4 I have _____ bread every day with meals.
5 Do you want _____ water?
6 No, I don't want _____, thanks.

74

B Complete the grammar box examples and rules 1–4 with *some* or *any*.

You want a piece of me,
I'm Mrs. Lifestyles of the rich and famous,
You want a piece of me.

6.2

There's **some** coffee and _____ tea here. And there's also **some** sugar.
Do you have **any** vinegar? Yes, but I don't have **any** salt or _____ pepper.
Do you want **some** cold juice? It's really hot!
Do we have **any** pasta? I want to make dinner.

1 Use _____ in affirmative sentences ⊕.
2 Use _____ in negative sentences ⊖.
3 Use _____ in questions when you think the answer is "yes."
4 Use _____ in questions when you think the answer is "no" or aren't sure.

➡ Grammar 6B p.148

Common mistakes

information
Do you have any ~~informations~~?
That was ~~a~~ bad news!
NB: The word *news* is an uncountable noun, not a plural.

C ▶ 6.8 Circle the correct form. Then listen to check. Are you similar to or different from Lucas?

Judy: So, Lucas, what do you usually have when you get up?
Lucas: I only have **some / any** water.
Judy: Wow! You don't eat **some / any** food?
Lucas: Well, I have **some / any** bread and **some / any** fruit two hours later.
Judy: Two hours later? And do you have **some / any** coffee? You know, to stay awake?
Lucas: I don't need **some / any** coffee. I don't get up until noon!

D 🙂 Make it personal In groups. What do you usually eat / drink in the morning? Whose morning diet is the healthiest?

I always drink some water when I get up.

③ Listening

A ▶ 6.9 Use the photos to guess what Amy is going to have for breakfast during her trip to Japan. Listen to Amy and her friend Bill to check.

B ▶ 6.9 Listen again. Choose the correct answers.
1 Amy's trip to Japan is for **vacation / work**.
2 Tourists usually like the **Western / Japanese** breakfast.
3 Bill **often / never** goes to Japan.
4 Miso soup **has / doesn't have** a lot of salt.
5 Green tea **has / doesn't have any** caffeine.
6 In Japan, you can buy coffee in a **bottle / can**.
7 A good way to go to your hotel in Tokyo is by **taxi / train**.
8 Amy **is / isn't** nervous about her trip.

C 🙂 Make it personal In pairs, compare your answers to these questions. Any surprises?
1 Would you like to try a Japanese breakfast? Why (not)? Any other unusual meals you like or would like to try?
2 What's your ideal breakfast, lunch, and dinner? Where, when, who with, what food?

My ideal lunch is me and Justin Bieber on a beautiful beach, eating fish and drinking coconut water.

My ideal lunch is me and my family eating my mom's home-cooked food!

6.3 How often do you eat chocolate?

1 Reading

A ▶6.10 Read the title of Nelly's blog. Do you think the answer is *yes* or *no*? Then read and listen to the blog and the article and see if the writer agrees with you.

Food & Life

HOME   ABOUT   RECIPES   MISC

Is Chocolate Really Good For You?
September 3rd by Nelly

I have a confession to make: I love sugar ❤. But I don't really eat a lot of candy. The secret to a "sweet" life 🙂 is quality, not quantity. When I really want some candy or a dessert, I always go for the most delicious and the most attractive that I can find. And they even say chocolate is good for you!

Maybe you're smiling because Nelly's blog sounds familiar. That's not surprising. Chocolate tastes good! And some claim it has health benefits, too.

- If you have a lot of pressure and stress in your life, chocolate can make you feel better mentally and physically. Chocolate gives you energy!
- Chocolate will reduce your appetite. If you eat a small quantity of dark chocolate before a big lunch, your appetite might be 15% less!
- Chocolate can improve your heart! Some even say your cholesterol may improve, too.
- Chocolate keeps your skin hydrated, and it also has anti-aging properties that help you stay young.
- Chocolate has a little caffeine, but much less than coffee. And it has some sugar. Be sure to check the ingredients before you buy. And make sure your chocolate is at least 85% chocolate.

So, is chocolate really good for you? No, not really! We usually eat it with a lot of fat and sugar, which aren't so good for you. But, the good news? A little chocolate now and again won't hurt you – and, of course, it tastes delicious!

B ▶6.10 How much can you remember? Complete the notes about chocolate. Listen to and read both texts again to check. Repeat the pink-stressed words.

People say:
1. It's good for pressure and _____.
2. It gives you _____.
3. Eat a little piece before a big _____, and you eat less.
4. It's good for your _____.
5. It makes you look _____.
6. But chocolate usually contains _____ and _____, so it's good to only eat a _____!

C 🙋 **Make it personal** Discuss the questions in groups.
1. Are you similar to or different from Nelly?
2. Does any information in the article surprise you? Anything missing?
3. Do you keep a blog or regularly read any blogs?

It doesn't mention the origin of chocolate. It comes from …

2 Grammar Quantifiers: *a little, a few, a lot of*

🎵 All I'm askin', (ooh) Is for a little respect when you come home (just a little bit).

A Circle the correct words in a–d and complete rules 1–3 with *a few*, *a little*, or *a lot of*.

a Nelly doesn't eat **a lot of / a little** candy.
b **A little / a few** chocolate satisfies her.
c If you have **a lot of / a few** stress, chocolate can make you feel better.
d We all have **a few / a little** bad habits.

1 Use _____ with countable nouns. It means a small number.
2 Use _____ with uncountable nouns. It means a small quantity.
3 Use _____ with countable and uncountable nouns. It means a large quantity or number.

➔ **Grammar 6C** p. 148

⚠ **Common mistakes**
I have a little ~~of~~ money in my purse.

3 Listening

A ▶ 6.11 Listen to Sandra and Joe talk about lunch at a Mexican restaurant. What do they decide to eat?

B ▶ 6.11 Listen again and complete the chart. Which meal would you choose? Why?

⚠ **Common mistakes**
six hundred~~s~~ fifty grams

NUTRITION FACTS
Serving Size: 1 burrito (198 g)

Quantity Per Serving	Chicken burrito	Meat burrito	Vegetarian burrito
Total Fat	____ g	5 g	4 g
Cholesterol	30 mg	____ mg	____ mg
Sodium	880 mg	890 mg	730 mg
Fiber	6 g	5 g	____ g
Protein	____ g	____ g	14 g

C 👥 **Make it personal** In pairs. Use the words in 1–6 and *a lot / a little / a few* to have short conversations about you and your friends. Any surprises?

1 eat / Mexican food
2 have / English-speaking friends
3 spend / money
4 do / exercise
5 download / songs
6 take / selfies

> Do you take a lot of selfies?
> No, only a few. I don't really like selfies.

6.4 How many meals do you cook a week?

1 Grammar *How much vs. how many*

A ▶ 6.12 Listen to and complete the conversation with *how much, how many, a lot, a few,* or *a little*.

Richie: OK, the chili's almost ready.
Grandpa: You can add some mushrooms, if you want.
Richie: _____ mushrooms?
Grandpa: I don't know! _____ if you like them or _____ if you don't.
Richie: OK – I get it. And how do I serve it?
Grandpa: With some rice.
Richie: _____ rice?
Grandpa: _____ if you're hungry, _____ if you're not.

B Circle the correct answers and complete the examples in the grammar box.

> 1 Use **how much / how many** with uncountable nouns: "_____ money do you have?"
> 2 There's always a plural noun after **how much / how many**: "_____ carrots are there?"
> 3 *A few* is an answer to **how much / how many**: "_____ eggs are there?" "A few."
> 4 *A little* is an answer to **how much / how many**: "_____ cheese is there?" "A little."
>
> → **Grammar 6D** p.148

⏱ Common mistakes

~~How many movie do you see a month?~~ → *movies*
~~How many time do you spend in the shower?~~ → *much*

C Complete the examples with *how much* or *how many*. In pairs, research these foods and role-play choosing something to eat.

a chicken burrito   a hamburger   a salmon burger
a veggie burger   a tofu burger

| fat | fiber | salt | cholesterol | protein |

Do you want a chicken burrito?   I'm not sure. _____ fat does it have?   Five grams.

And _____ grams of fiber does it have?   Only six.

D Complete 1–10 with *How much* or *How many*. Ask and answer in pairs.

1 _____ restaurants do you go to every month?
2 _____ coffee / tea / water / milk do you drink every day?
3 _____ people do you live / work / study with?
4 _____ hours do you work / study / exercise on the weekends?
5 _____ time do you spend studying English / listening to music / on social media a week?
6 _____ money do you spend on clothes / going out / traveling / food a month?
7 _____ meat / rice / fruit do you eat a week, on average?
8 _____ phones / computers / TVs / cars does your family have?
9 _____ texts / emails / Tweets, on average, do you send a day?
10 _____ times do you go out / go to the beach / play sports each month?

E 🗣 **Make it personal** Choose a topic 1–10 in **D**, and take a class survey. Share your answers with the class.

Most of us are on social media all the time, except Victor.

On average, we spend about X a month on clothes.

② Reading

🎵 *But she said where d'you wanna go?, How much you wanna risk?, I'm not looking for somebody, With some superhuman gifts.*

6.4

A In pairs, take the quiz, but don't read the article! Try to guess the correct answers.

HOW MUCH DO YOU KNOW ABOUT WHAT YOU EAT?
by Sally Larouche

1. Which of these foods doesn't have a lot of potassium?
   a potatoes   b beans   c bananas   d apples
2. Which of these drinks is the best way to rehydrate the body?
   a water   b tea   c sports drinks   d orange juice
3. Which of these drinks is really a food item?
   a tea   b coffee   c milk   d coconut water
4. Which of these vegetables has a lot of protein?
   a beans   b carrots   c spinach   d onions
5. Which of these foods is NOT rich in vitamin C?
   a strawberries
   b pears
   c kiwis
   d tomatoes

B ▶6.13 Skim the article and, in pairs, answer 1 and 2. Think of ten more cognates you know.
1. Words that are similar in two languages are called *cognates*. How many of the highlighted words in paragraph 1 do you recognize? Is the pronunciation similar or different in your language? Listen to check.
2. Examples can help you know the meaning of words, too. Can you guess the meaning of the highlighted words in paragraph 3?

How do we decide what to eat?

It's not easy because modern grocery stores offer many, many choices. The first step to a healthy diet is learning as much as we possibly can about the foods we eat. Let's look at the answers to the quiz.

1. Apples are good for you in many ways, but they're not rich in potassium like the other foods are. Potassium keeps our muscles strong and helps eliminate salt from the body. Apples are very nutritious, though, and have a lot of vitamin C and fiber.

2. As you've probably guessed, water is absolutely the best way to rehydrate the body. When it's hot out, drink, drink, drink, and always carry a bottle of water with you. Water also increases our energy, helps us concentrate, and prevents headaches.

3. Because it contains a lot of nutrients, including calcium, protein, and potassium, milk is a food. It's a food you can drink! But if you don't like the taste of milk, be sure to consider other dairy products, such as cheese and yogurt.

4. Do you remember Popeye? He loved spinach. Well, all of the foods in question 4 are good for you, but beans have a lot of protein, more than spinach, carrots, or onions. Maybe you eat beans often, but, if not, now is a good time to start. They taste good, too!

5. And finally, everyone knows that vitamin C is good for you, but which of these fruits is NOT rich in vitamin C? It's not the tiny strawberry. The answer is pears. The good news is that pears contain no fat and are a good source of fiber.

So ... happy, healthy eating! Please share my article with all of your friends. Thank you!

C ▶6.13 Listen to and read the article again. In pairs, take turns asking and answering the quiz in **A**. Check your answers in the article. Do you remember any interesting facts?

Here's one. Apples have a lot of vitamin C.

D 🗣 **Make it personal** In pairs. Ask and answer 1–4. Are your answers similar?
1. Do you Google information you don't know?
2. How many times a week do you check Wikipedia?
3. Did any answers to the quiz surprise you? Which ones?
4. Does it make you want to change anything about the way you eat?

I use Google a lot!

Me, too. I check Wikipedia every day.

79

6.5 Are you hungry?

ID Skills Scanning a menu

A Scan the menu. In pairs, answer 1–5.
1. What do the symbols ⓥ, 🌱, Ⓖ mean?
2. How many meat-free dishes are there?
3. What are the two types of starters?
4. How many main courses and desserts are there?
5. Write the price of each dish on the photos.

B ▶6.14 Listen to the ad for Fast & Fresh and check (✓) the dishes you hear on the menu.

C Read the menu again. True (T) or False (F)?
1. Croutons are bread and are only served in salads.
2. The fish and the steak are grilled.
3. There are three different kinds of potatoes.
4. The vegetables are fried.
5. The fruit salad has strawberries.
6. You can pay by cash or credit card.

D 🔴 **Make it personal** In pairs. Imagine you're at Fast & Fresh. Order a three-course meal.

For my starter, I'm having …   *And I'd like …*

6.5 What would you like for lunch?

 I am sitting in the morning, At the diner on the corner, I am waiting at the counter, For the man to pour the coffee.

ID in Action   Ordering food

A ▶ 6.15 Listen and check (✓) the items Marie and Phil order.

B ▶ 6.16 Listen and order the second part of the dialogue 1–10. Complete the dialogue with the food Phil and Marie order.

	Server:	OK. And you, sir?
	Marie:	Great, thanks.
	Marie:	Yes, please. I'd like the _____, please.
	Server:	OK. How are your starters?
	Phil:	Can I have _____, please?
	Server:	Would you like to order the main course now?
	Phil:	I'll have the _____, please.
	Server:	Any drinks with your meal?
	Server:	Sure. I'll be right back with those.
	Marie:	And I'll have _____, please.

C Read the dialogue in **B** again and find three different ways to order food in a restaurant.

D ▶ 6.17 Listen and check (✓) the desserts and hot drinks Phil and Marie order. What's the last thing Phil asks for?

E 👤 **Make it personal** Restaurant role-play in groups of four. **A**, **B**, and **C**: you're at Fast & Fresh for a three-course lunch. **D**: you're the server.

> Hi! I'm Gaby, and I'm your server today. What would you like to start?

> I'd like the soup, please.

> Excellent choice! And for your main course?

Common mistakes

I'd
✗ like pizza, please.
"I like pizza" = generally.
"I'd like pizza" = now.

I'll
✗ have a mint tea, please.

Writing 6 A food diary

Have some more chicken, have some more pie, It doesn't matter if it's broiled or fried, Just eat it.

My Life in Food

The healthy eater
Monica, age 22, personal trainer

I try to eat well, as I have a very active job. I believe there's a connection between what we eat and our physical health, so I like to eat food that's fresh and nutritious.

For breakfast, I usually have fruit juice, cereal with honey, and a cup of hot water. I drink a lot of water every day, because it's important to stay hydrated. I never drink sugary drinks. However, I love coffee, and I often have an espresso after lunch.

Mid-morning, I often have a snack, like a piece of fruit. I never eat chocolate or candy. I eat a lot of fruit and vegetables. I don't eat a lot of meat, but I do eat fish because it has protein without much fat.

I always eat lunch, as I need to maintain my energy level through the day. A typical lunch for me is a big salad, with tuna, bread, and more fruit. In the evening, I'm usually tired, so I eat something easy to prepare – for example, spaghetti with vegetables.

The junk food addict
Jude, 19, college student

I eat a lot of junk food, _____ I know it's bad for me and makes me put on weight.

I never eat breakfast _____ I always get up late, but when I get to college, I usually have a donut and a cup of coffee. I drink a lot of soda, _____ it's cheap and it tastes good, and the sugar helps me to stay awake in class.

I eat a lot of snacks through the day – _____, candy bars, chocolate, and potato chips. For lunch, I usually have a burger with some fries and a bottle of soda. I hate fish, and I don't eat fruit or vegetables; _____, I like banana ice cream!

I eat dinner alone _____ my mom works in the evenings. I usually get a take-out, _____ pizza, or sometimes Chinese food. I stay up late playing video games, _____ I often eat another slice of pizza or some chocolate at night. I'm surprised how unhealthy my diet is – I know I need to change it.

A Read what two people with very different diets eat in a typical day. Check (✓) the things they eat and drink.

	Monica	Jude	You
breakfast	☐	☐	☐
water	☐	☐	☐
coffee	☐	☐	☐
fruit	☐	☐	☐
vegetables	☐	☐	☐
fish	☐	☐	☐
meat	☐	☐	☐
soda	☐	☐	☐
chocolate	☐	☐	☐

B Read **Write it right!** In Monica's diary, circle the six connectors.

Write it right!

To improve your writing, use a variety of connectors.
- to give reasons: *because, as,* and *so*
- to give examples: *for example* (or *e.g.*), *like*
- to introduce a different idea: *however, but*

C Complete Jude's diary with *because, as, so, for example / e.g., like* and *however.*

D Complete the chart in **A** for you. Think about why you eat what you eat. Anything you need to change?

E **Make it personal** Write your own food diary in 150–180 words.

Before	Use your notes in D and the vocabulary in Unit 6.
While	Use connectors carefully.
After	Read a partner's diary and comment on her / his diet.

6 Party planners

1 Before watching

A Match 1–5 to their definitions.

1 split — be certain
2 tasting — small, red, sweet fruit
3 make sure — share
4 have no idea — not know at all
5 cherries — trying

B In pairs, guess where August and Andrea are, and what they're doing. Then watch to check.

I think they're sitting in …

2 While watching

A Listen and complete the extracts with *like, love, would like / 'd like*, or *will have*.

August: OK. I _____ to try the beef, for sure. But I do _____ chicken.
Andrea: That's OK. You get those. And I _____ to try the fish and vegetarian dishes. I'd also _____ a bowl of rice and a salad plate. So you could get the pasta and potatoes, OK?
Server: _____ you _____ to order dessert?
Andrea: Yes, please. I _____ the white chocolate cake. And also a cup of tea, please. Thank you.
August: And I _____ a slice of Black Forest cake and a coffee. Thanks.

B Complete 1–5 with *how much* or *how many*. In pairs, take turns asking and answering.

1 _____ food do they order?
2 _____ main and side dishes are there?
3 _____ slices of cake do they order?
4 _____ cups are there on the table?
5 _____ dishes does Andrea order?
6 _____ cake do they eat?

They both order a lot of food!

C Match food portions 1–4 to the correct group. Then add the food items to the groups.

| bread | cereal | coffee | pie |

1 A bowl of   paper, gum, _____
2 A cup of   pizza, cake, _____
3 A slice of   tea, hot chocolate, _____
4 A piece of   rice, pasta, _____

3 After watching

A True (T), False (F), or Not Given (NG)?

1 August and Andrea are at their favorite restaurant.
2 They're planning a surprise for their parents.
3 Andrea loves all red fruit.
4 August doesn't enjoy the Black Forest cake.
5 They thought they were trying the regular menu.
6 They don't have enough money to pay.

B Match questions 1–6 to the responses.

1 Are you ready to order?
2 What are you having?
3 Can I take your order?
4 What can I get you?
5 Can I get you anything else?
6 Would you like to see the menu?

☐ I'll have the chicken, please.
☐ Spaghetti and meatballs, please.
☐ Sure. Could I get the beef, please?
☐ Yes, thanks.
☐ Yes, I am. I'd like the fish.
☐ No, thanks. Just the bill, please.

C Complete 1–5 with expressions from the video.

1 _____ they don't know about the surprise party?
2 I think we have to try all of those things to _____ they're good.
3 Here comes the server … _____.
4 Dessert? _____ We have to try those, too.
5 _____ we just ate two main courses?

D 🅐 **Make it personal** In groups of three, role-play the situation. Eat a lot and pay too much!

Good evening sir, madam. A table for two?

83

R3 Grammar and vocabulary

A **Picture dictionary.** Cover the words on these pages and use the pictures to remember:

page	
58	8 places around town
60	10 free time activities
61	4 household chores
62	14 vacation activities
64	8 house sitting jobs
67	4 traffic signs
72–73	22 food and drink words
159	16 picture words for lines 1 and 2 of consonants

B **Make it personal** Play *Mime it!* Think of examples for 1–8. Mime them for a partner to guess. Were any of your choices the same?
1 Two spectacular animals.
2 Two useful *Can I ...?* questions.
3 Three boring activities.
4 Three relaxing places.
5 Three items in your fridge.
6 Two household chores.
7 Your favorite dessert.
8 One vegetable and one fruit.

No idea! Maybe a lion?

C Circle the correct alternative to complete 1–10.
1 _____ a good café with WiFi near here?
   a There is   b Is there   c Have
2 Today, _____ over 5 billion cell phones in the world.
   a there is   b there are   c there are some
3 Are there _____ cookies in the kitchen?
   a the   b a   c any
4 How _____ people are there at the party?
   a much   b a lot of   c many
5 _____ a great new store on the corner.
   a There is   b Is   c Is there
6 Can I have _____ water, please?
   a some   b any   c glass of
7 This vegetable soup has _____ salt.
   a much   b any   c a lot of
8 We _____ like watching TV.
   a same   b the two   c both
9 I love _____ to the gym and shopping.
   a go   b going   c goes
10 I hate cooking, but I don't mind _____ the dishes.
   a wash   b to wash   c washing

D ▶R3.1 Complete with *some* or *any*. Listen and check. Then in pairs, role-play using different food items.
Tina: I'm thirsty. Is there _____ juice in the fridge?
Carl: No, we didn't buy _____ juice this week. But, look, there are oranges. Do you want me to make you _____ juice?
Tina: Yes, thanks. Uh, and did we buy _____ cookies?
Carl: No, but there are still _____ cookies in the cabinet.
Tina: Great, thanks!

E Circle the correct words.
Dan: Do we have **a lot of** / **many** homework for next class?
Lee: No, just **a few** / **a little**. Maybe half an hour.
Dan: How **many** / **much** exercises?
Lee: I'm not sure, Dan. Only **a little** / **a few**. Why do you ask?
Dan: I have a party tonight and **much of** / **a lot of** my friends are going, so I don't have **many** / **much** time for homework! Hey, do you want to come, too?
Lee: Sure, why not? It sounds fun.

F Match the two parts to make activities.

cleaning	in rivers / in the ocean / in a pool
going	video games / soccer / cards
watching	museums / relatives / a friend
playing	the house / the bathroom / the car
taking	the sunrise / old movies / TV
doing	a class / a shower / a course
visiting	the dishes / the laundry / homework
swimming	online / out with friends / to the gym

G ▶R3.2 Complete with a pronoun. Listen to check.
1 Hi Mike, how are *you* ?
2 This is Nick and this is Steve, I work with _____.
3 Your coat is on the floor. Please put _____ on your chair.
4 That's Jessica. I go to school with _____.
5 This is David's phone. Can you give it to _____?

H Correct the mistakes. Check your answers in units 5 and 6.
1 A house sitter take care your house when you're away. (2 mistakes)
2 I love to walking in the beach. (2 mistakes)
3 To swim is good for you. (1 mistake)
4 I no really enjoy to do the dishes. (2 mistakes)
5 Do you know where is the soccer stadium? (1 mistake)
6 For dinner we ate a bread and a few yogurt. (2 mistakes)
7 You look hungry. Would like any biscuit? (2 mistakes)
8 It's my sister's book. Please give him to it. (2 mistakes)
9 I hate use maps, especially old maps. (1 mistake)
10 Stop! No do that! Please to sit down. (2 mistakes)

Skills practice

R3

🎵 There's a mountain top that I'm dreaming of,
If you need me you know where I'll be,
I'll be riding shotgun underneath the hot sun.

A 👤 **Make it personal** Do you like doing these activities? In pairs, compare. Anything in common?

hate — don't mind — like — love

clean the bathroom	cook	do the dishes
do the laundry	exercise	go online
play video games	read novels	
shop in malls / online	spend money	sunbathe
take selfies	tidy my room	water plants

> I don't mind doing the laundry, what about you?

> Oh, no! I hate doing the laundry.

B Try to match breakfasts a–f to the country they are typical of. Then read the blog to check your guesses.
1 Brazil   3 Japan   5 Norway
2 China   4 Mexico   6 The UK

What's your perfect breakfast?

"On the weekend I love to eat eggs, bacon, sausage, tomatoes, mushrooms, and toast. And lots of tea! I don't have time to make such a big, cooked breakfast from Monday to Friday."
Julia, London, UK

"My favorite breakfast is eggs in hot sauce with refried beans, tortillas, and some coffee."
Juan, Guadalajara, Mexico

"I eat the same thing every day - fruit, bread, pastries, some juice, and some coffee."
Milton, Salvador, Brazil

"On weekends or special occasions, I usually eat smoked salmon and scrambled eggs with some rye bread. Other days I just have some bread and cheese - and black coffee, of course! I don't usually eat much in the mornings."
Alexander, Oslo, Norway

"I always eat rice with some fish and soup for breakfast. I don't have time to eat again until the evening so a good breakfast is important to maintain my energy level through the day."
Kimiko, Tokyo, Japan

"Rice porridge with chicken is my best breakfast. I have this about three times a week."
Lin, Beijing, China

C Read again and name the person / people who …
1 eats the same thing every day? _____
2 has a different breakfast on weekends? _____
3 enjoys eggs with hot sauce? _____
4 eats meat for breakfast? _____
5 doesn't eat any meat or fish for breakfast? _____
6 eats rice for breakfast? _____

D ▶R3.3 Listen and follow the directions. Write the letter in the correct place on the map.
a the bookstore   c the mall
b the movie theater d the gym

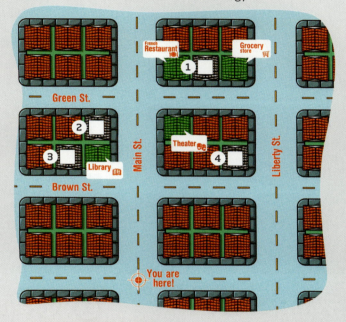

E 👤 **Make it personal** In pairs, are 1–5 True (T) or False (F) for your area? Any interesting differences?
1 There's a very good restaurant near my house.
2 There is a nice park at the end of this street.
3 There's no good shopping mall near here.
4 There are no interesting museums around here.
5 There aren't any cheap hotels in this area.

> There are a lot of excellent restaurants near my house.

> Really?! Lucky you! There aren't any near mine.

F 👤 **Make it personal** Question time.
In pairs, practice asking and answering the 12 lesson titles in units 5 and 6. Use the book map on p. 2–3. Where possible, ask follow-up questions, too. Can you comfortably ask and answer all the questions?

> Is there a mall in your hometown?   Yes, but it's only small.

> Do you go there often?   Not really.

7.1 Do you live in a house?

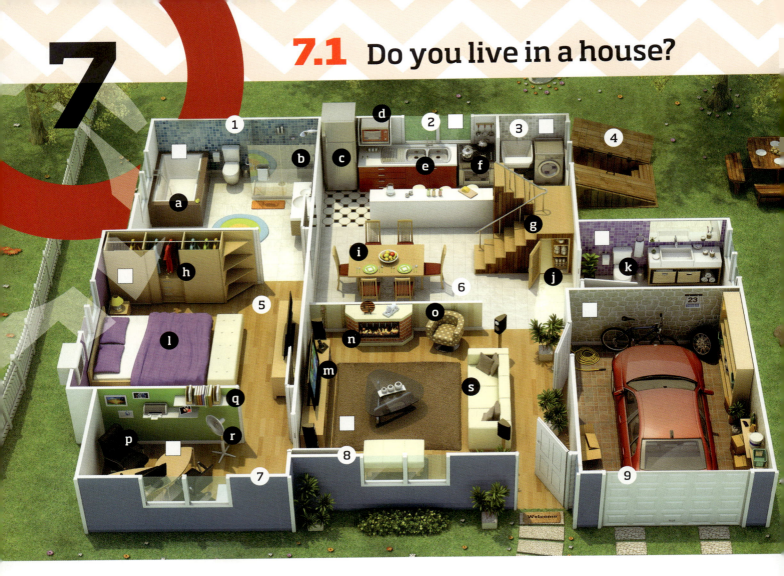

1. Take a shower in ...
2. You can cook in ...
3. You wash and dry clothes in ...
4. Store things you don't need in ...
5. You sleep in ...
6. People usually eat in ...
7. People work in ...
8. We watch TV in ...
9. We keep our car in ...

1 Vocabulary Rooms and furniture

A ▶7.1 Match clues 1–9 to the rooms. Listen to a guessing game to check.

- ☐ the basement ___
- ☐ the dining room ___
- ☐ the living room ___
- ☑ 1 the bathroom ___
- ☐ the garage ___
- ☐ the office ___
- ☐ the bedroom ___
- ☐ the kitchen ___
- ☐ the laundry room ___

B ▶7.2 Listen to Tom showing his house to Anna, a potential roommate. Number the rooms in **A** in the order you hear them, 1–6. Which three rooms in **A** are not mentioned?

C Match the words below to furniture a–s in the picture. First match the words on the left, then those on the right. How many of the words do you already use?

- ☑ a bed
- ☐ a sofa
- ☐ an armchair
- ☐ shelves
- ☐ a chair
- ☐ a table
- ☐ a bathtub
- ☐ a sink
- ☐ a closet
- ☐ a TV
- ☐ a fan
- ☐ storage space
- ☐ a refrigerator
- ☐ a toilet
- ☐ a fireplace
- ☐ a stove
- ☐ a shower
- ☐ a microwave
- ☐ the stairs

D 🔴 **Make it personal** In pairs, decide which items of furniture are essential at home and which are optional. Make two lists.

In my opinion, a bed is absolutely essential.

E ▶7.2 Listen again and list the furniture Tom mentions in each room. Do you think Anna likes the house? Why or why not?

F 🅐 **Make it personal** Give a tour of your home. Draw a floor plan and describe it to your partner. Are your homes similar?

This is the living room with a big sofa. And this is my bedroom.

2 Reading

A Look at the photo and guess what Jay says about his house. Then, read his blog post and answer the questions.

> Hi! I'm **Jay Shafer** and I live in a small house because it doesn't cause problems for the environment. Also, this way, I don't buy more things than I really need. My house is only 89 square feet (that's 8.3 m²). It has a very small living room, a tiny kitchen, a small bedroom, and bathroom. During the day, my bed is in the wall. You can have a small house, too! Dream big. Live small.

1 What rooms does Jay's house have?
2 What are some good things about a tiny house? Can you think of any others?

B ▶7.3 Watch the video with the sound off. In pairs, name everything you saw in one minute. Who remembered the most?

two chairs   *a toilet*

C ▶7.3 Watch again and circle the correct answers. Is his house comfortable?
1 Jay's living room has two chairs and a tiny **fireplace / sofa**.
2 The kitchen has a sink, stove, refrigerator, and a **dishwasher / toaster oven**.
3 The shower is **the bathroom / in the bathtub**.
4 Jay sleeps in **a bedroom / the loft**.
5 When it's hot, he uses **air conditioning / a fan**.

3 Grammar Past of *be*: *there was / there were*

A ▶7.4 Listen to Katie and Lenny talking about a tiny house. Complete the grammar box with *was, were, wasn't,* or *weren't*. How many syllables in *wasn't* and *weren't*?

	➕	➖	❓	Short answers
Singular	There _____ a window.	There was no stove. There wasn't a stove.	_____ there a bathtub?	Yes, there _____ . / No, there wasn't.
Plural	There were two closets.	There _____ any closets.	_____ there any bedrooms?	Yes, there _____ . / No, there weren't.

When something is negative, we use *there* _____ if it's singular, and *there* _____ if it's plural.

➡ **Grammar 7A** p. 150

🅒 **Common mistakes**

there
Was a bathtub?
There wasn't a
~~No had~~ garden in my old home.

B 🅐 **Make it personal** Imagine you're now living in a tiny house. In pairs, compare it to your "old home."

In my old home, there was a ... but now there's no ...!   *Were there any ... in your old home?*

7.2 Where were you last night?

1 Vocabulary Party items

A In pairs, name each item and its color.

a red teapot, colored invitations, ...

- [ ] coffee
- [ ] glasses
- [ ] plates
- [ ] presents
- [ ] juice
- [ ] a cake
- [ ] tea
- [ ] water
- [ ] balloons
- [ ] birthday cards
- [ ] candles
- [ ] invitations
- [ ] napkins
- [ ] snacks
- [ ] soft drinks

B ▶7.5 Listen to Liz, a party planner, talking about how to have a good party. Number the items in **A** 1–15 in the order she mentions them.

C ▶7.5 Listen again. What does Liz consider essential for a party that is not shown in **A**?

D 🔴 **Make it personal** In pairs, compare your last party. Which items in **A** and **C** were(n't) there?

My last party was fantastic!   *There were a lot of ...*

2 Grammar Past of *be*: statements and questions

A ▶7.6 Listen to Martha and Rob, and find Martha (1), Rob (2), Jane (3), and Rick (4) in the photos.

B ▶ 7.6 Order these words to make sentences. Who said them? Martha or Rob? Listen again to check.

1. was / I / party / great / at / yesterday / a / .
2. it / was / where / ?
3. was / it / Jane Foster's / at / home / .
4. birthday / was / it / her / .
5. there / Jane's / was / boyfriend / ?
6. he / yes, / was / .
7. parents / Jane's / there / were / ?
8. they / no, / weren't / .
9. boyfriend / I / before / Jane's / Rick / was / .
10. party / great / that / the / wasn't / .

'Cause we were just kids when we fell in love, Not knowing what it was, I will not give you up this time.

7.2

Common mistakes

Was your brother
~~Your brother~~ was at the party last weekend?

was
Were you alone? Yes, I ~~were~~.

C Read the grammar box and complete with *was*, *were*, *wasn't*, or *weren't*.

	+	**−**	**?**	**Short answers**
Singular	I was at home. You were … She / He / It was …	I wasn't there. You _____ … She / He / It wasn't …	Were you at home? _____ she / he / it good?	Yes, I was. / No, I _____. Yes, he / she / it was. No, he / she / it _____.
Plural	We were there. You _____ … They were …	We _____ there. You weren't … They _____ …	_____ you there? Were they …?	Yes, we _____. / No, they weren't.

Don't forget the pronoun with *Wh-* questions:
Where were you? I was at school.
When was Julia at school? She was there all day.

➔ **Grammar 7B** p.150

D Complete the email with the verb *be*. Where was Stacey yesterday?

To: **Martin** Today at 10:58
Subject: R U OK? All Mail

Hi Martin!

Where _____ you yesterday evening? Sleeping again? Well, I _____ at Lina's party, and it _____ amazing! There _____ some great music from the DJ, lots of dancing and the food _____ absolutely delicious! _____ you at home? Your cell phone _____ on all night, and I couldn't talk to you. That's why I _____ emailing you now. Are you OK? You _____ at school last week, and you _____ at the party. Where _____ you now??? 😕

I hope everything _____ OK.

Write back, text, or call me, please!

Stacey xx

E Complete the chart of past time expressions.

| afternoon | evening | Monday | month |
| morning | night | summer | weekend | year |

yesterday	last
evening	

Common mistakes

last Monday morning
I was at work ~~the last Monday in the morning~~.

all evening
We weren't at home ~~all the night~~.

F 🟢 **Make it personal** In five minutes, find out all you can about your partner's week. Use *Were you …?* or *When / Where were you …?* + past time expressions. Mime what you can't express in English. Change partners and report what you remember. Who had the most boring / interesting week?

Were you at home last night?   *Yes, I was, all evening. Where were you yesterday morning?*

89

7.3 Where were you last New Year's Eve?

1 Reading

A Which cities do the photos illustrate? What can you see in them?

The Opera House. That's in Sydney.

B ▶ 7.7 Who has good memories of New Year's Eve last year? Who doesn't? Read and write + or - next to what each person says. Listen to check.

New Year's Eve around the world

Billions of people globally welcome New Year's Eve with spectacular celebrations. How was your last New Year's Eve?

It was awesome! Our city was the first place in the world to really celebrate the New Year. And, of course, the first babies of the year were born here!
Kerry, Gisbourne, New Zealand.

Amazing! I'll never forget it. This was my first year in Sydney. There were fantastic fireworks, and there were hundreds of boats on the water!
Dave, Sydney, Australia.

It was cold! The music was good, but there were so many people along the River Thames! And there were no restrooms near us, so we didn't stay long!
Kirsty, London, England.

I was at the concert at the pyramids of Giza. It was magical! Incredible to think they're nearly 5,000 years old!
Habibah, Cairo, Egypt.

There were thousands of lights on the Eiffel Tower. It was absolutely beautiful!
Sabine, Paris, France.

It wasn't too good. I don't really like fireworks. But I was with a big group of friends. We were all asleep by 12:30!
Lindsey, Los Angeles, the U.S.

It was just like every other day. It wasn't really very special. The family was all together, and dinner was delicious, but it always is. My brother is a chef.
Larry, Santiago, Chile.

There were tons of confetti falling on Times Square. It was a fabulous sight. The snow was beautiful, too, but too many people, and all the trash on the streets wasn't very nice.
Kevin, New York, the U.S.

It was my birthday. It was New Year's Eve and then suddenly I was 12, too! Wonderful!
Jodie, Berlin, Germany.

Fantastic! I was on the beach all night. There was dancing, and then there was a terrific sunrise. Beautiful colors!
Luís, Guadalajara, Mexico.

C Answer the questions.

Who ...
1 was cold?
2 was on the beach?
3 was a child?
4 doesn't like fireworks?

Where ...
1 were the first babies born?
2 was there music along the river?
3 were there a lot of boats?
4 was there confetti?

D 🔲 **Make it personal** What happens in your town or city on New Year's Eve? In pairs, imagine you were together last year. Write a post to the website.

Traditionally here, people eat 12 grapes at midnight.

2 Listening

A ▶ 7.8 Where's the mouse? Listen. Match mice 1–10 to the prepositions.

- [ ] **ab**ove the TV
- [ ] **across from** the people
- [ ] **be**hind the TV
- [ ] **be**tween the sofa and the table
- [ ] **in front of** the TV
- [ ] **in** the bed
- [ ] **in** the box
- [ ] **next to** the sofa
- [ ] **on** the bed
- [ ] **un**der the table

🎵 *But here I am, Next to you, The sky's more blue, in Malibu.*

7.3

B ▶ 7.9 Listen to the couple and circle the seven mice they mention in the picture in **A**.

C ▶ 7.9 Listen again. Draw the mouse's new route on the picture. Describe the route to your partner using the phrases in **A**.

First, the mouse was under the table. Then it was ...

D 🙂 **Make it personal** In pairs, follow these steps.
1 A: Say where the mouse is.   B: Point to the correct picture.
2 A: Point to a picture.   B: Describe where the mouse is.
3 Close books and remember!

It's on the ...

💬 **Common mistakes**

I don't like the ~~mouses~~ *mice*.
mice = irregular plural, like *women*, *men* and *people*

3 Grammar Prepositions of place

A Read and complete the grammar box. Which are opposites? Mime one to test a partner.

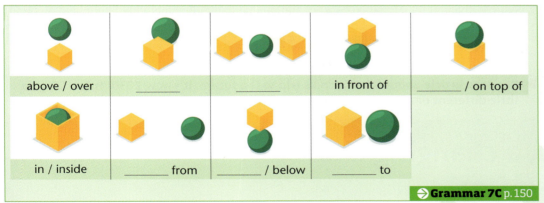

| above / over | _____ | _____ | in front of | _____ / on top of |
| in / inside | _____ from | _____ / below | _____ to | |

➡ **Grammar 7C** p.150

B In pairs, say where these items are in **2A**. Test each other with more items, too.
1 the pillow / sofa   3 the fruit / table   5 the CDs / TV
2 the plant / TV   4 the picture / TV   6 the bed / chairs

The pillow is on the sofa.

C 🙂 **Make it personal** Play a memory game in pairs. You each need five personal objects.
A: Close your eyes.   B: Move an object.
A: Look and say where the object was and where it is now.

The ... was next to the ... but now it's under the ...

Hmm ... Where was the ...? Now it's between ...

There was a ... in front of ... It wasn't behind ...

7.4 Was your hometown different 10 years ago?

1 Vocabulary Dates

A ▶ 7.10 Listen to and number the dates in the order you hear them. Then circle the correct options.

We say years like 1980 and 2017 as **two / three** numbers. For 2019, you can also say two **thousand / thousands** nineteen.

B ▶ 7.11 Listen to Núria describe her hometown. Write the dates.

I was born in Barcelona in _____. The city was very different then. In my neighborhood, there were a lot of old buildings and factories. Until _____, there were only two coffee shops (we call them "bars"), and there were no other restaurants on my street. By _____, the neighborhood was a little different, and by _____, there were many new businesses. Now it's _____, and there are families from all over the world. You can enjoy food from many countries, too!

C  **Make it personal** In pairs, describe a real or imaginary city on three different dates.

> It was very different. In ..., there was ...

2 Reading

A Is this photo of San Diego, California, from 1990 or 2018? In pairs, give three reasons. Which is the most convincing?

> I think it's 2018. There are a lot of tall buildings.

B Read the article about Bill Watson's trip to the future. It's now 2030! Is San Diego a little different or a lot different from his last visit? Does he like the city now?

San Diego, a changing city

by Bill Watson

As I arrive at my hotel in downtown San Diego in 2030, I am shocked. I was last here in 2018, and the city is very different. I almost think I'm in the wrong place!

Like many American cities, there has been urban renewal, and the downtown area has been renovated. It wasn't very nice when I was here in 1990, but, by 2018, visitors were able to enjoy good food, music and theater, or even a baseball game at Petco Park. Now, in 2030, the neighborhood near my favorite hotel is completely transformed!

There are new roads, a park, and new traffic lights. There wasn't so much traffic in 2018, but now traffic lights on every corner are essential. There were some good grocery stores downtown before, but now there are three new ones on my block where you can send your robot to do the shopping. And there's more! When I was here in 2018, there was a movie theater next to the bank. I went there often. But now, there's an enormous movie complex with six large theaters! And there are security cameras everywhere, but there weren't any in 2018. Maybe that's because there's a new school across from the movie complex. In 2018, there weren't any schools in this area.

My recommendation: This is a great city! Beautiful weather, clean, too, and there are a lot more cars in Los Angeles!

C ▶ 7.12 Read the article again and complete the chart about the neighborhood near Bill's hotel. Listen to check.

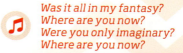

Was it all in my fantasy?
Where are you now?
Were you only imaginary?
Where are you now?

7.4

Back then, 2018	Today, 2030
1 There _____ so much traffic.	There _____ a lot of _____ lights.
2 There _____ some good grocery stores.	There are _____ new ones on the block.
3 There _____ a movie theater _____ _____ the bank.	There _____ a movie complex with _____ theaters.
4 There _____ no _____ cameras.	There are a lot of _____ cameras.
5 There _____ any _____ in the area.	There _____ a _____ across from the _____ _____.

D 🗣 **Make it personal** Imagine that you live in San Diego in 2030. In pairs, say which city you prefer, San Diego in 2018 or San Diego in 2030.

San Diego was great in 2018. It was so quiet!   *Yes, but there were no ...*

③ Listening

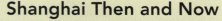

Shanghai Then and Now

A In pairs, use the photos of Shanghai, China, in 1992 and 2018 to find two things that are the same and two that are different.

There is a big lake in both photos.

B ▶ 7.13 Listen to a conversation about Shanghai then and now. Which changes are mentioned that you can see in the photos in **A**?

C ▶ 7.13 Listen again. Complete the chart on Shanghai. Write + (*a lot*), – (*not much / many*), or a number.

	1990	Today
Traffic		
Population		
Pollution		
Tall buildings		
Famous sights		

⚠ **Common mistakes**

There were ~~much~~ *many* more low buildings.

I/born in Quito. *was*

D 🗣 **Make it personal** Find out about your own city or town.
1 Google your hometown or another place you're interested in. Find five ways it was different 20 years ago. (Try to read online texts in English!)
2 In pairs, describe the changes. Mime what you can't express in English.
3 Share your information with the class. Who found the most interesting changes?

Twenty years ago, Curitiba was / wasn't very clean / big / busy.

There was / were / wasn't / weren't a lot of malls / traffic / people.

93

7.5 Do you enjoy weddings?

Skills Predicting from context

A Match the events to photos 1–5. What do you know about the five events?

☐ The 1985 Live Aid Concert   ☐ Prince Harry and Meghan Markle's wedding in 2018
☐ The 1970 World Cup   ☐ The 2016 Olympic Games in Rio
☐ The first Oscars in 1929

B ▶7.14 Read and listen to check your answers to **A**.

Dream tickets

It was at the Hollywood Roosevelt Hotel in Los Angeles, California, on May 16, 1929, and was a private dinner with 36 tables, and only 270 people. Believe it or not, tickets were only $5. Actors and actresses arrived at the hotel in luxury cars, and there were many fans waiting to greet them. It was not on radio or television. Douglas Fairbanks, president of the Academy of Motion Picture Arts and Sciences, was the host, and the ceremony was just 15 minutes long.

There were 600 people at the "small" ceremony and reception, but 1,200 guests came to greet the happy couple at Windsor Castle. An incredible 18 million people watched the event live on TV in the UK and 29 million in the U.S. The location of the honeymoon was secret!

It was the first World Cup in North America and the first outside South America or Europe. The Brazilian team were fantastic. Brazil beat Italy 4–1 in the final. It really was a great competition – the third World Cup victory for Brazil. It was Pelé's fourth and final World Cup. Pelé is about 80 years old now, but he's still considered the best player of all time.

This spectacular charity event was organized to raise money for the terrible famine in Ethiopia. There were two simultaneous concerts, one at Wembley Stadium in London, the other at JFK Stadium in Philadelphia. There were 72,000 people at the concert in London, and 100,000 in Philadelphia. On the same day, the event also inspired concerts in Australia and Germany. About 1.9 billion people, in 150 countries, watched it all live on TV. Artists included Queen, U2, David Bowie, and Paul McCartney.

C Cover the text. Uncover only line 1 and guess the word that comes next. Uncover line 2 to check, then guess the first word in line 3. Continue like this until the end. How many of your guesses were right?

D ▶7.15 *Race the Beep!* Listen to 12 numbers from the text in **B**. You have only 10 seconds to find the number and say what event it refers to.

E 🗣 **Make it personal** In pairs, follow these steps. Then change roles.
- **A:** Imagine you were at one of the events. How was it? Tell your partner. You can add any information you want!
- **B:** Ask your partner questions. What do you want to know?

I was at the … It was amazing! There was a lot of great music and dancing.

Were there a lot of people?

⚠ **Common mistakes**
million
two ~~millions of~~ people

7.5 How about a barbecue on Sunday?

This is an invitation across the nation, A chance for folks to meet, There'll be Dancing in the streets.

ID in Action Making invitations

A Read the invitations. What kind of event is each one for?

B ▶ 7.16 Listen and match conversations 1–6 to invitations a–f.
1 ____ 2 ____ 3 ____ 4 ____ 5 ____ 6 ____

C ▶ 7.16 Listen again and choose the expression you hear. Is the person making an invitation (M), accepting an invitation (A), or refusing an invitation (R)?
1 Can you and Sandy come? / Do you and Sandy want to come?
2 Sure. Sounds good. / Sure. Sounds great.
3 I'm sorry. We already have plans. / I'm sorry. We can't.
4 Great. I'd love to. / Sounds great.
5 Are you free on Friday? / Can you come on Friday?
6 Of course we can! What time? / Yes, we can! What time?

D 🗨 **Make it personal** In pairs, imagine an event and write the invitation. Go around the class and invite others. Note if they accept or refuse. Who has the most people going to their event?

We're having a Halloween party next weekend. Can you and your partner come?

We'd love to! What time?

Common mistakes

I'm going
~~I go~~ to a wedding this weekend.

I'm taking
Sorry, I can't go. ~~I go take~~ my mom to the hospital.
Use the present continuous, NOT the simple present for future plans.

Writing 7 An online review

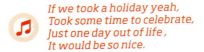

*If we took a holiday yeah,
Took some time to celebrate,
Just one day out of life,
It would be so nice.*

A Read the ad and underline the positive features of this city-center apartment.

Beautiful luxury apartment, with garage.
👤 2 guests 📶 Wi-Fi 🚗 Parking

Ideal for a weekend city break. In quiet location, only 10 minutes from city center and close to transportation. All modern conveniences, including superfast Wi-Fi, well-equipped kitchen, terrace with great views. Sheets and towels provided. $300 per night for two people.

B Read the review and circle the features in the ad that weren't good or weren't true.

Review by Alisha2001
🟢⚪⚪⚪⚪

Apartment sounds great, but was terrible – don't stay there!

My mom and I wanted a relaxing city break, but we were very disappointed. Yes, it's beautiful inside, but …

The first problem was car parking – the garage is over 100 meters away across a busy street!

Secondly, the ad says "close to transportation." That's true – kind of! There was a huge highway in front of the building, and a busy subway station at the back, too! Also, the apartment was not 10 minutes from the city center. Walking fast, it was over 30 minutes.

Then there were the "modern conveniences." There was a refrigerator and a microwave but no dishwasher or washing machine ... not even a toaster! Plus, the sheets weren't clean, and the Wi-Fi was really slow.

Finally, there was the noise. Unbelievable! Thousands of cars, and trains passing all night so we never opened the terrace doors!

C Read **Write it right!** and underline the connectors in the text in **B**.

> ✅ **Write it right!**
>
> In a review, start with a statement summarizing your feelings / opinion. Use connectors to:
> - sequence – *the first problem was, secondly, another thing was, then there was / were, finally.*
> - add information – *also, too, plus.*

D Use connectors from **Write it right!** to complete the review. Circle the eight problems.

My friends and I rented a camper van from ZZ Rentals last weekend – it was a disaster!

(1) _____ there was no record of our reservation.
(2) _____, there was only one very small camper available, so we had to take that.
(3) _____, because it was so small, there was no bathroom, and there wasn't a kitchen. It was (4) _____ dirty, and we had to ask for clean towels and sheets
(5) _____, when these were supposed to be included.
(6) _____ the insurance. There was an extra $100 per person to pay because we were all under 24. (7) _____, there was a deposit of $1,000 in case of damage!
(8) _____, when we were on the road, we realized there was no gas in the tank! I will never rent a camper van from this company again.

E 🎧 **Make it personal** Write a review of a bad experience at a hotel, in a restaurant, or on vacation.

Before	Use ideas from **B** and **D**, or your own experience.
While	Use a variety of connectors.
After	Check your review carefully and exchange it with a partner. Think of two questions to ask your partner about their experience.

7 House rules

 Café

1 Before watching

A 🔴 **Make it personal** In pairs, describe your home. Find six differences.

> Bea lives in a new apartment block, but I live in an old house.

B Match photos 1–5 to these words.
- ☐ an**ti**que furniture
- ☐ an **a**ttic
- ☐ a **ce**llar
- ☐ an indoor pool
- ☐ a lake house

C Complete 1–6 with the prepositions.

at behind in in front of next to on

1 August has a computer _____ his lap.
2 Andrea has a cell phone _____ her hand.
3 August's sitting _____ Andrea on the sofa.
4 The window's _____ the sofa.
5 Andrea and August are _____ home.
6 The sofa's _____ the window.

2 While watching

A Check (✓) the correct answer.
1 Andrea says they'll be the best ever …
  ☐ students ☐ owners ☐ renters.
2 Andrea and August are going to a lake house …
  ☐ on the ocean ☐ in the mountains
  ☐ on the beach.

B Check (✓) or correct all the rules they mention.
1 Don't sit on the furniture in the huge sitting room.
2 Don't go in the cellar.
3 You cannot go in the attic.
4 You can sleep in the master bedroom.
5 Don't swim in the lake.
6 Absolutely no parties.

C True (T) or False (F)? Correct the false sentences.
1 There are ten rules on the list.
2 August's status update doesn't mention the party.
3 Daniel says "My holiday is over."
4 Lucy says she'll clean the downstairs bedroom.
5 Andrea is sad because now they can't go to the beach.
6 Daniel says he'll put the dining room furniture back and **va**cuum.

3 After watching

A In pairs, describe the photo. Then complete 1–6 with was(n't) / were(n't).

> Three of them are sleeping. Andrea is …

1 It obviously _____ a small, quiet party.
2 There _____ probably a lot of people there.
3 There _____ probably a lot of food and drink.
4 Lucy _____ at the party, but Genevieve _____.
5 After the party, everyone except Andrea _____ sleeping.
6 All the rooms _____ very messy.

B Order the events, 1–6.
- ☐ The cleaning crew arrives.
- ☐ The crew goes upstairs.
- ☐ August sends an email to someone.
- ☐ August says he is selling his car.
- ☐ Everyone goes to the beach.
- ☐ They all start cleaning except August.

C 🔴 **Make it personal** In pairs, describe the last party you went to. Were your parties similar?

> My last party was at a hotel. It was my cousin's 15th birthday.

97

8

8.1 When did you start school?

1 Reading

A Name someone famous from the past. Your partner says something they know about that person. If they are correct, they get a point. Take turns.

Pablo Picasso. *He was an artist. I think he was Spanish.* *That's right!*

B ▶8.1 Match pictures 1–10 to a–j. Complete with *in*, *to*, or ⊘. Listen to check.

a marry _____ him
b learn how _____ tattoo
c want _____ go out with her
d stop _____ work (n.)
e be born _____ 1877
f die _____ 1961
g work _____ the circus
h agree _____ see him
i start _____ tattoo lessons at nine
j study _____ hard

C ▶8.2 Read and listen to Maud's biography. What were her two professions?

MAUD STEVENS WAGNER Famous … as a tattoo artist!

Maud Stevens was born in 1877 in Kansas in the United States. She was a circus performer who **worked** in the circus for many years, but that's not all. She was also a tattoo artist, the very first female tattoo artist in the U.S.

In 1909, Maud **married** Gus Wagner, who was a tattoo artist, too. His body was completely covered – there were tattoos all over it! When Gus first **wanted** to go out with Maud, she **didn't want** to go out with him. She only **agreed** to see him in exchange for a tattoo lesson. Maud **studied** hard, and soon she **learned** how to tattoo.

Maud **didn't stop** working in the circus, but she **covered** her body with tattoos. Soon, everyone wanted a tattoo from Maud. Maud and Gus's daughter Lotteva **started** tattoo lessons when she was only nine years old. They **toured** the U.S., giving tattoos to people everywhere. Finally, they **moved** to Lawton, Oklahoma, where Maud **died** in 1961 at the age of 84.

D ▶8.2 Write the verbs in the correct group, according to the pronunciation of their *-ed* endings. Read and listen again to check. Any surprises?

| agreed | covered | died | learned | married | moved |
| started | studied | toured | wanted | worked | |

/t/	/d/	/ɪd/
stopped	*lived*	*needed*

Common mistakes

/askt/
I asked /ˈaskɪd/ my teacher a question.

E In pairs, decide if 1–5 are True (T) or False (F). Then cover each paragraph in turn, and remember all you can from it.
1 Gus was a tattoo artist, but he didn't have any tattoos.
2 Maud wanted to go out with Gus, but Gus didn't want to go out with Maud.
3 She didn't learn how to tattoo before she married him.
4 Maud and Gus's daughter Lotteva didn't learn how to tattoo.
5 There were no female tattoo artists in the U.S. in 1877.

So wake me up when it's all over,
when I'm wiser and I'm older.
All this time I was finding myself,
And I didn't know I was lost.

8.1

Common mistakes

~~worked~~
Maud ~~work~~ in many places.
~~didn't live~~
She ~~no lived~~ in Mexico.

F 🙂 **Make it personal** Choose a famous person from the past. Research their life and write five sentences about them. Share your information with a partner.

> Avicii was a Swedish musician, DJ, and record producer. He died in Oman in 2018 when he was only 28. He didn't have any children. I loved his music, especially "Wake Me Up" and "Hey Brother".

2 Grammar Simple past regular verbs ➕ and ➖

A Complete the grammar box. Does the simple past in your language have more or fewer forms?

> Study the bold verbs in Maud's biography (and the negative verbs in **1E**). Complete the rules.
> 1 Positive and negative forms have **more than one / only one** form for all persons.
> 2 For negatives, use **doesn't / don't / didn't** + the infinitive.
> 3 To form the simple past tense:
>   the usual ending is _____.
>   when a verb ends in -e (agree, live, like), add only _____.
>   when a verb ends in -y (study, marry), change the y to _____ and add _____.
> 4 For positive -ed endings, there are three possible pronunciations: /t/, /d/, or /_____/.
>   The most common is _____.
>   Only add an extra syllable for -ed endings with verbs ending in the letters d and t.
>
> ➡ **Grammar 8A** p. 152

B ▶8.3 Write the simple past verbs. Then listen to information about the Mexican painter Frida Kahlo, and match the information to the dates.

1928	_was born_ in Coyoacán, Mexico City (**be born**)
1907	_____ in Casa Azul with her family (**live**)
1920s and 1930s	_____ to be a doctor (**want**)
1954	_____ to be a painter after a bus accident (**decide**)
1907 to 1928	_____ Diego Rivera, the world famous muralist (**marry**)
before 1925	_____ to the U.S. (**travel**), and _____ a unique style (**develop**)
childhood to 1954	_____ her entire life, and was famous for her self-portraits (**paint**)
1925	_____ in bed at the Casa Azul in Mexico City (**die**)

C ▶8.3 Listen again. Choose the correct answer.
Frida **enjoyed / didn't enjoy** her time in the U.S., but she **liked / didn't like** some aspects of American society. She **didn't travel / traveled** outside North America.

D In pairs, take turns telling Frida's story. Try to help each other with pronunciation.

E 🙂 **Make it personal** Write your own short biography using six of these verbs. Tell your story to the class.

| be born | decide | learn | live | marry | move | start | study | travel | work |

> I was born in Bogotá, Colombia. I lived there for five years before we moved to Baranquilla. I started school in 2009.

99

8.2 Did you go out last weekend?

a

b

c

d

e

f

1 Listening

A In pairs, guess which question goes with each picture.
How was your …?

| day off | day yesterday | summer | Sunday | Thanksgiving | weekend |

I think "How was your day off?" is "b."   *Really? I think it's "e."*

B ▶8.4 Listen and complete 1–6 with the words in **A**. Match them to the correct picture.

1 **A:** How was your _____ _____?
   B: Oh, perfect! I didn't do much. I **took** it easy and I **read** my book.
2 **A:** How was your _____ _____?
   B: I **slept** late. Then I **made** brunch and **had** a good time with my friends.
3 **A:** How was your _____?
   B: Great! My sister and her family **came** over, and we **ate** a lot!
4 **A:** How was your _____?
   B: Slow! I **didn't get up** until midday. Then I **met** some friends, and we **saw** a movie.
5 **A:** How was your _____?
   B: Fantastic! We **got up** late every day and then we **went** to the beach.
6 **A:** How was your _____?
   B: Saturday, I **went** shopping and **bought** some new jeans. I **did** chores all day Sunday.

C ▶8.5 Listen to the pronunciation of 14 common past tense irregular verbs and repeat.

buy – bought /ɔ/   go – went /ɛ/   say – said /ɛ/
come – came /eɪ/   have – had /æ/   see – saw /ɔ/
do – did /ɪ/   know – knew /u:/   take – took /ʊ/
get – got /ɑ/   make – made /eɪ/   think – thought /ɔ/
give – gave /eɪ/   meet – met /ɛ/

D 🎤 **Make it personal** Tell the class at least two things you did last weekend.

I met some friends and we decided to go to a nightclub. We had a great night.

2 Grammar Simple past irregular verbs ⊕ and ⊖

A Complete the grammar box.

1 Complete the sentences with the simple past ⊕ form of the verbs in parentheses.

	Subject	Verb	
1	I		my homework last night. (**do**)
2	You		me a really nice gift. (**give**)
3	He		really late after his final exam. (**sleep**)
4	She		good-bye at the airport. (**say**)
5	We		your parents at the mall. (**meet**)
6	They		some expensive clothes last weekend. (**buy**)

In the simple past, ⊕ irregular verbs only have one form for all persons.

2 Complete the rule for ⊖ sentences.
We saw Vero but she **didn't see** us.   Leo **didn't play** soccer because he **didn't feel** well.
Use the auxiliary _____ + infinitive for ⊖ regular and irregular simple past verbs.

➡ **Grammar 8B** p. 152

⚠ **Common mistakes**
~~have~~
We didn't ~~had~~ a class yesterday.

100

B Complete Laura's email to her friend Barbara with the simple past form of these verbs. Use each verb only once.

buy · come · get up · give · go ⊕ · go ⊖
know · make · meet · relax · see · sleep

🎵 *I knew it when I met him, I loved him when I left him. Got me feelin' like, ooh, and then I had to tell him, I had to go, Havana.*

8.2

To: **Barbara**
Subject: Hello!
Monday at 09:23

Hi Barbara,

How was your weekend? Mine was pretty good! Saturday I _____ _____ early and _____ shopping downtown with my brother. You _____ him at my party, remember? I _____ some new sandals, and I'm wearing them now! Then we _____ a really good movie. In the evening, my old school friend, Bill, _____ over, and I _____ dinner. And guess what? He _____ me a gift! I _____ he liked me! I _____ to the beach Sunday because I _____ until noon, and then it started raining ☹. So, I just _____ at home. Perfect!

Call me! Let's get together soon.

Laura xx

⚠ **Common mistakes**

Did you know my father?
                     met
Not really. I only ~~knew~~ him once.

C 😀 **Make it personal** List three things you did yesterday. Go around the class. Find at least two people who did the same things.

💬 *I ate pizza yesterday.* 💬 *Me, too!* 💬 *Oh, I ate fish.*

③ Vocabulary Ordinal numbers

A ▶ 8.6 In pairs, read the rules and practice saying the dates. Listen to check.

June 1st, 1996   March 2nd, 2001   December 3rd, 2018
February 4th, 1988   May 5th, 2016   August 6th, 2005
September 7th, 1803   January 8th, 1943   July 9th, 1994

> 1–3 are irregular: *first*, *second*, *third*. Other numbers add *-th*: *fourth*, *fifth*, *sixteenth*.
> Over 20: *twenty-first*, *thirty-seventh*.

B Add three family members to the chart. In pairs, share your information.

	Born on	Died on
My great grandmother	October 14th, 1861	April 3rd, 1961

💬 *My great grandmother was born on October 14th, 1861, and died on April 3rd, 1961.*

💬 *Wow! She was nearly 100 years old!*

C 😀 **Make it personal** Make a class birthday line. Which month and date have the most birthdays?

1. Stand up and ask "When's your birthday?" to form a class birthday line, from January 1st to December 31st.
2. Tell five classmates what you did on your last birthday. Any unusual celebrations?

💬 *What did you do on your last birthday?* 💬 *I had a big party.* 💬 *Lucky you! I didn't do anything special.*

⚠ **Common mistakes**

Miley Cyrus was born in 1992, ~~in~~ November 23rd.
on

101

8.3 Where did you go on your last vacation?

1 Grammar Simple past questions and short answers

A ▶8.7 In pairs, make sure you know the simple past of these verbs. Listen to the conversation, then complete David's blog about his vacation.

| be | drink | eat | go | have | meet | see | stay | take | travel | visit | walk |

On my last vacation, my girlfriend and I _traveled_ to Ilha Grande – that's Big Island in English! We _____ by car and then _____ the ferry. There are no cars there, so we _____ a lot! The island's incredible, the forest is really beautiful, and the smell of nature is absolutely fantastic. We _____ lots of beautiful beaches, too, and I _____ three dolphins! We _____ fresh fish every day. It _____ very hot, so I _____ a lot of cold soda, too! We _____ in a tiny hotel right across from the beach, and _____ some cool tourists from Argentina. We _____ a wonderful time, and I can't wait to go back.

B ▶8.7 Listen again. Which word is missing in these questions? How is it pronounced? Now complete the grammar box.

How _____ you get there?   What _____ you do?
What _____ you eat?   _____ you stay in a hotel?

Yes / No questions (ASI)

Auxiliary	Subject	Infinitive
Did	you	enjoy your vacation?
	she	go to Brazil?
	we	buy water?
	they	have a car there?

Short answers

	Subject	Auxiliary
Yes,	I	did.
	she	
No,	we	didn't.
	they	

Wh- questions (QASI)

Question word	Auxiliary	Subject	Infinitive
When	_____	you	go?
What	did	he	see?
Where	_____	she	stay?
	did	we	eat dinner?

To form simple past questions, use the auxiliary _____ . To answer Yes / No questions, use _____ ➕ or _____ ➖.

➡ **Grammar 8C** p. 152

⚠ **Common mistakes**

~~did~~ go
Where /she ~~went~~?
She went to Miami.

C ▶8.8 Listen and point to the four questions you hear. Which has more emphasis – _did you_ or the verb after it?

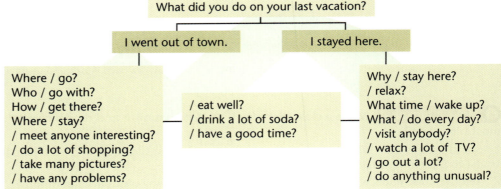

💬 What did you do on your last vacation?

💬 I traveled. / I stayed at home.

D 🔵 Make it personal In pairs, ask and answer about your last vacation.

102

② Reading

Oops, I did it again. I played with your heart, got lost in the game. Oh baby, baby.

8.3

A Quickly read a radio show interview and put the pictures a–e in order 1–5.

A BAD TRAVEL EXPERIENCE? Not really!

Travel the World: Next call, please.
Ms. Riggs: Hi! My name's Pamela Riggs.
TtW: Hi, Ms. Riggs. So, can you tell us about a bad experience you had on a trip?
Ms. R: Well, I don't usually have big problems on my trips, but here's an interesting story for you. Two years ago, I went to Turkey. It's a fantastic country – half European, half Asian!
TtW: Yes, it's amazing. Who did you go with?
Ms. R: Nobody. It was a business trip. Anyway, I got to Istanbul airport early in the morning, and I had a connection to Cappadocia, but the airline canceled the flight because of bad weather.
TtW: Really?
Ms. R: Yes, there was no flight until the next day!
TtW: Oh no! And what did you do?
Ms. R: Well … at first, I just cried! But then I saw a familiar face. It was Semir, my lovely neighbor from New York!
TtW: That's an incredible coincidence! What did he say?
Ms. R: He said, "I also had a ticket on that flight. But I need to get to Cappadocia tonight, so I rented a car. Do you want to come with me?"
TtW: So did you accept his offer?
Ms. R: Of course! But the trip took us around 13 hours.
TtW: But why did it take so long?
Ms. R: Well, Cappadocia is about 740 kilometers from Istanbul by car. And Semir knew the way very well, so we stopped a few times, and I saw some really interesting places. We also had a delicious Turkish meal at a fantastic restaurant in Ankara. We ate and talked for hours. It was great!
TtW: Wow … So the airline canceled the flight, but your trip to Cappadocia wasn't bad after all.
Ms. R: Not at all. On the contrary, I thought it was fantastic! It was one of the best trips of my life. And, um … I don't think I told you, I'm now married to Semir. Thanks to that bad weather!

B ▶8.9 Read and listen to the interview, and then complete 1–5 with two words. Do you know of any similar travel stories with a happy ending?

1. She arrived in Istanbul to _get a_ flight.
2. She cried because the airline _____ the _____ to Cappadocia.
3. Semir _____ a ticket for the same _____.
4. The trip to Cappadocia took around _____ _____.
5. She _____ a delicious Turkish _____ with Semir in Ankara.

C Circle the past tense verbs in the interview. In pairs, think of five past tense questions to ask Pamela Riggs in an interview.

Common mistakes
~~She arrived to the hotel late.~~ → *at*
She arrived at the hotel late.

D 👤 **Make it personal** In pairs, role-play the interview with Pamela Riggs.

> So, Ms. Riggs, where did you go for this trip?   I went to Turkey.   I see. Did you fly to the capital, Ankara?

③ Pronunciation *Did you*

A ▶8.10 Read the explanation. Then listen to six questions. Are they present or past? Compare in pairs. Then listen again to check.

> In rapid, informal speech, *did you* is often pronounced /dʒə/, but *do you* is pronounced /dəjə/. Can you hear the difference?

1. Where did you go?
2. Do you watch a lot of TV?
3. Did you relax?
4. Where did you stay?
5. Do you eat well?
6. When did you go on vacation?

B 👤 **Make it personal** In pairs. **A:** tell B about a trip. **B:** ask questions about it using *do / did you*. Then change roles.

> Last year I went to see my grandmother.   Oh, when did you go?

103

8.4 When do you listen to music?

1 Listening

A ▶8.11 Listen to an interview with Jay De La Fuente, a young songwriter. Order his actions yesterday 1–13.

- [1] He got up at about 6 o'clock.
- [ ] He took a shower.
- [ ] He played the keyboard and wrote a song.
- [ ] He ate breakfast.
- [ ] He answered 30 emails.
- [ ] He brushed his teeth.
- [ ] He had lunch.
- [ ] He turned on the computer.
- [ ] He ran a mile.
- [ ] He answered the rest of the emails.
- [ ] He went to sleep.
- [ ] He went to visit friends.
- [ ] He made coffee.

B ▶8.11 Listen again. In pairs, try to remember Jay's day.

What was the first thing he did? — *He got up at about 6 o'clock.* — *What did he do next?*

C ▶8.12 Listen to excerpts and number the "How to sound impressed" phrases in the order you hear them, 1–4.

D 🎤 **Make it personal** Interview role-play. **A**: interview **B**, a famous person, about yesterday. Sound very impressed! Then change roles. Who has the funniest interview?

What did you do first yesterday? — *I got up at about 5 o'clock.* — *Wow! So early. That's amazing!*

How to sound impressed
- [ ] You're kidding! That's incredible.
- [ ] Wow! That's amazing.
- [ ] That's fantastic!
- [ ] That's great!

2 Grammar Subject questions vs. object questions

A ▶8.13 How much do you know about music? Take the ID Pop Quiz and find out!

B ▶8.14 Listen to check. How many did you get right?

C Complete the grammar box. Choose the correct options. Is your language similar?

Object questions (QASI)

Who	does	Jay	live with?	He lives alone.
What	did	he	say?	He said he loves his job.
Where	did	he	go?	To a friend's house.

Subject questions (QV)

Who	sings	that song?	Michael Jackson.
Who	wrote	it?	Michael Jackson.
What	happened to	him?	He died in 2009.

1 In **subject** / **object** questions, you know the subject and want information about the action.
2 In **subject** / **object** questions, you know the action and want to discover who or what is responsible.
3 **Subject** / **Object** questions need an auxiliary.
4 Quiz questions 1-8 are **subject** / **object** questions.

➡ **Grammar 8D** p. 152

⚠ Common mistakes

What ~~did~~ happen^(ed) on Sunday?
What ~~said~~^(did) our teacher ~~?~~^(say?)

🎵 *Right now, I'm in a state of mind I wanna be in like all the time, Ain't got no tears left to cry.*

8.4

🆔 Pop Quiz

1. Who sold more than 100 million records and recorded the most songs?
   a Elvis Presley
   b The Beatles
   c Michael Jackson

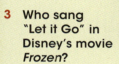

2. Who became the first artist to surpass 50 billion streams worldwide in 2018?
   a Drake
   b Coldplay
   c Justin Bieber

3. Who sang "Let it Go" in Disney's movie *Frozen*?
   a Celine Dion
   b Idina Menzel
   c Demi Lovato

4. Who wrote the first rap song to win an Oscar?
   a Eminem with "Lose Yourself"
   b Kanye West with "Stronger"
   c Jay-Z with "Run this Town"

5. Who made a massively popular music video in which the singer(s) walk and sing in the street, wearing colored suits?
   a Mark Ronson and Bruno Mars
   b Ed Sheeran
   c Maroon 5

6. Who had the first song in Spanish to surpass a billion views on YouTube?
   a Ricky Martin ("Livin' la Vida Loca")
   b Enrique Iglesias ("Bailando")
   c Luis Fonsi featuring Daddy Yankee and Justin Bieber ("Despacito")

7. Who was born when and where? Match the singer to their birthday and birth place.
   a Ariana Grande
   b Justin Bieber
   c Rihanna
   d Shawn Mendes

   • March 1st 1994; London, Canada
   • February 20th, 1988; St. Michael, Barbados
   • August 8th 1998; Toronto, Canada
   • June 26th 1993; Florida, the U.S.

8. Who didn't sing at President Barack Obama's inaugurations?
   a Beyoncé
   b Kelly Clarkson
   c Lady Gaga

9. Where did Reggaeton begin in the late 1990s?
   a Brazil
   b Colombia
   c Puerto Rico

10. What did Bob Marley say to his son, Ziggy, just before he died?
    a "Love one another"
    b "No woman, no cry"
    c "Money can't buy life"

D In pairs, take turns asking and answering subject and object questions about facts 1–5.

INTERESTING FACTS!
1. _____ landed on the moon in _____.
2. _____ directed *The Shape of Water* in _____.
3. _____ won their second soccer World Cup in Russia in _____.
4. _____ became U.S. President again in 2012.
5. _____ won five gold medals and one silver medal at the Rio Olympic Games in _____.

Answers: 1 Neil Armstrong / 1969 2 Guillermo del Toro / 2018 3 France / 2018 4 Barack Obama 5 Michael Phelps / 2016

Who landed on the moon in … I think … 1968?   *No, it was 1969, and I think it was Buzz Aldrin and ….*

E 🟢 **Make it personal** In groups, write five questions for a class quiz. Include at least three subject questions. Exchange with another group and take their quiz. Which group got more answers right?

Which driver won the 2018 Formula One Championship?

8.5 Can I use your phone?

Skills Understanding a story

Five common phone questions

1 I can't talk right now. Can I call you later?
2 Can I borrow your charger?
3 Can I use your phone? I left mine at home.
4 Is your phone working? I can't get a signal.
5 Can you tell me the Wi-Fi password, please?

A Do you remember the last time you asked 1–5?

I asked number 5 at a café last night.

B ▶8.15 Listen to the dialogue. Who's talking? Where are they? What's the problem?

C ▶8.15 Listen again and complete the dialogue. Predict what happens next.

Salesclerk: Hello, can I *help* you?
Customer: Yes, I _____ so. There's a _____ with my new phone.
Salesclerk: OK. I'll try to help. What _____ is the problem?
Customer: Well, I _____ to transfer the data and all my _____, but only _____ of them are here.
Salesclerk: Hmm … OK, _____ you have a _____ in the Cloud?
Customer: Yes, I _____ so.
Salesclerk: OK, just a _____ please.

D ▶8.16 Listen to the end of the dialogue. What does the customer do?

E In pairs, role-play the dialogue.
A: You're the salesclerk. B: You're the customer.

F ▶8.17 Number the pictures 1–5 to make a story. Then listen to check.

G ▶8.17 Listen again. What four questions does Mike ask Chris?

H 🗨 **Make it personal** Do you know any cell phone stories? Tell a story about something that happened to you or someone you know.

I left my cell phone in a taxi one day and …

8.5 Could you help me, please?

*Help! I need somebody,
Help! Not just anybody
Help! You know I need
someone, help!*

ID in Action Asking for favors

A ▶8.18 Match pictures 1–5 to favors a–e. Listen to five dialogues to check. Which favors did not happen?

 1
 2
 3
 4
 5

 a
 b
 c
 d
 e

B ▶8.18 Listen again and complete requests 1–7. Then match them to the responses.

Requests	Responses
1 Could you _____ who it _____?	☐ I'm really sorry. I have two parties to go to …
2 Could you _____ the _____ for me, please?	☐ Sure. There you go.
3 Can you please _____ the _____?	☐ Come on, I can do it tomorrow.
4 Could you please _____ the _____, Jim?	☐ Don't worry. I'll get it.
5 Could you _____ _____ this afternoon, please?	☐ Sorry, it's Brian's turn today.
6 Could I _____ you a _____?	☐ That de**pends**. What do you want?
7 Can _____ _____ my son with you this weekend?	☐ OK, I'll do it now.

Common mistakes

Could you ~~to~~ help me?
Could you ~~make~~ *do* me a favor?

C Read the requests and responses in B again and complete the rules with the words.

| can | could | 'll | will |

1 Use _____ or _____ to ask for favors. _____ is a little more polite.
2 Use _____ + verb for unplanned responses or decisions. The contraction is _____.

D 😊 **Make it personal** Role-play. **A:** Ask a favor 1–4. **B:** Respond and ask questions. Then change roles.
1 You're having a party next week, but you don't have any good music.
2 You can't read French, and you got an email from a customer in French.
3 You bought a new dog, but you're going away for the weekend.
4 You have to go to the airport really early tomorrow morning.

Hey, I'm having a party next week. Could you put some good music on my phone?

Sure, I'll do that, no problem. What type of music do you want?

107

Writing 8 A vacation message

*This is my message to you-ou-ou.
Singin' Don't worry about a thing.
'Cos every little thing gonna be alright.*

A Use the photos to guess where Tom went on vacation. Quickly read his email to check.

To: **Mom**
Subject: Hello!
Today at 16:03
All Mail

Hi Mom and Dad,

This is just a short email to tell you I'm OK. Monica and I are having a great time – there are so many things to do. The hotel is pretty basic, and there's no air-conditioning, but it's very cheap! The food's great, too – very hot and spicy! And the weather's excellent – it's much hotter than back home.

Last weekend, we visited a Buddhist temple in the jungle. We had to walk for two hours through the rainforest before we arrived. There were trees growing on the ruins and there were monkeys everywhere, too – it was beautiful. I took some fantastic photos – you can see them on my blog. After that, we rode an elephant – that was really cool.

Tomorrow, we plan to go kayaking in the bay – one of the most beautiful places in Vietnam … maybe the world! There are thousands of islands and secret beaches to explore – it's awesome and we're really excited!

Anyway, I have to go. Please say "Hi" to everyone, and don't forget to walk Toby!

Lots of love and see you soon,

Tom XXX

B Read again and answer 1–6.
1. Is their hotel comfortable?
2. What did Tom and Monica do last weekend?
3. Was it easy to get to the temple?
4. Did they see any animals?
5. How do Tom and Monica feel about kayaking tomorrow?
6. Who do you think Toby is?

C Which paragraphs answer 1–6? Complete the chart.
1. What are your plans for tomorrow?
2. What's the place / food / weather like?
3. Are you having fun?
4. What did you do before now? / How was it?
5. Where can we see your photos?
6. Do you have any other things to say?

Paragraph 1	Paragraph 2	Paragraph 3	Paragraph 4
		1	

D Read **Write it right!** How does Tom start and end his email? How does he start paragraphs 1 and 4? Underline five added comments.

> ✓ **Write it right!**
>
> Try to remember short phrases to start and end emails, or start paragraphs.
> Use — to add opinions or comments to a sentence.

E  **Make it personal** Write an email home in 150–180 words.

Before	Research a location for your vacation. Use the questions in **C** to help and imagine your answers.
While	Use starting and ending phrases, and write in paragraphs.
After	Check your email, then send it to a classmate to check again. Then send it to your teacher.

8 The favor

 Café

1 Before watching

A 🗣 **Make it personal** In pairs. Do friends sometimes ask you for favors? Do you ask, too? Any good stories?

> My friend asked me to help him with his homework.

B What's August doing? Then watch to check.
- [ ] He's waiting to be connected.
- [ ] He's listening to music.
- [ ] He's checking his voicemail.
- [ ] He's working on his in**ven**tion.

2 While watching

A Complete with the simple past of the verbs.

Genevieve: Hi, Rory. What's up?
Rory: Oh, hey, Genevieve. It's Rory. Oh, but right. You just _____ (say) ... Sorry, I _____ (not / know) you _____ my number. (have)
Genevieve: I'm a little busy here. Is there anything I can help you with?
Rory: August just _____ (call) me. He _____ (say) maybe you need help? With a music program or something?
Genevieve: Oh, I see. Yeah, I do need computer help.

B Order 1–7 to make sentences and questions. Some are two sentences / questions.
1. maybe / need / said / help / August / he / called / you / me / just
2. my / go / can't / I / day / there / it's / off
3. OK / anywhere / to / don't / you / need / go / it's
4. I / exercised / thanks / just / anyway / but
5. I / can / I / can / your / it / from / computer / here / fix / screen / and / see
6. weird / kind / of / sounds / safe / that / is / it
7. me / on / cup / and / your / first / coffee's / of

3 After watching

A Number the phrases in the order you hear them, 1–8.
- [ ] Call me back, OK?
- [ ] Could you do me a favor?
- [ ] Could you do something for me?
- [ ] He said maybe you need help?
- [ ] I need a favor.
- [ ] I really need your help.
- [ ] Is there anything I can help you with?
- [ ] What do you need me to do first?

B Who said it? August (A), Genevieve (G), or Rory (R)?

		A	G	R
1	Oh, sorry, yeah.			
2	Everything's fine.			
3	Tell her I'm sorry.			
4	Sounds simple!			
5	Put me on speaker phone.			
6	Oh, I see.			
7	What do you mean?			
8	That's all it was.			
9	Thank you so much.			
10	I really appreciate your help.			
11	You did me the favor!			

C Now check (✓) the things they did.

		A	G	R
1	asked for a favor			
2	called someone back			
3	fixed a computer			
4	listened to a voicemail message			
5	needed computer help			
6	thanked a friend			
7	didn't want to see Rory			

D In pairs, take turns asking and answering about what the characters did and said.

> Who said "..."?   Who asked ...?

E 🗣 **Make it personal** Help! Choose a situation and call a friend for help.
1. You don't know how to use your new phone.
2. You need a babysitter for tonight.
3. You're in bed sick with no food at home.
4. You have a job interview today and your best suit is dirty.

> David? Help! I have a big problem. Could you do me a favor?
>
> What is it Marta? How can I help?

109

R4 Grammar and vocabulary

A Picture dictionary. Cover the words on these pages and use the pictures to remember:

page	
86	9 rooms and 19 furniture words
88	15 party items
91	13 prepositions of place
97	5 more *house* words
98	10 verb phrases
103	Ms. Riggs' story
107	5 favors
159	16 picture words for lines 3 and 4 of consonants

B Circle the correct alternative to complete 1–7.
1. Forty years ago, _____ no cell phones.
   a there were b there was c was
2. How many people _____ at the party?
   a were they b there were c were there
3. It _____ my sister's birthday yesterday.
   a is b were c was
4. _____ you at school last week?
   a Are b Were c Was
5. When was she _____?
   a born b is born c was born
6. Who _____ the Mona Lisa?
   a did paint b painted c was painted
7. What _____ Leonardo da Vinci paint?
   a did b was c is

C Complete stories 1 and 2 using the simple past of the verbs in parentheses. In pairs, compare. Do you know any similar stories?

1 I love Beyoncé, so when I _____ (**read**) about a writing competition to win tickets for her show I _____ (**be**) really excited. I _____ (**write**) about how her songs make me happy or sad and I sent the letter. I ____ (**not think**) about it anymore, but imagine my surprise when, two weeks later, a letter _____ (**arrive**). I couldn't believe it! I _____ (**win**) two tickets to the show. I _____ (**take**) my sister and we ____ (**have**) a really good time. She _____ (**give**) an unforgettable show.

2 I _____ (**see**) BTS about two years ago when they _____ (**visit**) my city, and the best thing was – I _____ (**have**) a VIP pass! The band _____ (**come**) on and they _____ (**start**) with a song from their new album. Not everybody _____ (**know**) the words, but I _____ (**do**) and I _____ (**sing**) really loudly. They _____ (**finish**) with an old song. After the show, I _____ (**go**) backstage and _____ (**meet**) the band. They _____ (**be**) fantastic. I _____ (**get**) all their autographs.

D It's Monday morning. Put expressions 1–8 in the timeline.
1 the day before yesterday
2 tomorrow afternoon
3 Tuesday evening
4 last Friday
5 tonight
6 next Thursday
7 yesterday morning
8 last Thursday

Monday morning

E Complete the questions for the answers given.
1. Who _____ a famous second world war diary?
   Anne Frank.
2. Where and when _____ born?
   On June 12, 1929, in Frankfurt, Germany.
3. When _____ die?
   In March 1945.
4. Who _____ these sunflowers?
   Van Gogh.
5. When _____ this picture?
   He painted it in 1888.
6. How many sunflower pictures _____?
   He painted five of them.

F Play *Past tense tennis!* Take turns "serving" a verb for your partner to "return" in the simple past.

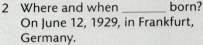

G Correct the mistakes. Check your answers in units 7 and 8. What's your score, 1–10?
1. Some years ago, had two movie theaters in my town. (2 mistakes)
2. You was at school today? (2 mistakes)
3. A: Was your dad on vacation the last week? (1 mistake)
   B: No, wasn't. He was sick all the week. (2 mistakes)
4. Five years behind, there were a lot trees here. (2 mistakes)
5. I finished the school when I had eighteen years. (3 mistakes)
6. I no went to college. I get married and had children. (3 mistakes)
7. What did Ms. Riggs saw from her trip to Turkey? (2 mistakes)
8. What did happen to her there? (1 mistake)
9. With who did she traveled? (2 mistakes)
10. Could you to open the door for me? (1 mistake)

Skills practice

You're everything I need and more, It's written all over your face, Baby, I can feel your halo, Pray it won't fade away.

R4

A Read the fact files. True (T) or False (F)?

The Olympics

The first modern Olympics were in Athens, Greece, in 1896, but there are many differences between the early days of the games and the Olympics today. In the first games, there were 245 sportsmen from only 14 countries, only nine different sports, and 43 events. Nowadays, the whole world participates and there are approximately 17,000 competitors from 205 countries, and 306 events – that's an enormous change! Another big social change is in the number of women involved. In 1896, there were no women at all. Today, there are sportswomen in all the Olympic sports.

The soccer World Cup

The first World Cup was in 1930 in Uruguay. There were only 13 teams and all of the games were in Montevideo. There were four European countries, eight came from South America, plus the U.S. In the final, Uruguay beat Argentina 4-2. These days, over 200 teams try to qualify, but only 32 teams get through to the finals of the competition. There are other differences, too. Until 1970, there were no red or yellow cards. Nowadays, teams that don't get many cards can win the Fairplay award, and there are other awards, too. In 1930, there were only the winner's cup and the Golden Ball for the best player. Today, there are also the Golden Boot for the top goal-scorer and the Golden Glove for the top goalkeeper.

1 There weren't any women in the first Olympics. _____
2 There were more sports than countries in Athens, in 1896. _____
3 In 1930, there weren't World Cup games in different cities. _____
4 Argentina won the first World Cup. _____
5 The winner's cup is the only award teams can get in the World Cup. _____
6 There is the same number of countries in the World Cup finals as in the Olympics. _____

B ▶R4.1 Read the blog about a visit to Amsterdam and number the paragraphs 1–5 in the correct order. Listen to check.

C Read again and complete 1-6. Which attraction would you like to visit most?

1 It <u>wasn't</u> cheap to rent a _____.
2 The bike tour _____ perfect because the bike _____.
3 They thought the Anne Frank museum _____.
4 They _____ to check out of the hotel before _____.
5 The journey to the airport was _____.
6 Their visit to Amsterdam _____ more positive than _____.

At last we were in Amsterdam! We were really excited to see everything the city has to offer, even though we were there for only a few days. We saw a lot! Here's what we did:

___
The next day, it rained all day and we got very wet in the morning! So, in the afternoon, we avoided the rain and went to some of the fabulous art galleries and museums in the city. My favorite was the Van Gogh Museum, where we saw hundreds of original Van Gogh paintings and learned a lot about his life. It was fantastic. After that, we ate in a tourist restaurant near the museum. It was a bad choice – the food was terrible, and it was very expensive, too.

___
First, we took a bike tour of the city. Amsterdam is famous for its bikes – people ride bikes everywhere, and it's definitely the best way to see the sights. It was more expensive to rent a bike than we expected, though. We had a great time riding around on the bike paths and narrow streets along the canals. But then I got a flat tire! We were a long way from the place where we rented the bikes, and we couldn't fix the tire, so we walked all the way back. It took ages and it wasn't the best way to end our first day.

___
We had to check out of our hotel at noon on our last day, so we left our bags there and found a cheap Vietnamese restaurant close to the hotel for lunch. It was great! There were lots of locals eating there, as well as tourists. Then we walked around and did some shopping for souvenirs, before collecting our bags and getting the train to the airport. It's a really easy journey by train.

___
I recommend Amsterdam for a visit. There were a couple of disappointments, but overall it was a really good experience.

___
On our second day, we got tickets for a canal cruise. This is a great way to see the city from the water. In the old part of the city, the canals are lined with amazing tall, narrow houses that are hundreds of years old. We stopped at different places and went to Anne Frank House, which is where she hid with her family in World War II and where she wrote her diary. The house is now a really interesting museum, but we all felt a little sad thinking about what she and her family suffered during the war.

D How many stars (from 1–5) do you think the blogger gave the visit? In pairs, compare and say why.

I think it was probably 3 stars because …

E 🎤 **Make it personal** Question time.
In pairs, practice asking and answering the 12 lesson titles in units 7 and 8. Use the book map on p. 2–3. Where possible, ask follow-up questions, too. Can you comfortably ask and answer all the questions?

Do you live in a house?   *No, I don't. I live in an apartment.*

How many bedrooms do you have?   *Just two, but there's an enormous terrace!*

111

9

9.1 How did you get here today?

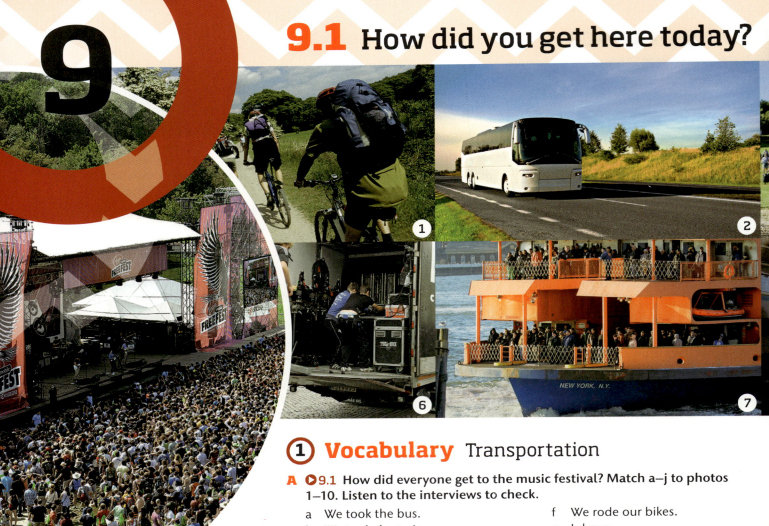

1 Vocabulary Transportation

A ▶9.1 How did everyone get to the music festival? Match a–j to photos 1–10. Listen to the interviews to check.

a   We took the bus.
b   We took the train.
c   We took the ferry.
d   They took a helicopter.
e   I rode my motorbike.
f   We rode our bikes.
g   I drove.
h   I drove the band's truck.
i   I flew.
j   We walked.

B In pairs, take turns asking and answering about the photos.

A: Point at a photo and ask "How did (they) get there?"
B: Answer.
A: Confirm and rephrase.

> He went by motorbike.   That's right, he rode his motorbike.

C **Make it personal** In pairs, ask and answer the questions.

1   What's the best way for you to get to:
   a   the nearest shopping mall?
   b   this English class?
   c   your favorite restaurant?
   d   your local airport?
   e   a good beach?
   f   a place with snow?
2   How did you get:
   a   here today and how are you getting home?
   b   to school when you were a child?
   c   to your last vacation destination?

> What's the best way for you to get to the nearest shopping mall?
> By car. I live 20 kilometers away, so I always drive.

Common mistakes

did you get / come
How ~~you arrived~~ here?
         on
I came ~~by~~ foot.

112

🎵 *Oh, I want to get away, I want to fly away, Yeah, yeah, yeah.* 9.1

② Listening

A ▶9.2 Guess which transportation problems a–f go with sentences 1–6. Listen to check. Were you right?

1 The train was late.
2 My plane was de**layed**.
3 My bus had a flat tire.
4 There was a traffic jam.
5 I made a wrong turn.
6 I had an accident.

B ▶9.3 Listen to two conversations at a party. Which problems in **A** does each person have? Which ones have you experienced?

Conversation 1   Conversation 2

C ▶9.3 Match the questions to the answers. Listen again to check.

1 Did you just get here?
2 Where do you live?
3 How did you get here?
4 How's it going?
5 What happened?

a Pretty good, thanks. How about you?
b I had an accident. Nothing serious.
c Yes, actually.
d Right now? In Chicago.
e I took the bus.

D 🗣 **Make it personal** Imagine you're at a party. Invent a character. In pairs, role-play a "problem" conversation. Then change partners. Who had the biggest problem?

Hi Bob! Great to see you! How's it going?   *Hi Jane! Sorry I'm late ... I lost my car keys.*

> 🔸 **Common mistakes**
> Where are you working these days?
> ~~Right now?~~
> ~~Actually?~~ In New York.

113

9.2 What do you do?

1 Reading

A Guess the answers to questions 1–4. Then read the article quickly to check.
1. What's the man in the photo doing?
   a He's going to work.   b He's training for a marathon.
2. What's his job?
   a He teaches sports.   b He's a doctor.
3. How far is his commute to work and home?
   a eight miles   b two miles
4. Why does he commute like this?
   a He can't drive and is afraid to ride a bike.   b He wants to stay in shape.

An Unusual Commute

Most people commute by bus, or they drive, but not Ted Houk, from Towson, Maryland. For five years, Dr. Houk rode his bike to work, but then he decided to run, instead, because he wanted even more exercise. Then, for 15 years, Dr. Houk always ran to his internal medicine practice from his home in Lutherville, and back again every day. It's about four miles (around six and a half kilometers) there and four miles home, but he ran when it was sunny, when it was raining, and even when it was snowing. He ran if it was hot or cold, and if it was light or dark.

He always ran with a big bag in his hand. In the bag were his clothes, his stethoscope, his phone, and about two pounds of fruit and vegetables. His full bag weighed about ten pounds (around four and a half kilograms). When Houk got to work, he always rubbed alcohol on his body to remove perspiration. But sweat is not really a problem, he says, because "your sweat is clean."

Then, in 2013, Dr. Houk had a serious accident as he ran. He was seriously injured when a car hit him, and he was in the hospital for two months. Fortunately, he recovered and now works – and runs – again.

B ▶9.4 Listen and read again. True (T) or False (F)? Do you agree with Ted's ideas?
1. Dr. Houk lives next to his workplace.
2. He takes the bus to work if it rains or snows.
3. The bag he carried was empty.
4. He went by bike to work before he started running.
5. He thought the sweat on his body was a problem.
6. Dr. Houk started to run again after his accident.

C 🔴 **Make it personal** Do you know anyone with an unusual commute or way to exercise? What do your classmates do to keep in shape?

My aunt swims five kilometers every day.   *I never use elevators.*

114

2 Vocabulary Jobs

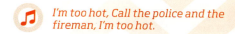

9.2

A ▶9.5 Match photos a–j to the jobs. Which words are easy for you to recognize? Listen to students discussing the photos to check.

- a cab driver
- a computer programmer
- a cook
- a dentist
- a firefighter
- a flight attendant
- a hairdresser
- a personal assistant
- a photographer
- a police officer

B ▶9.6 Look at picture k. What job do you think each person has today? Listen to two of the friends talking about the group to check.

C In pairs, decide which sentences 1–7 apply to the jobs in **A**. Which are the best professions? Why?

1. You can / can't make a lot of money.
2. It's interesting / boring / dangerous work.
3. You work with other people / alone.
4. You work / don't work long hours.
5. You help / don't help a lot of people.
6. It's a job of the past / future.
7. It's a job I'd like / I wouldn't like to do.

> I think computer programmer is the best job because you can make a lot of money, and it's interesting.

D **Make it personal** What's your occupation? What do you like about it? What don't you like? What's your dream job?

> What do you do?

> I'm a student. I enjoy it because my teachers are good, but I don't have any money!

Common mistakes

I'm a student at City College.
~~in~~

Doctors earn / make a lot of money.
~~win~~

115

9.3 Where are you going to be in 2025?

1 Listening

A ▶9.7 Listen to Kelly and Michael discussing future plans and check (✓) the correct answers.

	Profession interested in?	Need to go to grad school?
Michael	☐ financial advisor ☐ pet psychologist	☐ yes ☐ no
Kelly	☐ financial advisor ☐ pet psychologist	☐ yes ☐ no

B ▶9.7 Listen again. Who says 1–8, Michael (M) or Kelly (K)?

1 That sounds boring. ____
2 You can make a lot of money. ____
3 You help people. ____
4 You can be your own boss. ____
5 Your parents are going to be happy. ____
6 I don't want to be a veterinarian. ____
7 It's going to be fun. ____
8 Tell me what that dog is thinking. ____

C 🗣 **Make it personal** Which job do you prefer? Why?

I think I prefer the pet psychologist because I love animals, too.

2 Grammar *going to* for future

A ▶9.8 Listen to these sentences from the conversation in **1A** and complete 1–7. Then complete the grammar box.

1 What are you _____ to do?
2 I'm _____ to _____ a financial advisor.
3 Your parents _____ going to _____ happy.
4 _____ going _____ be a pet psychologist.
5 It's _____ going to _____ easy, but it's what I want.
6 You can meet lots of people. _____ going _____ be fun.
7 I know I'm _____ going _____ be rich, but that's OK.

Common mistakes

It isn't going /be easy. → *to*
Why you are going to do that? → *are you*

Subject	A	⊖	*going to*	I	
I	'm			go	to grad school.
You	're	(not)	going to	like	it.
She / He / It	____			make	a lot of money.
We / They	____			study	psychology.

Q	A	S	*going to*	I		⊕⊖ Short answers
What	are	you	going to	do?		
	Are			go	to grad school?	Yes, I am. No, I'm _____.

Use *going to* to talk about predictions and future intentions. In ⊖ sentences, use contractions.

1 I _____ not going to like the movie.
2 She _____ going to be late.
3 My parents _____ going to be happy.

➡ Grammar 9B p.154

B Order these questions. Then find someone who has the same answers.

🎵 *I'm gonna swing from the chandelier, from the chandelier, I'm gonna live like tomorrow doesn't exist.*

9.3

1. you / are / going / what / evening / do / this / to / ?
   _____
2. you / going / tonight / are / TV / watch / to / ?
   _____
3. year / going / you / to / go / vacation / are / on / next / ?
   _____
4. are / where / celebrate / next / birthday / going / you / to / your / ?
   _____

C 👤 **Make it personal** Where are you going to be in 2025? Discuss your answers in groups. Who has the most original answer?

> *I'm going to be in space. I want to be an astronaut.*   *Wow! How do you learn to do that?*

③ Reading

A ▶ 9.9 Read the article and write the name of the person who talks about these topics. There's one extra topic.

1. buildings _____
2. education _____
3. politics _____
4. space travel _____
5. conservation _____
6. transportation _____
7. shopping _____
8. technology _____

THE FUTURE?

What is work going to be like for young people? We asked some high school graduates for their plans and predictions for the world of work. This is what they told us.

"I'm not going to be like my parents. They have an online movie rental business. I want to open a physical store like in the old days!" **Saul, 17**

"We're all going to live on the moon, so I'm going to be a space pilot and fly people to the moon and back." **Mariana, 16**

"We're not going to educate our kids in the same way in the future. We're going to use video games to teach kids. I'm going to be an educational video-game designer." **Laisa, 18**

"Humans are not going to use cars forever. I think we're going to be able to teleport pretty soon." **Margarita, 17**

"I'm not going to work in an office. With technology, everyone can already telecommute, and more people are going to do it." **Chris, 19**

"Politics is a career that's not going to change. Even if you don't like politicians, this is an important job and it's what I'm going to do." **Javier, 16**

"Because we can print in 3D now, soon we're not going to need construction workers, and we'll be able to "print" new houses. I'm going to work in this business." **Marco, 18**

④ Pronunciation

A ▶ 9.10 Listen to the sentences. Check (✓) the ones that are pronounced "gonna" /gənə/ in rapid speech. Then listen again and repeat.

1. a ☐ b ☐   2. a ☐ b ☐   3. a ☐ b ☐   4. a ☐ b ☐

⚠️ **Common mistakes**

I ~~'m~~ not going to be rich.
Are you gonna ~~to~~ be famous?

B 👤 **Make it personal** Which predictions in 3A do you agree / disagree with? In pairs, compare answers.

> *I don't agree with Mariana. We're not gonna live on the moon in the future.*

> *I'm not so sure. The future is a long time, and the population is growing fast!*

117

9.4 What are you going to do next year?

1 Vocabulary Life changes

A ▶9.11 Listen to Mr. James and complete phrases 1–11. Match six of the phrases to pictures a–f.

1 leave college.
2 find a g_____.
3 get e_____.
4 get m_____.
5 leave h_____.
6 start a (new) j_____.
7 start a f_____.
8 get d_____.
9 m_____.
10 lose a j_____.
11 retire (from a j_____).

B ▶9.11 Listen again to check. In pairs, what is one mistake that Mr. James made?

C 🔴 **Make it personal** In groups, discuss at what age people usually do these things in your country. Do you all agree?

learn to drive   leave home   go to college   get married   start a family

> We usually go to college when we're 17 or 18.   People usually start a family when they're about 30.

2 Reading

A Quickly read Alex's blog. What eight changes is he going to make?

New Year's Resolutions!

Well, I had a long talk with my dad the other day, and he convinced me. We're very different, but I love him. So, I'm going to make a few changes in my life. And, anyway, today is a new year, so time for a new start!

First, I'm going to exercise more. I ate too much over the holidays! Then I'm going to get a new job. I'm a server in a restaurant, and I hate my boss. He makes me stay late and keeps my tips! I want to be a web designer, so I'm going to go back to school, get my bachelor's, and show them all! I'm going to learn a new language, too. I want to learn to speak Mandarin.

I'm also going to move out of my mom's house and get an apartment with some friends. I think it's time, don't you? And I'm going to buy a new car. Then I'm going to find a new girlfriend – I'm so lonely! So … "How are you going to do all this?" I hear you asking.

Here's my plan: Well, after lunch, I'm playing basketball with my friend, Carl, and then tonight, I'm having dinner with my mom to tell her I'm leaving home. Next week, I'm talking to a career specialist, and I'm starting a class in Mandarin. And … I'm going on a date tomorrow night. Wow! Wish me luck! What do you think of my plan? Thanks for reading!

comment:
Hi Alex! I think this is a good plan. But why are you going to learn Mandarin? Why don't you learn Spanish or Portuguese?

B ▶9.12 Listen to and read the blog again and complete the chart.

> ▶ **Common mistakes**
>
> ~~are you doing~~
> What ~~do you do~~ after class?
> I'm going   I'm working
> I ~~go~~ home. I ~~work~~ tonight.

Intention	Reason
1 do more exercise	he ate too much over the holidays
2 get a new job	
3 go back to school	
4 move from his mom's house	
5 get a new girlfriend	

C 🔴 **Make it personal** What do you think of Alex's plan? Follow the models above and below, and write a blog comment to encourage him.

Hi Alex! I think your plan sounds great! I studied Mandarin, too, last year. It's not easy, but I really enjoyed it!

118

3 Grammar *going to* vs. present continuous

Ooh, love, no one's ever gonna hurt you, love. I'm gonna give you all of my love. Nobody matters like you. So, rockabye baby, rockabye.

9.4

A Are 1–4 in the present continuous (PC) or do they use *going to* (GT)?

		PC	GT
1	I'm going to leave this job when I find a better one.		
2	After lunch, he's meeting his teacher.		
3	Tonight, he and his mother are having dinner.		
4	I think we're going to win tonight.		

B Answer the question in the grammar box.

I'm going to do all my homework this weekend.	= an intention in the future
I'm starting a new job tomorrow.	= a fixed plan in the future

Use the present continuous to talk about a fixed plan in the future. For intentions or predictions, use *going to*.

Which sentences in **A** are intentions / predictions or fixed plans?

➡ **Grammar 9C & 9D** p. 154

C In Alex's blog in **2A**, find four examples of intentions and four examples of fixed plans.

D Complete 1–5 with the present continuous or *going to*.
1 I'm _____ (**travel**) to Rio next week to see my mom. I got my ticket online yesterday.
2 They say it _____ (**rain**) tomorrow. I hate the rain!
3 My brother says he _____ (**save**) for a new car next year. He wants an electric one.
4 I think they _____ (**win**) the election.
5 Sofía _____ (**not / go**) to the movies with us on Saturday. She has a dance class.

> **Common mistakes**
>
> ~~going to go to sleep~~
> I'm ~~sleeping~~ early tonight.
> When *go* is the main verb or is part of an expression, always include it.

E 🗣 **Make it personal** In pairs, talk about:
1 your plans for the weekend.
2 things you intend to do next year.
3 predictions for your future (jobs, marriage, retirement).

> *I'm meeting my friends on Saturday. We're having a party at the beach.*

> *I'm taking my grandmother out for dinner. It's her birthday!*

4 Listening

A 🔊 9.13 Listen to four phone messages. What are these people going to do? Match 1–4 to the correct answers.

1 Carla's brother   move to a warm place ☐
2 John's parents   get engaged ☐
3 Julia   go back to school ☐
4 Martin   live in France ☐

B 🔊 9.13 Listen again and choose the main reason why each person is calling. Who do you think is going to be most surprised?
1 Carla wants Ronnie …   ☐ to cook dinner.   ☐ to help with packing.
2 John wants Melissa …   ☐ to give him information.   ☐ to move to Costa Rica.
3 Julia wants to tell her mom …   ☐ that she graduated.   ☐ some important news.
4 Martin wants Lucy …   ☐ to go to work.   ☐ to celebrate with him.

C 🗣 **Make it personal** Imagine it's New Year's Eve. Write a post about the changes you are going to make in your life next year.

> *Well, next year I'm going to …*

9.5 Would you like to be a nurse?

ID Skills Making connections

Reading

A ▶9.14 Match jobs 1–6 to their area of work a–f. Listen to the talking dictionary to check.

1 a civil engineer
2 a dentist
3 a financial advisor
4 a market research analyst
5 a nurse
6 a software developer

a computers
b money and finance
c teeth
d health and medicine
e bridges and roads
f what people buy

B Read the article and match the jobs to the paragraphs 1–6.

computer specialists   engineers   nurses
dentists   financial advisors   market research analysts

THE BEST JOBS FOR THE FUTURE

What professionals are we going to need in the future? Here are predictions for the six jobs that are going to be in demand in the U.S. in 10 years.

1 _____

We will need more people to help the millions of workers who are going to retire in the next 10 years. Many people are going to ask experts to help them plan what to do with their money.

2 _____

People over the age of 65 are going to keep more of their own teeth, so there are going to be more professionals to show them how to keep their teeth healthy.

3 _____

What are we going to do about all the cars and buses? With more traffic, we need more roads and bridges, for example. We need more people who can build these large structures.

4 _____

Companies need people to help them understand what people want to buy. They want people who can analyze what customers want and tell them what products to make.

5 _____

People with IT (information technology) degrees and extensive computer experience are going to be in high demand, to make new software.

6 _____

There are going to be a lot more people over the age of 90 because of progress in medicine. This means we are going to need more people to help to look after them.

C ▶9.15 Listen and read again and circle the best answer.
1 When people retire they **don't need / need** help with their money.
2 People **always / don't always** know how to take good care of their teeth.
3 We need to build roads because of more **traffic / people.**
4 Companies want information about why people **buy / sell** things.
5 You will need a degree **or / and** experience to make software.
6 Medicine is going to be **good / bad** for people over 90.

D 👤 **Make it personal** In pairs, do you agree with the six predictions? Which of the jobs would you most / least like to do?

I completely agree with number 1. People will need help to save money.   *I don't really agree with number …*

120

9.5 Could I borrow your pen?

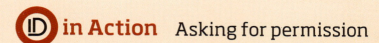

Lend me your ears and I'll sing you a song, and I'll try not to sing out of key. Oh, I get by with a little help from my friends.

ID in Action — Asking for permission

A Guess what the people in photos a–d are asking for. Use these ideas.

- to borrow the car
- to borrow some money
- to close a window
- to leave work early
- to take the day off
- to turn on the air conditioning

I think in photo "a" the man is asking to …

B ▶ 9.16 Listen to dialogues 1–4 to check, and match them to photos a–d.

1 ☐   2 ☐   3 ☐   4 ☐

C ▶ 9.16 Listen again. Complete the questions and circle the responses you hear.

Asking for permission	Giving permission	Saying no
Can I ask you something?	That's fine.	No, I'm busy.
Could _____ take the day off?	Sure. Go ahead.	Maybe next time.
Can I _____ the car?	Of course. No problem.	No, I'm sorry, you can't.
Could _____ lend me some _____?	Help yourself.	I'm sorry, but …
Do you mind if I turn _____ the _____ conditioning?	Not at all.	I'm sorry, but it's too cold.
		Sorry, I'm meeting a friend.

Common mistakes

Can I borrow ~~you~~ *from you* a pen?
Could you ~~borrow~~ *lend* me a pen?

D Role-play conversations for photos 1–4. Change roles. Be difficult sometimes!

Do you mind if I borrow your laptop? *I'm sorry, but I'm going home. And I'm working tonight.*

E 🧑 **Make it personal** Choose something you could ask for permission to do. Go around the class and ask. How many positive responses did you get?

Could you lend me your phone for a minute? *I'm sorry. I left it at home.*

Can I borrow some money for a coffee? *Sorry, I only have my credit card with me.*

Writing 9 A reply to a blog post

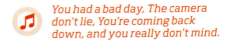
You had a bad day, The camera don't lie, You're coming back down, and you really don't mind.

A Read Michael's blog entry and answer 1–3.
1. Why did Michael have a bad day? (3 reasons)
2. What does he want people to do? (2 things)
3. What advice can you give him?

Michael's Blog

Today was terrible, seriously, one day to completely forget! I got to work a little late. OK, it wasn't the first time, so, of course, my boss didn't believe a word I said, and he fired me immediately. Yes, I actually lost my job! Can you believe it? Well, I hated that job anyway, but the thing is – what am I going to do now? I'm 25, I'm a smart guy (I graduated from college two years ago), I'm getting married next year, but I just don't know what to do. Come on blogosphere, give me some advice and tell me your plans! I need to make some money! Maybe I can get a few ideas from you guys.

B Read three replies. Which advice do you agree with?

Hi, Michael. What a horrible day – are you OK? I think you need to find your dream and work hard for **it**! **That**'s what I'm doing. I want to go back to college to study medicine. I'm working as a personal assistant and living with my parents so I can save for it. When I graduate, my dream is to work as a doctor for a charity in Africa. Why not go back to college?
Megan, 20

Sorry to hear about your job. I don't like **mine**, either. Why don't you take a course in your free time? I'm taking **one** in the evenings so I can get a promotion or do something different. You see, I work in a bank and I spend all day, every day **there**. But I want to work with customers in other countries, and for **this** I need to improve my English. **That**'s why I'm not going out until I pass this course! Go for it, Michael!
Jorge, 23

Man, that is bad luck. I know how you feel, I really can't decide what I'm going to do, either. My teachers say I'm good at most school subjects. **They** say I'm ready to go to college, but I don't want to go right now. I'm going to Europe in the summer! I want to travel **there** and try lots of different jobs so I can see which **ones** I like, then … who knows? Do you want my advice? Take a break and go traveling, too.
Leon, 19

C Reread the replies. Circle the words or phrases that the **bold** words refer to.

D Complete the rules with the **bold** words in **B**.
1. *This*, *that*, and *it* all refer back to a thing or a situation.
2. _____ refers back to more than one person or thing.
3. _____ refers back to a place.
4. _____ or _____ replace countable singular or plural nouns.
5. _____ replaces *my* + noun.

✓ Write it right!
Use pronouns to avoid repetition.
I like red apples, but I don't like green ones.

E **Make it personal** Write a reply to Michael.

Before	Use your ideas from **A**. Include your own experience, what you're doing now, and your future plans.
While	Use the highlighted phrases to introduce your advice. Use pronouns to refer back to nouns and ideas.
After	Send your ideas to your classmates. Which is the best advice?

9 The sky's the limit

 Café

1 Before watching

A Complete 1–4 with the words in the box.

climatology   internship
meteorologist   tornado alley

1 A _____ is a person who researches weather patterns.
2 In the Midwest of the U.S. they call the states of Iowa, Kansas, and Nebraska _____ because of all the strong wind storms.
3 He's applying for an _____ in a science department.
4 The study of the Earth's climate is called _____.

B In pairs, guess what Daniel is looking at, doing, and thinking in the photo. Write a thought bubble for him. Watch the start of the video to check.

I think he's ...   I don't think so. I think he's ...

2 While watching

A Order the phrases 1–10 as you hear them. Complete the missing words.

☐ I think this is g_____ t____ b____ an important program for climatology.
☐ I wanna invent a m_____ or a p_____ that can tell people when a storm is coming.
☐ I'd like to go to grad school and then w_____ a____ an environmental reporter.
☐ I'll s____ y_____ the program as soon as I can. Express mail.
☐ So where do you s____ y_____ in five years?
☐ Thank you for a_____ t____ this interview.
☐ That's incredible. Could you let me k____ h____ that goes?
☐ Can you tell me a l_____ m_____ about your Storm Tracker?
☐ You a____ n____ a paid intern of the Foundation for Environmental Advancement.
☐ You'll be part of my r_____ s_____.

B Complete with the *going to* form of the verbs. Which ones would also be correct in the present continuous?

1 Daniel _____ (talk) on the phone in a few minutes.
2 Dr. DiChristina _____ (track) a tornado in Kansas.
3 His storm tracker _____ (be) useful for scientists.
4 Dr. DiChristina _____ (recommend) Daniel for a full, paid internship.
5 She _____ (email) him the address.
6 Daniel _____ (start) his internship after the semester ends.

C True (T) or False (F)? Correct the false sentences.

In the video ...
1 Daniel is waiting nervously to make a call.
2 Daniel and the doctor are meeting for the first time.
3 Only the doctor is asking questions.
4 Daniel is giving a video presentation of his Tracker.
5 Daniel talks about his past and his future dreams.
6 She asks him to send her his invention to test it.
7 She offers him a job.
8 He sends her his address.
9 He says he's going to contact her again soon.

3 After watching

A Cover the photo of Dr. DiChristina. In pairs, describe her office.

On the left, there's a window and some ...   Is there a plant?

B Make five *Wh-* questions using the words in 1–5.

1 you / plan / after school
2 time / start / she / the interview
3 he / wait / for the phone call
4 they / do / after / their conversation
5 you / talk to / this evening

C 🔵 Make it personal In pairs, ask and answer the questions in B. Add some follow-up questions.

Where are you planning on going after school?

First, I'm going home, and then ...

D 🔵 Make it personal In groups, speculate about your lives in 10 years. Any big differences?

In 10 years' time, I'm going to be married with a baby!

Really? Who are you going to marry?

123

10

10.1 Do you look like your mom?

1 Vocabulary The body and face

A ▶10.1 Label the photos with these words. Listen to a sports science class to check. Point to the part(s) of your body as you hear each word.

| arms | back | chest | fingers | foot / feet |
| hands | head | legs | stomach /k/ | toes |

B In pairs, say which parts of the body you use to do activities 1–8.

1 to think
2 to run
3 to swim
4 to ride a bicycle

5 to play soccer
6 to write
7 to do yoga
8 to learn English

You need your legs and your feet to run.   And you need your arms, too.

Common mistakes

I need warm socks because ~~the toes~~ are cold.
  my toes
       your
You need ~~the legs for~~ to run.

124

C ▶10.2 Look at the photo and label these parts of the face. Listen to check.

ears lips
eyes mouth
eyebrows nose
hair teeth

I feel it in my fingers, I feel it in my toes, Love is all around me, And so the feeling grows.

10.1

1
2
3
4
5
6
7
8

D What part(s) of the face do you associate most with these verbs?

- [ ] eat
- [ ] listen
- [ ] look
- [ ] kiss
- [ ] read
- [ ] see
- [ ] smell
- [ ] speak
- [ ] watch

E 👤 **Make it personal** In pairs, think of more activities you can do with the parts of the body and face in **A** and **C**. Which pair has the most activities?

You need your arms to get a taxi in the street.   *You have to have fingers to use a cell phone.*

2 Listening

A ▶10.3 Listen to descriptions of three suspects. Write the name, Adam, Charlie, or Mark, under the correct person.

B ▶10.3 Write the number of the suspect 1–3 for each item. There are four items for each suspect. Then listen again to check.

Weight
- [ ] average build
- [ ] overweight
- [ ] slim

Height
- [ ] average height
- [ ] short
- [ ] tall

Eyes
- [ ] blue eyes
- [ ] brown eyes
- [ ] green eyes

Hair
- [ ] long dark hair
- [ ] short dark hair
- [ ] short fair hair

C Spot the suspect! **A:** Describe one of the suspects. **B:** With your book closed, say who it is. Change roles.

He has … hair and he is …

D 👤 **Make it personal** Describe a "suspect" in the class. Use "this person," not "he" or "she." Can your classmates guess who it is?

This person is tall with long, dark hair. This person is wearing …

Common mistakes

What does he look like?
~~How is he?~~

         's
He ~~/~~ tall.
He has ~~the~~ long hair.

125

10.2 Are you like your dad?

1 Reading

A ▶10.4 Read the article and complete the information about Kelly. Listen and read again to check.

An extraordinary athlete

Kelly Bruno is tall and slim with long dark hair and brown eyes – she loves sports and she's an excellent athlete. She looks like a lot of young women, but Kelly is different. Born in North Carolina on March 23, 1984, Kelly was six months old when doctors amputated part of her leg. Three months later, she got a prosthetic leg and she began to walk at the age of only 13 months. She was very athletic in school and was good at sports, especially baseball, soccer, and running. She was also courageous and determined, and wanted to succeed. Now she is a champion triathlete. In a triathlon, she has to swim 1,500 m, ride a bike for 40 km, and run 10 km. She won the New York City Triathlon in 2008, and she also competes in ultramarathons – races of over 160 km.

Kelly became a doctor in 2017. Her father was a doctor, and he inspired Kelly to study medicine before he died in 2010 in an earthquake in Haiti. He was working there for an organization called "Food for the Poor."

What does Kelly think about her leg? "It's just an obstacle," she says. "Everyone has their own obstacles. Whatever yours is, just don't quit."

Full name: Kelly
Description:
Hobbies:
Occupation:

B ▶10.5 Read again and complete Kelly's timeline. Listen to a conversation to check.

6 months old	9 months old	13 months old	2008	2010	2017
doctors amputated part of her leg					

Is that thin? No, I know, slim!

⚠ **Common mistakes**
~~is~~
What does she like?

C In pairs, match words 1–3 to definitions a–c. Then take turns miming a word from the article for your partner to say.

1 to quit
2 an earthquake
3 to succeed

a when the ground shakes
b stop, give up, abandon
c be successful

D 👤 **Make it personal** What do you think of Kelly's experiences and attitude? Choose three words to describe her. Compare your choices in groups. Do you know anyone like her?

| active | athletic | courageous | determined | extraordinary |
| energetic | heroic | ordinary | strong | |

Which words did you choose?

I think she's strong, determined, and heroic. My grandfather is like her.

2 Grammar Comparatives with -er and more   10.2

🎵 *What doesn't kill you makes you stronger, Stand a little taller, Doesn't mean I'm lonely when I'm alone.*

A ▶10.6 Listen to Maggie and Steve. Then match photos 1 and 2 to the adjectives.
☐ boring ☐ happy ☐ interesting ☐ sad ☐ short ☐ tall

B ▶10.6 Listen again and complete 1–4 with the word(s) you hear.

| happier | interesting | sadder | shorter | taller |

1 Scott is _____ than Jake.
2 Jake is _____ than Scott. Scott's _____.
3 It doesn't matter that he's _____ than Scott.
4 Scott is more _____ than Jake.

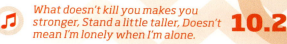
1 Jake 2 Scott

C Complete the grammar box.

> Match 1–4 to a–d to make rules.
> 1 Adjectives of one syllable: a *good → better; bad → worse*
> 2 Adjectives of two or more syllables: b use *more* plus adjective
> 3 Adjectives of two syllables (ending in -y): c change -y to -i and add -er
> 4 Irregular comparatives: d add -er.
>
> Spelling adjectives that end consonant + vowel + consonant (CVC), double the final consonant: "Russia is bigger than Canada." "It was hot yesterday, but today it's _____."
>
> ➡ **Grammar 10A** p. 156

⏱ Common mistakes
~~more bad~~ **worse**
My writing is ~~more bad~~ than my speaking.
~~more big~~ **bigger**
Our apartment is ~~more big~~ than Sheila's new house.

D Write eight comparative sentences with your opinions. Choose from the adjectives below or others of your own.

| bad | friendly | happy | interesting | relaxed |
| expensive | good | hard | nice | sad |

1 work / school *School is more relaxed than work, I think!*
2 summer / winter
3 museums / movies
4 evenings / mornings
5 shoes / sandals
6 my mother / my father
7 the news in [country] / the news in [country]
8 rock music / hip hop music

E 👤 **Make it personal** In groups, share your opinions in D and give reasons.

> *I think winter is nicer here because there aren't a lot of tourists.*   *Yes, but it's cold!*

3 Listening

A ▶10.7 Listen and identify Brad's sisters Zoe and Rebecca in the pictures.

B ▶10.7 Listen again. Complete these sentences with Zoe (Z) or Rebecca (R). Are you more similar to Zoe or Rebecca?
1 _____ is friendlier than _____.
2 _____ is more generous than _____.
3 _____ is more timid than _____.
4 _____ is calmer than _____.
5 _____ is more intelligent than _____.
6 _____ is more organized than _____.

C 👤 **Make it personal** Use adjectives from 2A, 2D, and 3B (and others that you know) to compare yourself with someone in your family.

> *My dad is friendlier than me. He likes to go to parties and meet people. I'm a little shyer.*
> *Do you look like him?*   *Not really. He's a lot shorter.*

10.3 Who's the most generous person in your family?

1 Reading

A ▶10.8 What is an enneagram, definition 1 or 2? Read the introduction to the website and choose the best answer. Then read and listen. Pause after each type and repeat the pink-stressed adjectives.

1 A new system to label positive and negative people.
2 A diagram that represents nine personality types.

Which type are you?

The enneagram is an ancient symbol used to describe personality types. It is a circle with nine points. Each of them represents a different personality type with both negative and positive characteristics. The enneagram says that we move between these negative and positive characteristics. All of us have one of nine basic personality types. Here is an example of each type:

 I'm **type 1**. I'm a perfectionist and I'm idealistic. My negative side is that sometimes I'm very critical of other people.

 Type 4 people are romantic and want to understand other people. That's me! I like to understand how people feel, but sometimes I can be moody.

 I love to have fun and be spontaneous. I'm **type 7**, and I'm usually happy, but I can be disorganized when I'm trying to have fun!

 I love to help people and I'm very generous, but if you're my friend, I don't want to share you! I can be very possessive. I'm **type 2**.

 I'm a solitary person, and I want to try to understand what's happening in my world. That's **type 5**. Sometimes I feel depressed and that's my negative side.

 Type 8 people are strong, and they want to do important things for the world – that's me. My negative side is that I can get angry when you don't agree with me!

 Well, I'm **type 3**. I am ambitious and good at things. If I do things well I can become more arrogant – this is my negative side.

 I'm very loyal to my friends, and I'm very responsible. My negative side is that I can be suspicious. This is **type 6**.

 I'm **type 9** and I hate conflict, so I always try to be calm. The negative part of this is that I'm a little passive and accept things, just because I don't want any problems.

B Work in groups of three. Each student reads three personality types from **A** and completes their part of the chart with adjectives.

Student	Type	Positive side	Negative side
A	1	idealistic	
	2		
	3		

🔴 **Common mistakes**

Don't stress suffixes -ive, -al, -ous, or -ic.
possessive, passive, critical, loyal, ambitious, generous, idealistic, romantic

C ▶10.9 Listen to a conversation to check your answers. Which type(s) do you like best?

D 🗣 **Make it personal** What enneagram type are you? In groups, describe yourselves using adjectives from **A**. Similar or different?

Well, I think I'm type 1. I'm idealistic, but I'm also critical.

Me, too. I think I'm more critical than you.

2 Grammar Superlatives with -est and most

🎵 Don't give up, I won't give up,
Don't give up, no no no,
I'm free to be the greatest, I'm alive, I'm free
to be the greatest here tonight, the greatest.

10.3

A ▶10.10 What can you see in the photos? Read the quiz and answer the questions. Listen to check. Is the suffix -est pronounced /ɪst/ or /est/?

> Well, the highest is … so the second highest has to be …

Who came second?

We always remember the winner, but what about second place?

1 What's the second highest mountain in the world? ☐
   a Kilimanjaro   b Everest
   c K2

2 What's the second most-spoken language in the world? ☐
   a English   b Spanish
   c Mandarin Chinese

3 What's the second most populated city in the Americas? ☐
   a São Paulo   b New York City
   c Mexico City

4 What's the second most successful movie of all time? ☐
   a Star Wars (1977)   b Avatar
   c Gone with the Wind

5 What is the second closest planet to the sun? ☐
   a Venus   b Mercury   c Earth

B Complete the grammar box.

Their **Greatest** Hits by The Eagles is the **best**-selling album in history. 6 ☐
The **most successful** national soccer team is Brazil. 7 ☐
Salzburg is **the prettiest** city in the world. 8 ☐

Match the halves of the rules.
When an adjective …
   a has one syllable,   good → the best, bad → the worst, more → the most
   b has two or more syllables,   put *most* before the adjective.
   c ends in *-y*,   change *-y* to *-i* and add *-est*.
   d is irregular,   add *-est*.

Spelling adjectives that end consonant + vowel + consonant (CVC), double the final consonant: "The **biggest** airport is in Atlanta, Georgia."

Which rule a-d do the superlatives in the quiz questions in **A** and the three examples above follow?

➡ Grammar 10B p. 156

> **Common mistakes**
>
> Home is the ~~most nice~~ *nicest* place in the world.
> She is the ~~most~~ happiest person I know.

C Put these words in order to make questions. Then, in pairs, take turns asking and answering as many as you can.
1 the / what / largest / your / is / city / country / in / ?
2 the / in / expensive / are / what / most / your / restaurants / town / ?
3 highest / what / the / town / your / is / building / in / ?
4 most / in / country / popular / beaches / your / what / the / are / ?
5 mountain / what / the / is / country / highest / in / your / ?
6 most / world / people / famous / the / in / are / who / the / ?
7 youngest / your / in / who / the / is / class / person / ?

D 🗣 **Make it personal** In pairs, write five questions for a trivia quiz. Then find someone who can answer each question correctly.

> What age is the oldest person in the world?
>
> I really don't know, but it's definitely over 100.

129

10.4 What's the best place in the world?

1 Reading

A Do you know the places in photos 1–9? Find examples of these things in the photos.

a canyon	a cave	a forest	an island
a lizard	a mountain	a river	
an underground river	a volcano	a waterfall	

B ▶10.11 Quickly scan the article and match the places to photos 1–9. Then listen and read. Any pronunciation surprises?

C In pairs, try to answer 1–9. Then read again to check. Which place:
1. is in nine different countries?
2. has many different flowers?
3. has caves and lakes?
4. has an underground river?
5. is in two countries?
6. contains a volcano?
7. is a very deep canyon?
8. is home to a famous animal?
9. is a mountain over five kilometers high?

D 🔵 **Make it personal** Do you agree with the choices? Which of the places do you most want to visit? Why?

> *I want to visit Table Mountain. I really want to go to South Africa, plus I love flowers.*

2 Pronunciation Sentence stress

A ▶10.12 Watch the video and say which two of the nine places in the photos are not mentioned.

B ▶10.12 Watch again and number the places 1–7 in the order you hear them. Notice the most stressed words. Then read the pronunciation rules.

> We normally stress words that carry the message. Other words are often unstressed, reduced, and said faster. If you don't hear them, you can still understand the meaning.
>
> • • • •
> The Pacific is the largest ocean on Earth.

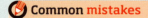

⚠️ **Common mistakes**

the most common language in
English is ~~the language most common~~ of the world.

C ▶10.13 In pairs, listen and underline the stressed words in each sentence.
1. The biggest lizard in the world is in Indonesia.
2. The Amazon rainforest is the largest in the world.
3. The River Nile is longer than the Amazon.
4. The Arctic is the world's smallest ocean.
5. The Amazon River goes through six countries.

D 🔵 **Make it personal** In pairs, search the Internet to find five surprising facts and say them, stressing the most important words. Then share the facts in groups. Which are the most interesting?

> *Look at this one! An astronaut wrote his daughter's initials on the moon!*
>
> *You're kidding!*

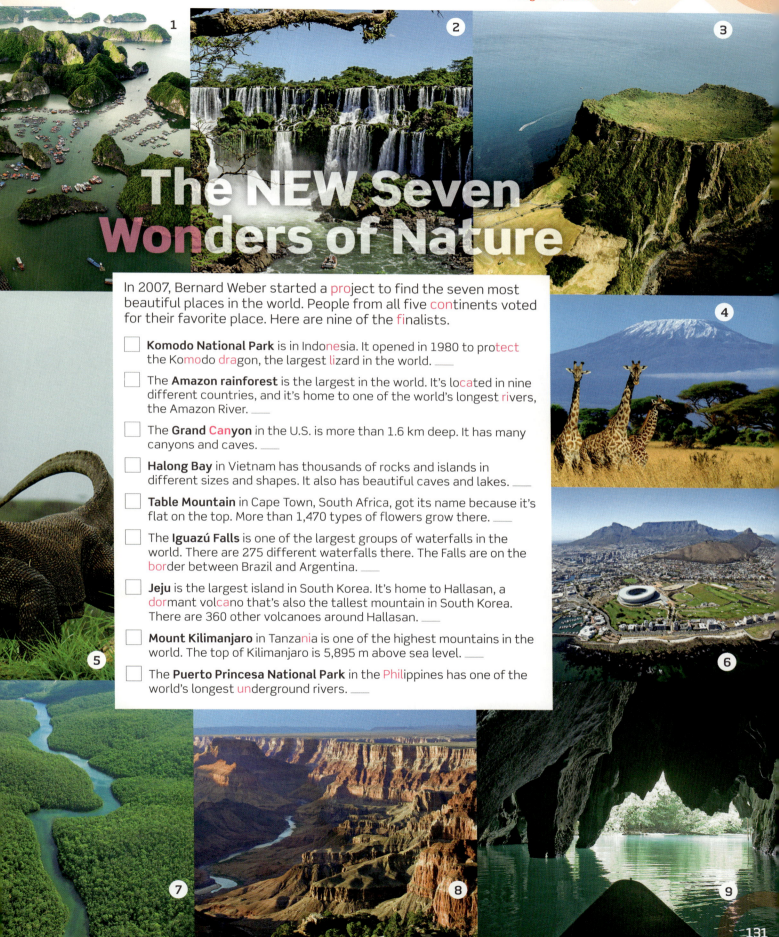

Tropical the island breeze, all of nature wild and free, This is where I long to be, La Isla Bonita.

10.4

The NEW Seven Wonders of Nature

In 2007, Bernard Weber started a project to find the seven most beautiful places in the world. People from all five continents voted for their favorite place. Here are nine of the finalists.

☐ **Komodo National Park** is in Indonesia. It opened in 1980 to protect the Komodo dragon, the largest lizard in the world. ___

☐ The **Amazon rainforest** is the largest in the world. It's located in nine different countries, and it's home to one of the world's longest rivers, the Amazon River. ___

☐ The **Grand Canyon** in the U.S. is more than 1.6 km deep. It has many canyons and caves. ___

☐ **Halong Bay** in Vietnam has thousands of rocks and islands in different sizes and shapes. It also has beautiful caves and lakes. ___

☐ **Table Mountain** in Cape Town, South Africa, got its name because it's flat on the top. More than 1,470 types of flowers grow there. ___

☐ The **Iguazú Falls** is one of the largest groups of waterfalls in the world. There are 275 different waterfalls there. The Falls are on the border between Brazil and Argentina. ___

☐ **Jeju** is the largest island in South Korea. It's home to Hallasan, a dormant volcano that's also the tallest mountain in South Korea. There are 360 other volcanoes around Hallasan. ___

☐ **Mount Kilimanjaro** in Tanzania is one of the highest mountains in the world. The top of Kilimanjaro is 5,895 m above sea level. ___

☐ The **Puerto Princesa National Park** in the Philippines has one of the world's longest underground rivers. ___

10.5 What's your blood type?

And we danced all night to the best song ever, We knew every line, Now I can't remember.

🆔 Skills Understanding facts

Vocabulary

A Match these words to pictures a–g. Which two words rhyme?

☐ a beard ☐ blood ☐ a brain ☐ a heart
☐ a lung ☐ fingernails ☐ a tongue

a

e

b

f

True or false? How much do you know about the human body?

1. The brain is more active at night than during the day.
2. Hair grows faster on your face than on other parts of your body.
3. Toenails grow faster than fingernails.
4. On average, women's hearts beat faster than men's.
5. Your right lung is smaller than your left lung.
6. Food is more important to humans than sleep.
7. The tongue is one of the strongest muscles in the human body.
8. The most common blood type in the world is Type A.

c

g

d

B ▶10.14 In pairs, take the quiz. Listen to check. Which fact is not illustrated?

C ▶10.14 Listen again and complete the words in 1–8. Which is the most interesting fact?

1. Your b_____ is very a_____ when you s_____.
2. It says that if m_____ don't shave, a b_____ can g_____ to more than 10 meters long!
3. Your t_____ grow slower than your f_____.
4. Women are s_____ than men, so their h_____ needs to move the blood f_____.
5. The h_____ needs a lot of s_____.
6. The l_____ time a person can go with no s_____ is 11 d_____.
7. When you eat or t_____, you are using your t_____.
8. The most c_____ blood type is _____.

For me, the most interesting fact is …

D 🔵 **Make it personal** **Memory test!** **A:** Ask a question from the quiz. **B:** Cover the quiz, answer, and give a reason. Google another fact of your own.

Is the brain more active at night than during the day?

Yes, it is. The brain is very active when we dream.

132

10.5 Is your English better than a year ago?

10.5

ID in Action   Making choices

A ▶10.15 Listen and match conversations 1–3 to three of the photos a–d. Check (✓) the option they choose. Which of the three was the easiest to understand?

☐ Strawberry
☐ Chocolate
☐ Vanilla
☐ Coconut

B ▶10.15 Listen again and read AS 10.15 on p. 168 and try to remember all you can.

C In pairs, look only at the photos in **A** and practice the three conversations from memory. Create a similar one for the fourth picture.

So, which movie do you want to watch?

Hmm, the actors in the comedy are much better than in the others …

But the action movie looks so much more exciting!

D 🔴 **Make it personal**   In pairs, discuss which of the three options in each of the situations below you'd like to do. Use any adjectives from this unit and make a decision.
Go and see Ed Sheeran, Taylor Swift, or Drake.
Continue studying English, start learning Chinese, or give up learning languages.
Go for a coffee, go home, or go out to dance.

Let's go see Ed Sheeran. He's the best.   *No, I prefer Taylor Swift. She's a better singer.*

133

Writing 10 A family profile

🎵 *You're simply the best, better than all the rest, better than anyone, anyone I ever met.*

A Read the family profile and complete Karina's family tree.

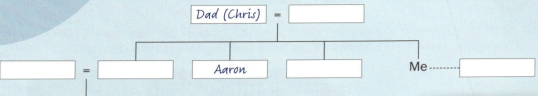

We're a close family. My dad, Chris, is an engineer. He's a big guy, a little taller than both my brothers. He's around 50, with gray hair and a beard, and he's strong and very calm. My mom, Kathy, works at the hospital as a nurse. She's quite short, with dark hair, and she's always busy – she's far more energetic than anyone I know.

My sister Rachel is the **ol**dest. She's tall and slim with long dark hair, and she's the most athletic one in the family. She does triathlons – that's how she met her husband, Victor. He's a firefighter. They've been together for about five years and have a little girl, Salma. She's 15 months old and very cute.

My older brothers are twins. They look almost i**den**tical and are both very tall, approximately 1.95 m. In fact, Aaron is a little taller, and Ben is a bit heavier. Aaron is serious, ambitious, and idealistic; he can be moody and critical, but he's the most intelligent person I know. Ben is more spontaneous and very disorganized. He's less ambitious than Aaron, but a lot more fun.

Finally, there's Max the dog. He's 10 years old, which is around 70 in dog years! He has big brown eyes and long ears. He's very loyal and he's my best friend.

B Which member of the family:
1. is 10 years old?
2. is always busy?
3. is the most athletic?
4. is the tallest?
5. is fun to be with?
6. is the most intelligent?
7. is the youngest?
8. has the most energy?

C Read **Write it right!** and underline the connectors in the text in **A**.

> ✓ **Write it right!**
>
> To show approximation, you can use: *approximately, around*.
> To make a comparison more accurate, you can use: *a lot, much, a little*.

D Order these words to make sentences.
1. much / me / brother / heavier / my / than / is / .
2. know / I / he's / person / the / ambitious / most / .
3. romantic / think / boyfriend / far / is / more / than / her / people / her / .
4. a little / than / expected / exam / that / was / easier / I / .
5. her / than / Anya / much / is / ambitious / sister / less / .
6. men / stronger / is / a lot / some / than / she / .

E Answer the questions in **B** about your family, or a family you know.

F 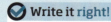 **Make it personal** Write a family profile.

Before	Use your notes from **E**. Think of two more pieces of information about the family.
While	Use words / expressions to show approximation and more comparisons.
After	Check your writing carefully. Give it to your partner to check. Then email it to your teacher.

10 Geminis

 Café

1 Before watching

A Complete 1–5 with these words.

| attitude | genius | horoscope |
| tattoo | twins | zodiac sign |

1 My sister has a bad _____. She thinks she doesn't have to work hard.
2 She has a _____ on each arm.
3 I read my _____ online every morning.
4 My _____ is Leo. My birthday is in August.
5 August is Gemini, and he thinks he's a _____.
6 I don't know any identical _____. Do you?

B 🗨 **Make it personal** In pairs, modify the sentences in A so they are true for you. Any similarities?

> My son has a positive attitude to school. He's never late.

C Complete the song lines with the comparative or superlative of the adjectives.
1 I'm your _____ (**big**) fan, I'll follow you until you love me, paparazzi. (Lady Gaga)
2 It seems to me, that sorry seems to be the _____ (**hard**) word. (Elton John)
3 Never mind, I'll find someone like you, I wish nothing but the _____ (**good**) for you. (Adele)
4 Just like a pill instead of making me _____ (**good**) you keep making me ill. (Pink)
5 Today this could be, the _____ (**great**) day of our lives. (Take That)

D Look at the photo. In pairs, predict four topics Lucy and Andrea will talk about. Watch to check.

> I think they'll talk about their plans for the weekend.

> Yes! Or … the celebrities in their magazines.

2 While watching

A Check (✓) the words you hear in the first part of the video.
☐ a beauty salon   ☐ magazines
☐ fashion and design ☐ pictures of celebrities
☐ your horoscope   ☐ outfit
☐ hair

B Complete with the comparative or superlative you hear.

Andrea: Can you believe her? That is _____ (**ugly**) outfit. No, no, this is _____ (**ugly**) outfit. And this is _____ (**bad**) nose job ever!
Lucy: Or, look at this one.
Andrea: No, no. That's ridiculous. She looked way _____ (**good**) before.
Lucy: I know. Her lips were already big and now she has _____ (**big**) lips in Hollywood.

C Watch the next part of the video. In pairs, remember what they say about:
1 the actress   3 Zoey
2 the girl   4 August

D Watch the final part of the video. True (T) or False (F)? Correct the false sentences.
1 Marlena was really nice to August at school.
2 She worked as an actress in scary movies.
3 She had the most wonderful voice and really positive attitude.
4 She wasn't mean to anyone.
5 The girls thought they saw Marlena in the salon.
6 Lucy's impressed by Andrea's love for her brother.
7 Andrea and August got their Gemini tattoos after the science fair.
8 August won the fair but then Marlena broke his experiment.

3 After watching

A In pairs, remember what these superlatives refer to.
1 the ugliest   3 the biggest
2 the worst (x 2)   4 the most annoying

B 🗨 **Make it personal** In pairs. Do you know anyone who has made changes to their physical appearance (cosmetic surgery, tattoos, piercings, etc.)? What do you think about them?

> Lady Gaga has lots of tattoos.

> Yes, you're right. My cousin has one of a dragon! I think it's cool.

135

R5 Grammar and Vocabulary

A **Picture dictionary.** Cover the words on these pages and use the pictures to remember:

page	
112	10 methods of transportation
115	10 jobs
118	6 life changes
121	4 short dialogues for photos a–d
124	10 parts of the body
125	8 parts of the face
125	descriptions of the 3 suspects
132	7 more parts of the body
159	16 picture words for lines 5 and 6 of consonants

B Read the chart and circle the correct alternatives in 1–5.

	Canada	China	Russia
Size in km²	9,984,670	9,598,086	17,098,242
Population	37 million	1,415 million	144 million
Life expectancy	82 years	76.5 years	71 years
Highest point	Mount Logan, 5,959 m	Mount Everest, 8,848 m	Mount Elbrus, 5,642 m

1 Russia is **smaller** / **larger** than China.
2 China has a **bigger** / **smaller** population than Russia.
3 Canada is **more** / **less** populated than Russia.
4 People live longer in China than in **Russia** / **Canada**.
5 Mount Logan is higher than **Everest** / **Elbrus**.

C **Make it personal** In pairs, ask and answer 1–4 with superlatives about your country.
1 Which country is the _____ (**small** / **big**)?
2 Which country has the _____ (**large** / **small**) population?
3 Where do people live the _____ (**long** / **short**)?
4 Which is the _____ (**high**) mountain?

D In pairs, ask and answer 1–6 about the picture.
1 What is Mark saying? And the chef's answer?
2 Are Fred and Rory honest? Why (not)?
3 What's Scott going to do? What's Laila going to say?
4 Is the floor going to get messy? Why?
5 Are Rachel and Owen happy? Why (not)?
6 Which character do you like best? Why?

E ▶R5.1 Order requests 1–6, adding a verb to each. Listen to check.
1 you / mind / / do / your / if / bike / I / ?
 Do you mind if I borrow your bike?
2 a / / could / pen / me / you / ?
 _____
3 door / I / / the / can / ?
 _____
4 mind / I / / pizza / this / you / do / if / ?
 _____
5 your / can / / laptop / I / ?
 _____
6 earlier / home / / I / could / today / ?
 _____

F In pairs, practice 1–6 in **E**. Vary your questions and answers.

 Could I borrow your bike this afternoon?
 No, sorry. I'm doing a triathlon next week. I need to train!

G Play *Describe it!* In groups of three, take turns describing an item from units 9 and 10 for your partners to guess. How many can you describe and guess in four minutes?

 It's the opposite of (thin).
 It's what you say when (you meet somebody).

H Correct the mistakes. Check your answers in units 9 and 10.
1 My mom is great cooker. (2 mistakes)
2 I'm student in UCLA and I'm an unemployed. (3 mistakes)
3 Sales assistants don't win a lot money. (2 mistakes)
4 I don't do anything special next weekend. (2 mistakes)
5 Are you gonna to go to the party? (1 mistake)
6 Could you borrow me your charger? (1 mistake)
7 We run the New York marathon the next week. (2 mistakes)
8 She looks like slim with the long curly hair. (2 mistakes)
9 I'm more big then my father. (2 mistakes)
10 It's the most old city of the country. (2 mistakes)

Skills practice

R5

🎵 *Work it Harder, Make it Better, Do it Faster, Makes us Stronger, More than Ever.*

A In teams, play *Give us a clue!* **Team A:** cover card 2. **Team B:** cover card 1. Give one clue at a time. You score three points for a correct answer after clue a, two after clue b, or one after clue c. Write one extra question with three clues.

OK, number one.   *The first clue is …*

Uh, we don't know. Give us the next clue.

CARD 1

1 People in this job:
  a studied a lot for their job.
  b usually wear a white coat to work.
  c work with animals.
2 People in this job:
  a wear a uniform.
  b have a dangerous profession.
  c look for criminals.
3 This type of transportation is:
  a common in big cities.
  b a kind of train.
  c under the streets.
4 This type of transportation is:
  a good for you.
  b free.
  c faster than walking.
5 a You have two of them.
  b They're part of your head.
  c You listen with them.

CARD 2

1 People in this job:
  a wear a mask.
  b are often unpopular with children.
  c care for our teeth.
2 People in this job:
  a serve people.
  b travel a lot.
  c work on a plane.
3 This type of transportation:
  a is large.
  b carries people.
  c travels on the road.
4 This type of transportation:
  a travels on the road.
  b is dangerous.
  c in heavy traffic, is faster than a car.
5 a You have lots of them.
  b They are part of your legs.
  c They are shorter than your fingers.

B 🔴 **Make it personal** In pairs, ask and answer 1–3. Do you agree?
1 Which profession in **A** is the best paid / the most interesting / the most difficult / the most dangerous? Why?
2 Do you use the methods of transportation from the quiz? Which do you prefer? Why?
3 Which is more important to you: your eyes, ears, or hands?

C 🔴 **Make it personal** In pairs, use the chart to ask and answer ten superlative questions. Do you agree?

Who / What is the	(bad) (delicious) (exciting) (famous) (funny) (good) (interesting) (young)	food restaurant singer actor writer student model cook politician	in the world? in this country? in this neighborhood? in our class?

D Read Laila's email. True (T), False (F), or Not mentioned (N)?

Hi Jenna!

All good with you? I hope so! Well, me, I'm finishing grad school soon and I have to start making plans now! I'm taking a vacation first. I'm going to Thailand with Scott for two weeks, I can't wait! But, before that, I'm moving out of my apartment, so right now I'm busy packing everything. I'm actually looking for a new apartment at the moment. Do you know anywhere I could stay? Fingers crossed! 🙂 Then when we get back from vacation, I'm going to find a job. Wish me luck!

Love, Laila

1 Laila left grad school recently. _____
2 Scott is Jenna's boyfriend. _____
3 After her vacation, she's leaving her apartment. _____
4 She's going to find a place to live alone. _____
5 She has a job to go to when she gets back. _____

E ▶ **R5.2** Listen to Laila and Jenna and answer 1–3.
1 Which room does Jenna offer to Laila?
2 When is Laila going to fly to Thailand?
3 How long does she need the room for?

F 🔴 **Make it personal** Question time.
In pairs, practice asking and answering the 12 lesson titles in units 9 and 10. Use the book map on p. 2–3. Where possible, ask follow-up questions, too. Can you comfortably ask and answer all the questions?

How did you get here today?   *I came by car.*

Did you drive?   *No, I came with a friend.*

137

Grammar Unit 1

1A Verb *be* +/- and *Yes* / *No* ?

The verb *be* only has three forms: *am, is, are*.
Use contractions when you speak or write informally.

+		Contractions	
I *am*		I'm	a student.
You (singular) *are*		You're	Latin American.
He / She / It *is*		He's / She's / It's	Panamanian.
We *are*		We're	from Brazil.
You (plural) *are*		You're	students.
They *are*		They're	British.

−	
I'm not	Colombian.
You're **not** or **aren't**	Asian.
He's / She's / It's **not** or **isn't**	Spanish.
We / You / They're **not** or **aren't**	Canadian.

	Short answers	
?	Yes	No
Are you from the U.S.? Are you American?	Yes, I am. Yes, I'm Texan.	No, I'm not.
Is he a great player? Is she an OK actor? Is it a Chinese phone?	Yes, he is. Yes, she is. Yes, it is.	No, he's not. / isn't. No, she's not. / isn't. No, it is not. / isn't.
Are you students?	Yes, we are.	No, we're not. / aren't.
Are they actors?	Yes, they are.	No, they're not. / aren't.

We usually answer *Yes / No* questions with a short answer.
Are you Spanish? Yes, I am. NOT *Yes, I'm.*
Do not use contractions with + short answers.

1B Adjectives and *a / an* + noun

a	an
She's **a** good person.	He's **an** interesting person.

Use *a* before a consonant sound / *an* before a vowel sound.

Adjectives

article adjective noun	article adjective noun
Neymar's a Brazilian soccer player.	Jennifer Lawrence is a fantastic actor.
Buenos Aires is a great city.	This is a green book. Those are green books.

In English, the adjective comes *before* a noun, and doesn't have a plural form.

1C Verb *be*: *Wh-* ?

- **What**'s your address?
- **Where** are you from?
- **Why** are they here?
- **When**'s your birthday?
- **Who**'s he?
- **How** are you?

Wh- question words come before the verb *be*.
Remember to invert in questions.
Where are you from? NOT *Where you are from?*

1D Demonstrative pronouns

Use *this / these* for things or people that are with you or near you (here).
- **This** is my pen. (It's with me.)
- **These** are my keys. (They're here.)

Use *that / those* for things or people that are with other people or distant from you (there).
- **That**'s my pen. (It's on the table.)
- **Those** are my keys. (They're there.)

Remember to invert in questions.
Is this your book? NOT *This is your book?*
Use pronouns in answers.
Yes, it is. NOT *Yes, this is.*

1E Possessive adjectives

Subject pronoun	Possessive adjective
I	**My** car is blue.
You	**Your** green glasses are on the table.
He	**His** new laptop is fantastic.
She	That's **her** teacher.
It	This is my dog. Oh, what's **its** name?
We	**Our** friends are here.
You	Please turn off **your** cell phones.
They	**Their** city is really cool.

Possessive adjectives only have one form.
Possessive adjectives go before a noun or an adjective + noun.
My new shoes. NOT *Mys shoes news.*

*Hi, I'm **your** teacher. **My** name's Bruno.*

Unit 1

1A

1 **Complete 1–5 with verb *be*. Use contractions when possible.**
   1 He _____ not from the U.S. He _____ Canadian.
   2 We _____ not Hawaiian, we _____ Mexican.
   3 It _____ not an Irish flag, it _____ an Italian flag.
   4 They _____ from NY, but the statue _____ from France!
   5 Her name _____ not Emma. It _____ Emily.

2 **Complete 1–5 with verb *be*. In pairs, ask and answer. Remember to use short answers when possible.**
   1 _____ you Chilean?
   2 _____ Christ the Redeemer statue in Spain?
   3 _____ Justin Bieber American?
   4 _____ you and Neymar friends?
   5 _____ Idris Elba and Emily Blunt British?

1B

1 **Correct the mistakes.**
   1 She's a girl cool.
   2 They're not actors terrible.
   3 Rio de Janeiro is a city excellent.
   4 You're a player fantastic.
   5 Is it a car Korean?

2 **Order the words to make sentences.**
   1 interesting / is / San Francisco / an / city / .
   2 actor / intelligent / an / Antonio Banderas / is / .
   3 players / are / they / important / soccer / .
   4 is / a / ridiculous / it / movie / .
   5 excellent / I / student / an / am / .

1C

1 **Order the words to make Wh- questions.**
   1 the name of / what / in Mexico / 's / that place / ?
   2 are / when / home / you / ?
   3 who / your / 's / friend / best / ?
   4 you / why / are / here / ?
   5 email / 's / what / address / your / ?

2 **Correct the mistakes.**
   1 How's her name?
   2 What's your favorite actor?
   3 Is where his laptop?
   4 Why you're in this class?
   5 What's your favorite cities?

1D

1 **Look at the examples and write questions and answers.**
   What are those?   Those are …
   What's this?   This is …

2 **Complete with the correct demonstrative pronoun.**
   1 _____ is a blue bookbag.
   2 Is _____ your friend Tina?
   3 _____ are my friends, Dan and Mary.
   4 _____ is not my homework. _____ is my homework.
   5 _____ is my email address.

1E

1 **Correct two mistakes in each.**
   1 Her name is José and she's from Spain.
   2 I think his name is Mary. She's american.
   3 Is we in the same English class?
   4 These is our teacher, Ms. Jones. We are in his class.
   5 That not my phone. The my phone is black.

2 **Complete with the correct possessive adjectives.**
   1 _____ name is Daniel and I'm from Mexico.
   2 This is my friend. _____ name is Karina.
   3 We are in English class together. _____ school is in California.
   4 This is our new teacher. _____ name is Bruno.
   5 These are my parents. _____ names are David and Marcia.

139

Grammar Unit 2

2A Simple present ⊕ ⊖

The simple present only has two forms:
1 The infinitive, used for *I / You / We / They*
2 The infinitive + *s* used for *He / She / It*

Use the simple present:
– for routines, habits, repeated actions
– for facts
– for scheduled events
– with time phrases (*every morning, sometimes,* etc.)

▸ *I wake up at 7 a.m. every day.* (routine)
▸ *You never study before tests.* (habit)
▸ *Banks don't open on weekends.* (fact)
▸ *We have a meeting today at 2 p.m.* (scheduled event)

Subject	⊕	
I / You / We / They	live	in Paris.

Subject	⊖	
I / You / We / They	do not / don't live	in Ecuador.

⊕ Use *I, you, we,* and *they* + the infinitive. (I)
⊖ Use *do* + *not* before the verb. Contraction = *don't*.
We don't have a car. NOT ~~We have no car.~~

Third person singular: *she, he,* and *it* + *s*

Subject	⊕	
She / He	plays	volleyball.

Subject	⊖	
She / He	doesn't play	golf.

Spelling rules:
Most verbs add -*s*: *knows, speaks, loves.*
Verbs ending in -*ch*, -*sh*, -*ss*, -*x*, or -*o*, add -*es*: *ch – watches; sh – finishes; ss – kisses; x – mixes; o – goes.*
Verbs ending in consonant + -*y*: change *y* to *i* and add -*es*: *study – studies.*

Notes:
do ends with *o*, so it is spelled -*es* (*does*) in the third person.
When we use the auxiliary, the main verb is always an infinitive:
▸ *He works here. – He doesn't work here.*
▸ *She goes to school. – She doesn't go to school.*

Why does Superman have an ?
Because he is the *third person*.
*He hate**s** kryptonite, he love**s** Lois, and he do**es**n't like bad guys!*

2B Simple present ❓

A	S	I (O)	Short answers
Do	you	**like** sports?	Yes, I do. / No, I don't.
Does	he	**live** here?	Yes, he does. / No, he doesn't.
Does	she	**play** tennis?	Yes, she does. / No, she doesn't.
Do	they	**work** near here?	Yes, they do. / No, they don't.

To form a *Yes / No* question use:
Auxiliary (*do / does*) + **S**ubject + **I**nfinitive (+ object) = **A S I (O)**.
Short answers use: *do / does* or *don't / doesn't*.

Q	A	S	I (O)
When	do	you	get up?
What	does	Joe	do in the evenings?
Why	does	Sue	work at night?
How	do	they	go to the beach?

To form a *Wh-* question use:
Question word + **A**uxiliary (*do / does*) + **S**ubject + **I**nfinitive (+ object) = **Q A S I (O)**.

2C Frequency adverbs

100% → **always** → **usually** → **often** → **sometimes** → **occasionally** → **rarely** → **never** → 0%

▸ How **often** do you drink coffee?
   I **always** have two cups for breakfast.
▸ How **often** does he exercise?
   He **rarely** exercises.

Adverbs of frequency go before the main verb.

Use **time expressions** to say how many times something occurs.

▸ When do you go to the gym?
   I go to the gym at 7 a.m. on Mondays and Wednesdays.
   = I go to the gym **twice a week**.
▸ I go out every Saturday. = I go out **once a week**.

2D Prepositions of time

▸ *I sometimes go to work **at** around 5:15 p.m.*
▸ *We never go out **at** night.*
▸ *Dad usually visits me **at** Christmas.*

Use *at* with times, night, and holidays (without day).

▸ *Our vacation is always **in** January.*
▸ *See you **in** the morning / afternoon / evening.*

Use *in* with months and parts of a day (except *night*).

▸ *I do yoga **on** Tuesdays / Tuesday nights.*
▸ *I rarely work **on** Friday (evenings).*
▸ *We go shopping **on** weekends.*

Use *on* with days, day + part of a day, and *weekend*.

Unit 2

2A

1 Match the verbs to the people. Then complete 1–6.

| drive | exercise | have breakfast |
| leave home | live | walk |

1 Jane _____ at 8 a.m.
2 Mr. Jones _____ to work every day.
3 Andy _____ Jane to school by 8:30.
4 Mary and Jack _____ at 8 a.m.
5 Miguel _____ in the morning.
6 They all _____ in houses.

2 Make negative sentences about the people in 1.

1 Miguel _____ 8 a.m. (**not leave home**)
2 Jane _____ on weekdays. (**not exercise**)
3 Andy and Jane _____ at 8 a.m. (**not have breakfast**)
4 Mary and Jack _____ to work. (**not walk**)
5 Mr. Jones _____ to work every day. (**not drive**)
6 Mary _____ with Andy. (**not live**)

3 Circle the correct auxiliary.

1 What time **do / does** they usually get up?
2 When **do / does** he leave for work in the morning?
3 **Do / Does** you live with your parents?
4 Where **do / does** people go shopping in this neighborhood?
5 **Don't / Doesn't** we have school in December?
6 Where **do / does** their dog live?

2B

1 Order the words to make *Wh-* questions.

1 have / breakfast / you / do / when / ?
2 go / where / he / morning / does / every / ?
3 out / usually / time / what / she / does / go / ?
4 at / they / gym / often / exercise / the / how / do / ?
5 who / visit / when / go / you / do / you / Texas / to / ?

2 Complete the dialogue with auxiliaries.

A: Wow, you're here! _____ you always come to class this early?
B: No. I _____ always get here this early on Mondays.
A: I see. Well, _____ the class always start on time?
B: Hmm, sometimes it _____, but occasionally it _____. We never know.
A: Hey, _____ that girl always sit at the back of the class?
B: Yes, she _____. And she always listens to music before class.
A: I _____ that, too.

2C

1 Match the frequency adverbs to sentences 1–5.

1 They study on Mondays, Tuesdays, Fridays, and Sundays.
2 She goes to the office on Tuesdays and Thursdays.
3 He likes to relax and play video games every day.
4 They don't travel together.
5 We visit our parents twice a year.

☐ never ☐ always ☐ often
☐ rarely ☐ sometimes

2D

1 Circle the correct preposition.

1 We are always in class **at / in / on** 3 p.m.
2 Jackie is never **at / in / on** time for work.
3 You can complete this language course **at / in / on** 15 hours.
4 His birthday is **at / in / on** Monday. Let's have a party!
5 They start the semester **at / in / on** January.

141

Grammar Unit 3

3A Present continuous ⊕ ⊖

Subject	Present of *be*	Verb + *ing* + object	
I	am / am not 'm / 'm not	reading	this box.
You / We / They	are / are not 're not / aren't		
She / He / It	is / is not 's not / isn't	walking	right now.

Use the **present continuous** for actions in progress now.
Do not contract *am* + *not* (~~I amn't~~).

Spelling

Present participle (-*ing*)	Spelling rule
She's **listening** to a song. They're **playing** a game.	Most verbs, add -*ing*.
I'm **making** a cake. Our train's **arriving**.	Verbs ending in -*e*, change -*e* to -*ing*.
They're **running** a race. I'm **sitting** alone.	Verbs ending in consonant + vowel + consonant (CVC), double the final C + -*ing*.
Look! Mike's **boxing** now.	Don't double consonants *x* or *w*.

3B Present continuous ❓

Yes / No ❓

Present of *be*	Subject	Verb + *ing* + object	
Am	I		
Are / Aren't	you / we / they	listening	to the news?
Is / Isn't	she / he		
Is / Isn't	it	raining	now?

We usually answer Yes / No questions with a short answer.
▸ *Aren't you coming with me?*   *Yes, I am. / No, I'm not.*

Wh- ❓

Wh-word	Present of *be*	Subject	Verb + *ing* + object	
Who	am	I	talking	to?
Why	are	you / we / they	driving	fast?
When	is	she / he	running	that marathon?
Where	is	it	raining	now?

We often use contractions in questions and responses.
▸ *What's she doing?*
She's watching the weather report.

Present continuous for things happening around now

At the moment	Around now
I'm watching TV right now.	I'm watching TV a lot these days.
Look! He's taking her money!	I'm taking dance lessons this semester.

It is very common to use the **present continuous** to talk about things that are happening around now.

3C Simple present and present continuous

Use the **simple present** for a daily habit, routine, facts, or scheduled events.

Use the **present continuous** for:
▸ an action happening at the moment or a break in a routine.
▸ processes in progress but not necessarily happening right now.
I'm doing a degree in Engineering (but I'm not studying today).
▸ for future plans/arrangements. (see Unit 9)
What are you doing after class?
I'm going home, then I'm working. NOT ~~I go home then I work.~~
Are you coming out later?
No, we're staying home all weekend.

Other future time expressions; *in a few minutes, this evening, tonight, tomorrow* (*morning*), *next week, this semester, in the summer*, etc. (See Unit 9)

Routine / Habit	Now, developing, or breaking routine
It never snows in March.	Look, it's snowing! (now)
I go to the salon every Saturday.	I'm driving to the salon. (now)

Adverbs of frequency and time phrases can help you decide when to use **simple present** or **present continuous**.

Simple present	Present continuous
always, sometimes, usually, often, every day, occasionally, never, first, next, then, rarely	at the moment, at this moment, just, right now, just now, now, still

Verbs for emotion, senses, or mental states

adore, appear, be, believe, dislike, hate, have, know, like, look, love, mean, prefer, remember, see, seem, smell, sound, surprise, understand, want.

Use the **simple present** not the present continuous with these verbs.

Correct	Incorrect
He believes you.	He's believing you.
She doesn't understand.	She's not understanding.
They like this party.	They're liking this party.
Do you remember it all?	Are you remembering it all?

Note: Phrases like "I'm loving it!" or "I'm liking this." are now used in informal conversation.

Unit 3

3A

1 Complete 1–6 with the present continuous.
1. Look, it _____ today. But it's really windy. (**not / rain**)
2. Why _____ her homework? (**not / do**)
3. Are you _____ a friend and _____ to me at the same time? (**text**) (**talk**)
4. Excuse me, I _____ the subway station. (**look for**)
5. Where _____ the other students _____ after class? (**go**)
6. I think they _____ for a coffee. (**meet**)

2 Look at the example and write sentences about the picture.

Victor is sleeping.

3B

1 Order 1–6 to form questions, then ask and answer in pairs.
1. right now / what / you / doing / are / ?
2. you / are / at the moment / with your family / living / ?
3. doing / much exercise / you / these days / are / ?
4. working / at the moment / where / are / you / ?
5. another / Chinese / are / or / studying / you / language / ?
6. learning / you / why / are / English / here / ?

2 Do 1–7 refer to right now (RN), around now (AN), or future (F)?
1. I'm watching a great show on TV, so I can't chat.
2. We're watching a lot of TV at the moment, usually around three hours a day!
3. I'm not coming on Monday, I'm going to the dentist's.
4. I'm working in Paris at the moment, lucky me!
5. I'm still working, so I can't come to the movies with you.
6. The sun is shining and we're sitting on the beach.
7. We're leaving early tonight to avoid the traffic.

3C

1 Correct the mistakes.
1. Hey. What do you do? Are you busy?
   No. I have lunch right now. What do you think of doing?
2. Where is she buying her clothes? I am wanting to go there, too!
   Yeah! She looking great. I think about buying the same dress!
3. Hey, where does he go? We having a meeting in a few minutes.
   I am not knowing. He talk on his cell phone in the hall.
4. I'm not believing you all finally here. Wow!
   Yeah, and we stay at a great hotel! We love New York in the summer.
5. I'm have a salad. Are you just eat a hamburger?
   No, I'm not. I'm always ordering French fries and a soda.

2 Circle the correct form of the verb.
1. I **'m talking** / **talk** to you on the phone and walking.
2. We often **are cooking** / **cook** dinner before watching TV.
3. I **'m hating** / **hate** talking about politics in class.
4. She **'s riding** / **rides** a bike to work, because her car is at the mechanic's.
5. He's not at the office, so he **emails** / **'s emailing** us from his smartphone.
6. I **'m not going** / **don't go** out tonight. I'm too tired.

143

Grammar Unit 4

4A Definite article *the*

English has only one definite article: *the*. The form never changes.
Use *the*
- to refer to something already mentioned.
  *I rent a place here. **The** apartment's very nice.*
- when you imagine there's only one.
  *Where's **the** bathroom?*
- before superlatives and ordinal numbers.
  *"Uptown Funk" is **the** best Bruno Mars song.*
  *These are **the** first mangoes of the year.*

Do not use *the*
- with plural nouns.
  I love beans.
- with uncountable nouns.
  We often eat rice.
- to talk about things in general.
  I don't like politics, I enjoy watching detective movies.

4B Can

Can: ⊕ ⊖

Subject	Modal	Infinitive (+ object)
I / You	can	play the piano.
He / She / It	can't /	drive a truck.
We / They	cannot	speak English.
		dance well.

Can is a modal auxiliary verb with the same form for all persons. It is followed by infinitive without *to*.
We can swim. NOT *We can to swim.*
It means "be able to" or "know how to":
- *I **can** play tennis. = I'm able to play tennis.*
- *I **can't** drive = I don't know how to drive.*

Use *well*, *very well*, (*not*) *at all* to describe the level of ability.
- *He **can't** ride a bike **very well**, but he **can** run.*
- *We **can't** play the piano **at all**, but we **can** sing **well**!*
- *She **can't** play golf, but she **can** play soccer **very well**.*

Can: Yes / No ❓

Modal	Subject	Infinitive (+ object)	Short answers
Can / Can't	I / you / she / he / we / they	sing? come to the party? ski?	Yes, _____ can. / No, _____ can't.

- *I **can** speak English, but I **can't** speak Japanese.*

Can: Wh- ❓

Q	A modal (*can*)	S	I (+ object)
What	can	you	play on the piano?

Other meanings of *can*

Can has many different uses. Here are a few:
- **Possibility**: *You **can** read about the school on their website.*
- **Requests**: *Can I please see your passport and ID?*
- **Permission**: *You **can** use my car, but you have to come home by 10 p.m.*
- **Favors**: *Please can you pick me up at the airport?*

4C Possessive pronouns

Possessive adjective	Possessive pronoun
This is not **my** jacket.	**Mine**'s blue.
I think **your** keys are on the table.	These keys aren't **yours**.
Are those **his** glasses?	No, these green glasses are **his**.
Is that **her** phone?	No, this white phone is **hers**.
These are **our** sandwiches.	But those cookies aren't **ours**.
I think **your** coats are over there.	Are they **yours**?
Their house is beautiful.	Which house is **theirs**?

English only has six possessive pronouns. *Yours* is both singular and plural. A **possessive pronoun** substitutes a possessive adjective + noun.
Use *Whose* to ask about possession.
- *Whose book is that? Whose books are those?*
NOT *Of who is this book?*

4D Possessive 's

1. Add 's to names and nouns to indicate possession.
   That's the teacher's chair. NOT *That's the chair of the teacher.*
- *That book is Jenna's. → It's hers.*
- *Isn't that Nina's car?*
- *This is someone's money, but not mine.*

2. Names ending in -s, use 's or just an apostrophe after the letter (s').
- *It's James's iPad. = It's James' iPad.*

3. Regular plurals add an apostrophe after the s.
- *Isn't that your parents' house?*

4. Irregular plurals add 's.
- *Which are your children's toys?*

Unit 4

4A

1 Circle the correct article in 1–10 (θ = no article).
1. I love **a** / **the** / **θ** dogs, but I hate **a** / **the** / **θ** cats.
2. We live in **a** / **the** / **θ** small house. My grandmother lives on **a** / **the** / **θ** same street.
3. Excuse me. Can you tell me where **an** / **the** / **θ** elevator is?
4. I need **a** / **the** / **θ** chocolate! Where's **a** / **the** / **θ** nearest grocery store?
5. My brother lives on **a** / **the** / **θ** first floor of that building. It's **a** / **the** / **θ** great apartment.
6. I never eat **a** / **the** / **θ** French fries at **a** / **the** / **θ** home.
7. **a** / **the** / **θ** Camila's sister has **a** / **the** / **θ** green eyes and **a** / **the** / **θ** beautiful dark hair.
8. I love **a** / **the** / **θ** sports and I'm really enjoying **a** / **the** / **θ** sports documentary series on Channel 5.
9. I never eat **a** / **the** / **θ** breakfast on **a** / **the** / **θ** weekends.
10. I hate **a** / **the** / **θ** messy people!

4B

1 Complete 1–5 with *can* / *can't* and the verbs.

drive	play	ride	swim	use

1. He loves American football. He _____ very well.
2. Is that your new bike? _____ you _____ it? It looks too big!
3. This hotel has an amazing pool. It's too bad I _____.
4. I don't know how she's a writer. She _____ a computer!
5. _____ you _____? I need to get home quickly!

2 What can / can't each person in the pictures do? Use your own ideas.
1. Lee can _____, but he can't _____.
2. Martin can't _____, but he can _____.
3. George can't _____, but he can _____.
4. Janice can _____, but she can't _____.
5. May can't _____, but she can _____.

3 Write *Wh-* questions for answers 1–5.
1. We can be at the train station by 6 o'clock.
   What time can you be at the train station?
2. You can take the train from Central Station.
3. He can't play soccer or baseball.
4. My mother can cook Italian food really well!
5. We can serve your breakfast from 7 to 10 a.m.

4 Are 1–5 ability (A), possibility (P), or request (R)?
1. Can you come to a party on Saturday night? _____
2. Can we open the window, please? _____
3. Can't we get tickets for the movie tonight? _____
4. Can I use your car this weekend? _____
5. Can she play the piano and sing? _____
6. Can you watch my bike for a moment, please? _____
7. Can you read that page without your glasses? _____
8. Can you help me with my homework, please? _____
9. Can you tell me how to get to Fifth Street? _____
10. Can you explain that word, please? _____

4C

1 Complete 1–5 with a possessive pronoun.
1. I'm a musician. That guitar is _____.
2. Marcy is always talking to somebody! I think that phone is _____.
3. Your sneakers are blue, not red. Are you sure these are _____?
4. It's really cold in here. Are those _____ sweaters?
5. It looks like Joe's wallet, but I don't think it's _____. He's traveling.

4D

1 Add the possessives ('s) or (').
1. Those are not my shoes, those are Marcus.
2. Where is your grandparent house?
3. My sisters new pants are yellow and blue.
4. That is Charles desk. His dad office is over there.
5. Her friends phone numbers are in her contact list.
6. My mom favorite album is *Queen Greatest Hits*.

145

Grammar Unit 5

5A There is / are ⊕ ⊖ ❓

There is / are ⊕ ⊖

	⊕	⊖	
Singular	There is a park near the river.	There's no / There isn't a	mall near here.
Plural	There are 20 people in the room.	There are no / There aren't any	animals in there.

Use *there is / are* to express "existence" in a physical space.
For negatives, use *there 's / is / are* + *no* or *there isn't / aren't* + *a / any*.

There is / are ❓

❓			Short answers
Is	there	a bank near here? an answer to the question?	Yes, there is. No, there isn't.
Are		any tourists here? any good restaurants in this area?	Yes, there are. No, there aren't.
Isn't		a swimming pool around here?	Yes, there is. No, there isn't.
Aren't		any cups on the table?	Yes, there are. No, there aren't.

Do not use contractions in ⊕ short answers.
Yes, there is. NOT ~~Yes, there's.~~

5B like / love / hate / enjoy / not mind + verb -ing

I	love	to swim / swimming
You	like	to camp / camping
Tom	likes	to read / reading novels.
Nina	doesn't mind	waking up early.
We	hate	cleaning the house.
You	enjoy	listening to music
My brothers	hate	playing baseball.

I don't mind going out on weekends. NOT ~~I don't mind to go out ...~~

Note: Use the gerund (verb + -ing which functions as a noun) as the subject of a sentence.
▸ *Swimming is my favorite sport.*
▸ *Playing tennis is awesome.*
▸ *Studying on the weekend is boring!*
Speaking English is important. NOT ~~To speak English is important.~~

5C Object pronouns

Subject		Object
I love animals, but I don't think they like		me.
You're always trying to help. But who's helping		you?
Martin says people don't understand		him.
Marta's not coming. But why don't you call		her?
Your bag's on the floor. Please put		it on a chair.
Don't worry, we're OK. Everything's fine with		us.
The windows are open, can you close		them, please?

English only has seven object pronouns. Use an **object pronoun** to substitute the **object** of the sentence.
It and *you* (singular and plural) have the same form for both subject and object pronouns.
The other five have different forms.
The object pronoun comes after the verb.
She loves him but he doesn't love her. NOT ~~She him loves but he doesn't her love.~~

Note: We usually refer to an animal with a name as **he / him** or **she / her.**
▸ *Our dog, Bart, is great. He's really friendly! We all adore him.*

5D Imperatives ⊕ and ⊖

⊕	⊖
Sit down.	Don't sit down.
Stand up.	Don't stand up.

Use **imperatives** to give orders or make requests.
▸ *Go away!* (order)
▸ *Don't touch that!* (order)
Imperatives only have one form for all persons.
Use *please* to make a request and sound polite.
▸ *Please be quiet.*
▸ *Don't talk here, please.*
There is no subject in an imperative sentence.
Don't go! NOT ~~Don't you go!~~

5E Comparatives and superlatives

To form comparatives and superlatives with long adjectives use **more / less + the most / the least** + adjective
▸ *You're more adventurous than me.*
▸ *I'm less intelligent than you.*
▸ *Joao's the most adventurous in our class.*
▸ *Who's the least intelligent?*
See p. 156 for more rules.

Unit 5

5A

1 Complete 1–5 with verb *be*. Contract when possible.
1 There _____ a racetrack in Belmont, Long Island.
2 There _____ very important horse races at the track.
3 We're happy because there _____ a new movie theater near us.
4 There _____ three nice hotels and two museums in this city.
5 In our city, there _____ a famous monument next to the station.

2 Order 1–6 to make sentences. Then change them so they're true for you.
1 city / is / football / there / an / enormous / stadium / my / in / .
2 this / restaurants / neighborhood / any / around / aren't / there / .
3 exhibition / is / good / our / local / museum / a / at / there / art / .
4 in / mall / no / there / is / neighborhood / this / .
5 street / my / there / swimming / a / on / isn't / pool / .
6 in / river / a / middle / city / of / our / clean / 's / the / there / capital / .

5B

1 Circle the correct alternative.
1 My son really loves **reading** / **read** comic books.
2 My little sister doesn't mind **to take** / **taking** piano lessons twice a week.
3 All our friends love **playing** / **play** and enjoy **watch** / **watching** international soccer.
4 I really like **go** / **going** to the movies, but it's expensive.
5 We hate **shop** / **shopping** and **to doing** / **doing** the laundry.

2 Correct two mistakes in each.
1 Anna loves wash dishes and to clean the bathroom.
2 I hate to reading novels. I like read biographies or true stories.
3 He doesn't mind to see a romantic movie sometimes, but he not enjoy horror movies.
4 We love to eating out on the weekend. We doesn't like cooking at home.
5 They hate to doing laundry, but don't mind to do dishes.
6 On vacation, I enjoy to hiking and snorkel, but I never go kayaking.

5C

1 Circle the correct object pronouns.
1 Ranger Juan works at this station. Please respect **him** / **her** / **it**.
2 There are bears in the park. Please don't feed **it** / **them** / **us**.
3 Cars are not allowed. Leave **their** / **they** / **them** in the parking lot.
4 Don't leave garbage at the campsite. Throw **him** / **her** / **it** in the trash.
5 We're here to help. Tell **us** / **we** / **me** what we can do for you.

2 Complete the dialogue with object pronouns.
A: I often come to this park. I really love _____.
B: Same here! Ranger Juan is so friendly. I like _____ a lot.
A: Yeah, and there are bears in the forest, but we never see _____.
B: Let's find someone who can help _____ see a bear.
A: Ranger Sarah gives bears medicine and food. Let's talk to _____.

5D

1 Which of 1–5 are orders (O) and which are requests (R)?
1 Please don't open the window. _____
2 Don't eat all the pizza! _____
3 Be quiet! _____
4 Open the door, please. _____
5 Listen to me! _____

2 Write the opposite instruction.
Come in. / Go away.
1 Sit down.
2 Listen to what I'm saying.
3 Please close your eyes.
4 Don't look at the board.
5 Please translate word for word.

147

Grammar Unit 6

6A Countable and uncountable nouns

Countable (C) nouns

Singular	Plural	Singular	Irregular plural
an apple	ten apples	a child	two children
a banana	three bananas	a foot	two feet
a bottle	two bottles	a man	five men
a box	eight boxes	a mouse	ten mice
a baby	four babies	a person	three people

C nouns can be singular or plural, regular, or irregular.
Most plurals are formed with *-s*, but also *-es* or *-ies*. There are a few irregular plurals.
Singular C nouns need an article (*a, an, the*), or quantifier (*some, any,* etc.)

Uncountable (U) nouns
U nouns have only one form.
Food-related: beer, bread, butter, cheese, chocolate, coffee, coke, ice, meat, milk, oil, pasta, pepper, rice, salad, salt, soup, sugar, tea, water, wine, yogurt.
Substances, materials: alcohol, deodorant, detergent, gasoline, gold, paper, perfume, plastic, metal, money, oil, wood.

1 To count U nouns use *a / an / number + portion + of*:
   a piece of bread; *two bottles* of water; *four spoons* of sugar.
2 Some U nouns have only a plural form and take a **plural verb**:
   glasses, gloves, jeans, pants, shoes, shorts, etc.
▸ *My jeans are* new. This is a new pair of jeans.

6B Quantifiers: *some* and *any*

Countable ⊕	Uncountable ⊕
We have **some** apples on our tree. (unspecified number)	I have **some** money for a tip. (enough to pay)

Countable ⊖	Uncountable ⊖
There aren't **any** children in the playground. (zero)	There isn't **any** water in the bottle. (zero)

Countable ?	Uncountable ?
Do you want **any** potatoes? (a portion)	Do you want **any** meat? (a portion)

Use **some** in questions when you expect the answer "yes":

Countable ?	Uncountable ?
Do you want **some** apples?	Do you want **some** cake?

Use **any** in questions when you expect the answer "no" or aren't sure:

Countable ?	Uncountable ?
Are there **any** tomatoes?	Is there **any** milk?

Use:
any with C nouns and the verb in the negative.
▸ *There aren't any* pens on the table.
no with C nouns and the verb in the affirmative.
▸ *There are no* pens or pencils on the table.
any with U nouns and the verb in the negative.
▸ *There isn't any* information on their website.
no with U nouns and the verb in the affirmative.
▸ *There's no* gas in the car.

6C Quantifiers: *a little, a few, a lot of*

Countable ⊕	Uncountable ⊕
I only eat a **few** fries on weekends.	There's a **little** cereal in the box.
There are **a lot of** donuts.	They eat **a lot of** pasta in Italy.

Countable ?	Uncountable ?
Do you eat a **few** cookies a day?	Can we eat a **little** ice cream?
Does he have **a lot of** tomatoes in his garden?	Does she eat **a lot of** bread for breakfast?

Countable ⊖	Uncountable ⊖
There aren't **a lot of** tickets available.	There isn't **a lot of** news online today.

6D *How much* and *how many* ?

Question (*how much*)	Answer ⊕
How much **time** do you have?	There was **a lot of** information on the web.
How much **sugar** do you want?	Just **a little**, please.
How much **exercise** do you get?	I work out **a lot**.
Question (*how many*)	**Answer** ⊕
How many **dresses** does she have?	I know she has **a lot of** dresses. More than 20.
How many **eggs** do we need?	Only **a few**.
How many **people** are in the class?	**A lot.** Over 15!
Question (*how much / how many*)	**Answer** ⊖
How much **meat** do you want?	I don't want **any** meat. / I want **no** meat.
How much **homework** do you get?	Not much.
How many **apps** do you use?	I use **no** apps. / I don't have **any** apps.
How many **friends** do you have?	Not many.
How many **watches** do you have?	None. I use my phone.

Use:
how many to ask about **plural C nouns**.
how much to ask about **U nouns**.
any with a ⊖ verb, and **no** with a ⊕ verb in ⊖ answers.
any and **no** with the noun in the **plural (C nouns)**.

Unit 6

6A

1 Circle the correct words in 1–5.
1. I'm buying some **cookies / cookie** for dessert.
2. I need some **information / informations** before I can go.
3. Remember to buy some **cheeses / cheese**, please.
4. Can you put some **breads / bread** in the toaster?
5. I'd like some **egg / eggs** for breakfast.

2 C or U? Cross out the odd word.
1. bread water apples milk
2. information books computers magazines
3. paper metal children rice
4. men women perfume bananas
5. eggs money dollars euros
6. news information paper ideas

6B

1 Complete 1–5 with some or any.
1. I'm looking for organic pasta, but I can't find _____.
2. There isn't _____ cheese for our sandwiches, so we're cooking _____ eggs instead.
3. There isn't _____ information about the restaurant online, so let's stay home and order _____ pizza.
4. I can't see _____ healthy dishes on the menu.
5. I don't eat meat, but I do eat _____ fish occasionally.

2 Complete questions 1–5 using some or any.
1. Is there _____ chocolate?
   No, of course not!
2. Do you want _____ of this delicious chicken?
   Yes!
3. Are there _____ tomatoes in this pie?
   No! It's a banana pie!
4. I know you don't like pasta, but do you want _____?
   No way, you can have it all.
5. It's your favorite cake, do you want _____?
   Yes, of course I do!

6C

1 Circle the correct quantifier.
1. I'm buying **a few / a little** sugar because I don't have **many / much** left.
2. Dad wants to cook **some / any** pasta, but he has **no / none**, so we're having potatoes instead.
3. There's **many / a lot of** meat, but not **much / many** milk in the refrigerator.
4. For breakfast, I like **a little / a few** eggs, but I don't drink **much / many** juice.
5. There's **no / any** fruit in the refrigerator for after dinner, just **a few / a little** chocolate.

2 Correct the mistakes. Are 1–5 true or false about you?
1. I don't eat a little meat, just once a week.
2. I drink a few juice for breakfast.
3. In my family, we eat a little bananas every week.
4. I don't drink a few coffee – about two cups a day.
5. I sometimes eat a few junk food, especially on weekends.

6D

1 Circle the correct words in 1–5.
1. How much **sugar / apples** do you want?
2. How many **pies / bread** is Mom cooking for dinner?
3. I don't know **how much / how many** coffee you drink, but I made a lot.
4. How much **money / dollars** did all this chocolate cost? You bought a lot!
5. He didn't know **how much / how many** eggs were in the refrigerator.

2 Complete 1–5 with how much or how many and match them to pictures a–e.
1. Please, tell the baker _____ cupcakes you'd like.
2. Let me know _____ people you're bringing to the party.
3. Look at this! _____ chocolate did you buy this time?
4. _____ slices of pie did they order?
5. _____ ice would you like in your drink?

149

Grammar Unit 7

7A There was / there were ⊕ ⊖

	⊕	⊖
Singular	There **was** a car in front of the house.	There was **no** gas in the tank. There wasn't **any** gas in the tank.
Plural	There **were** two cars on the street.	There were **no** parking spaces. There weren't **any** parking spaces.

Use: *there was / there were* for "existence" in a place in the past.
Form: *there* + past tense *be* + quantifier + noun phrase.
There was an accident in my street. NOT ~~It was an accident …~~
There weren't any police officers. NOT ~~Had no police officers.~~

There was / there were ❓

Past of *be* ⊕ ⊖		Object	Short answers ⊕ ⊖
Was / Wasn't	there	a gas station near here?	Yes, there was. / No, there wasn't.
Were / Weren't		a lot of people at the party?	Yes, there were. / No, there weren't.

Remember to invert in questions.
Were there any special offers? NOT ~~There were any special offers?~~
Note: Use *a lot of* + noun for large quantities.

7B Past of *be* ⊕ ⊖

Subject	Past of *be* ⊕	Past of *be* ⊖	Object phrase
I / She / He / It	was	was not / wasn't	at the party yesterday.
We / You / They	were	were not / weren't	

Be in the past tense has only two forms and two contractions.
Note: Be careful with *you* singular and plural.
▸ You were late. Yes, I was. Sorry.
▸ You were late. Yes, we were. The traffic was horrible.

Common past time expressions:
▸ She **was** here **a few minutes ago**.
▸ I **wasn't** at home **last night**.
▸ We **were** at the concert **last Saturday**.
▸ They **were** in Italy **in 2017**.

In time expressions, don't put *the* before *last* or *next*.
I was ill last night. NOT ~~the last night~~
See you next week. NOT ~~the next week~~

Yes / No ❓

Past of *be*	Subject	Phrase
Was / Wasn't Were / Weren't	I you	in your class? at the party?
Was / Wasn't	she he it	at the gym? in class? a good party?
Were / Weren't	we you they	in your class? in school? at work?

Short answers ⊕ ⊖
Yes, I was. / No, I wasn't.
Yes, you were. / No, you weren't.

Yes, she was. he it	No, she wasn't. he it

Yes, you were. / No, you weren't.
Yes, we were. / No, we weren't.
Yes, they were. / No, they weren't.

7C Prepositions of place

▸ The armchair is **between** the window and the fireplace.
▸ The box is **on** the armchair.
▸ The cat's **in / inside** the box.
▸ The picture's **above / over** the TV.
▸ The skateboard's **under** the armchair.
▸ The sofa's **across from / opposite** the TV.
▸ The phone's **in front of** the TV.
▸ The fireplace is **next to** the armchair.
▸ The fan's **behind** the TV.
▸ The TV's **below** the picture.

150

Unit 7

7A

1 Correct the mistakes in 1–5.
1. No had television when dad was a child.
2. In my last house, there wasn't any closets.
3. There no was food in that kitchen yesterday.
4. Were not there two bathrooms and a toilet downstairs?
5. No was there sofa or chair in that hotel room?

2 Order 1–5 to make sentences.
1. wasn't / furniture / any / her / in / apartment / there / .
2. balloons / there / no / at / party / his / birthday / were / .
3. snacks / table / the / on / were / there / .
4. was / kitchen / the / lemonade / there / in / .
5. napkins / any / there / on / table / the / weren't / .

7B

1 Order 1–5 to make questions and cross out the extra word in each.
1. were / at / park / on / you / last weekend / the / ?
2. yesterday / what / were / 6 p.m. / where / at / you / ?
3. there / who / with / you / where / was / ?
4. on / was / movies / there / any / were / last night / interesting / TV / ?
5. you / in / where / last Saturday / were / ?
6. in / your / country / family / this / were / last / the / summer / ?

2 Complete the dialogue with the past of verb *be*.
A: When _____ you in Seattle? I _____ there last year!
B: Wow! I _____ there in August. _____ you at the music festival?
A: No, I _____ . _____ there any good bands at the festival?
B: Yes, two local bands and one _____ from Australia.
A: Really? Cool. What _____ the name of the band?

7C

1 Look at the picture. True (T) or False (F)? Correct the false sentences.
1. The cell phone is under the desk.
2. The bed is opposite the desk.
3. There are shoes between the bed and the desk.
4. The night table is next to the desk.
5. There are books on the box.

2 Now circle the correct preposition.
1. The lamp is **in front of** / **behind** the alarm clock.
2. The poster is **above** / **on** the bed.
3. There are two boxes **under** / **behind** the desk.
4. The bed is **next to** / **opposite** the night table.
5. The socks are **on** / **under** the bed.
6. The light switch is **below** / **next to** the door.
7. The two shelves are **on** / **in** the wall, **over** / **below** the table.
8. There are lots of shoes **on** / **across from** the floor.

151

Grammar Unit 8

8A Simple past

Simple past ⊕ ⊖

⊕	⊖
Steve Jobs **lived** in California.	Jobs **didn't study** hard at school.
He **produced** the iPhone and iPad.	He **didn't finish** college.

Use the **simple past** to talk about completed past events. The simple past has only one form for all persons except *was / were*.
▸ I / You / She / He / It / We / You / They **lived** in Mexico City.
▸ I / She / He / It **was** born in Puebla.
▸ You / We / You / They **were** born in Cuernavaca.

Form the negative using *did not / didn't* + infinitive.
▸ Jobs didn't live with his parents. He was adopted.

Common past time expressions include:
▸ a few moments / minutes ago, an hour ago
▸ last night / Monday / week / month / year / century
▸ yesterday evening / afternoon / morning
▸ in 2017, in 1974

Simple past regular verbs – spelling rules

	Spelling rule
They **played** tennis yesterday.	Most verbs: verb + *-ed*.
She **danced** a lot at the party.	Verbs ending in *e*: + *-d*.
The car **stopped** at the traffic lights.	Verbs ending in consonant-vowel-consonant (**CVC**): double the final consonant + *-ed*.
They **tried** to talk to you last Monday.	Verbs ending in **consonant +** *y*: change *y* to *i* and add *-ed*.

8B Simple past irregular verbs

Irregular verbs don't end in *-ed*. They only have one form for all persons.

Most frequent irregular verbs

Infinitive	Past	Infinitive	Past	Infinitive	Past
become	became	hold	held	run	ran
bring	brought	keep	kept	say	said
buy	bought	know	knew	see	saw
do	did	leave	left	sit	sat
feel	felt	lose	lost	speak	spoke
forget	forgot	make	made	stand	stood
get	got	mean	meant	take	took
give	gave	meet	met	tell	told
go	went	pay	paid	think	thought
have	had	put	put	write	wrote
hear	heard	read	read		

Irregular verbs have no formation rules. For a complete list go to the Richmond Learning Platform.

8C Simple past ❓

Yes / No ❓

A	S	I	O
Did	she	go	to the concert?
Did	you	visit	your mom?
Did	they	call	him before the class?
Did	Fred	buy	a new laptop?

Did she call you this morning? NOT ~~She called you this morning?~~

To ask ⊖ questions, use the contracted form *didn't*:
▸ **Didn't he call** yesterday?

Short answers are the same for all persons.
▸ Yes, we did. / No, they didn't.
▸ Yes, she did. / No, he didn't.

Wh- ❓

Q	A	S	I	O
Where	did	you	go	last weekend?
What	did	she	do	last night?
When	did	they	get up	yesterday?
Why	did	he	stay	there?

8D Subject questions

Question word	Simple past	Object
What	happened was	yesterday? that noise?
Who	broke wrote went	the glass? the book? with you?

Subject questions ask for / about the **subject of the answer**. Use **Wh-** words, but **don't** use the auxiliary *did*.
Who helped you? NOT ~~Who did help you?~~

Unit 8

8A

1 Complete with the verbs in parentheses.

Carmen Miranda was born in 1909, on February 9. She _____ (**live**) in Portugal until the age of one when she _____ (**move**) to Brazil with her parents in 1910.

In 1929, Carmen _____ (**record**) her first single and in 1932 she _____ (**appear**) in her first movie. She _____ (**arrive**) in the U.S. in May, 1939, and became a media sensation. She _____ (**become**) the most famous Latin American in the U.S. She _____ (**die**) at 46 of a heart attack on August 4, 1955.

2 Correct 1–5 by making them negative.
1 Carmen Miranda lived in Portugal all her life.
2 She moved to Brazil alone.
3 She recorded her first single in 1932.
4 She appeared in her first movie in 1939.
5 She arrived in the U.S. in 1955.

8B

1 Circle the correct forms in 1–5.
1 Bruce Lee **taught** / **teached** martial arts and **starred** / **stared** in movies in the 1970s.
2 His son Brandon Lee **didn't liked** / **didn't like** school and he didn't finish it.
3 Brandon **taked** / **took** a special test to get his high school diploma.
4 Brandon **studied** / **studied** acting and **makes** / **made** a few movies.
5 Brandon **get** / **got engaged** just before he **dead** / **died**.

2 Complete the story with these verbs.

be	not buy	dance	eat
get	go	have	look	love
see / not see	rain	walk		

I love London! On our first day it <u>rained</u> all day, and we _____ very wet! But, we _____ to the fabulous British Museum and _____ all types of amazing objects from around the world, including many from our country! I _____ the Egyptian mummies! It's huge, so we _____ more than 10% of what's there. After that, we _____ down Oxford Street and _____ in all the shops. I _____ anything as it was so expensive. That night, we _____ dinner in a pub. There _____ a cool band and we _____ for hours. A great day, even with the rain!

8C

1 Order 1–5 to make questions. Take turns asking and answering.
1 do / you / did / Saturday / last / what / ?
2 your / go / with / did / friends / you / ?
3 went / did / to sleep / what / do / you / before / you / ?
4 did / eat / last / what / you / night / ?
5 vacation / last / did / go / where / you / ?

2 Match answers 1–5 to questions a–e.
1 I went out of town last weekend for a few days.
2 I saw some old friends from college.
3 I really didn't spend any time in the city.
4 It rained all weekend, so we stayed in!
5 We watched TV and ate at the restaurant.

a What did you see downtown?
b What did you do at the hotel?
c Who did you meet up with?
d Where did you go for the holiday?
e What was the weather like?

8D

1 Complete dialogues 1–5 with the simple past of these verbs. Which are subject questions?

| announce | give | go | happen | pay | tell |

1 A: Hey, what _____? I heard they canceled your flight!
   B: Yes, they canceled it because of bad weather. Who _____ you that?
2 A: Sylvia saw it on TV. When _____ the airline _____ it?
   B: They didn't do it until 6:30 p.m. And my flight was at 7.
3 A: That's terrible. So, where _____ you _____ after that?
   B: I took a taxi back home with all my bags!
4 A: Gee … And who _____ for the taxi?
   B: Oh, at least the airline paid for it.
5 A: _____ they _____ you a new ticket?
   B: Yep, they gave me one for tomorrow morning.

2 Subject question (S) or object question (O)? Find the answers to the questions.
1 When did The Beatles start playing? _____
2 Who invented the name of the band? _____
3 What type of music did they play? _____
4 Why did the band finish? _____
5 Who composed the hit "Help!"? _____

153

Grammar Unit 9

9A Articles + jobs

Use an indefinite article in front of professions.
▸ *She's an engineer and he's a doctor.*

This becomes definite when we know who the person is.
▸ *The dentist I visit is very professional.*

Note: Don't use an article before adjectives with no nouns.
My father's retired. OR *My father's a retired firefighter.* NOT *My father's a retired.*

9B Future with *be + going to* ➕ ➖

Subject	➕	➖		Infinitive + object
I	'm	'm not		win this game tonight.
You	're	aren't		sing with the band tonight.
She / He	's	isn't	going to	get engaged when he finds a job.
We	're	aren't		visit you next week.
They	're	aren't		study English next year.

Going to is the most common future form in spoken English. Use *be + (not) + going to + infinitive* to talk about:
– general future plans: *I'm going to get married before I'm 30.*
– intentions: *We're going to study English next year, too.*
– predictions: *Look at those clouds. It's going to rain.*

Pronunciation of *going to* in informal speech is often *gonna*.

Be + going to – Yes / No ❓

Verb *be*	S		I + O	A
Am	I		finish my homework tonight?	Yes, I am. / No, I'm not.
Are	you		go out tonight?	Yes, I am. / No, I'm not.
Is	she	going to	find a job?	Yes, she is. / No, she isn't.
Are	we		travel to the U.S. next year?	Yes, we are. / No, we're not.
Are	they		work this weekend?	Yes, they are. / No, they're not.

Be + going to – Wh- ❓

Q	Verb *be*	S		I + O
What	are	you		do tonight?
When	is	she	going to	travel to Spain?
Why	are	they		study Mandarin?
How	are	you		get home?

9C Present continuous as future
➕ ➖ ❓

S	Verb *be* ➕ ➖	V + -ing + O
I	'm (not)	running the marathon next year.
You	're / aren't	leaving for Houston tomorrow.
She / He	's / isn't	taking a French class next semester.
We	're / aren't	having fish for dinner tonight.
They	're / aren't	visiting their grandparents in Europe in June.

Q	S	V + -ing + O	Short answers
Am	I	coming to your birthday party?	Yes, I am. / No, I'm not.
Are	you	watching the game tonight?	Yes, you are. / No you aren't.
Is	she / he	taking the bus to Mexico City?	Yes, she / he is. / No, she / he isn't.
Are	we	doing our homework at your house later?	Yes, we are. / No, we aren't.
Are	they	driving to the beach in the morning?	Yes, they are. / No, they aren't.

9D *Going to* and present continuous as future

Use both *going to* and **present continuous** to talk about future actions / events which are already decided or planned.
▸ *We are going to get a new car.*
▸ *We are getting a new car.*
There's only a subtle difference in meaning.

Going to

Use *be + going to + infinitive* for predictions and intentions.
▸ *I think they're going to win the election.* (prediction)
▸ *I'm going to do all my homework this weekend.* (intention)
▸ *Ted's going to try to take the day off on Friday.* (intention)

Present continuous for future

Use the **present continuous (present of *be* + verb + -ing)** for fixed plans, or personal arrangements with other people. (e.g., things you put in your calendar)
▸ *I'm leaving on the midnight train tomorrow.* (fixed plan = I have a ticket)
▸ *She's having dinner with her mom tomorrow!* (personal arrangement with other people)
▸ *We're buying Terry's car next week.* (personal arrangement with other people)

To differentiate from actions that are happening now, use a **future time expression**.
▸ *I'm leaving.* (**now**)
▸ *I'm leaving in half an hour.* (**future**)

Unit 9

9A

1 Complete the sentences with a / an / θ (θ = no article).

1 Tina's _____ actor.
2 Charlie's _____ flight attendant.
3 I'm _____ unemployed, so I'm going to look for a job.
4 Jack's going to be _____ cook.
5 You're not going to be _____ artist!

9B

1 Look at the picture. Are predictions 1–5 True (T) or False (F)? Look at the example and write sentences about the people in the picture.

1 Charlie's going to cook dinner. _____
2 The cat's going to eat the fish. _____
3 Tina's going to have dinner. _____
4 The kids are going to play games. _____
5 Jack and Jane are going to sleep. _____

Charlie's not going to cook dinner. He's going to wash the dishes first!

2 Circle the correct form in 1–5. Mark intention (I) or prediction (P).

1 People **is** / **are** going to buy flying cars in 10 years. _____
2 I **am going to** / **am going** be a pilot. _____
3 Food **is not** / **are not** going to be more expensive in five years. _____
4 Politicians **are not going** / **are not going to** have a salary. _____
5 I heard Walter and Jen **is** / **are** going to travel to Europe. _____

9C & 9D

1 Look at Rob's diary for next week. True (T) or False (F)? Correct the false ones. Look at the example and write some more sentences about Rob's week.

MONDAY	TUESDAY	WEDNESDAY	THURSDAY	FRIDAY	SATURDAY	SUNDAY
Dentist 9 a.m.	Coffee with Juan	Work	Work	Sofia's party 7 p.m.	Gym	Lunch with Mom and Dad.

1 He's seeing the dentist on Tuesday. _____
2 He isn't working on Monday. _____
3 He's working out at the gym on Saturday. _____
4 He's having dinner with his parents on Wednesday. _____
5 He isn't having coffee with Juan next week. _____

He isn't seeing the dentist on Tuesday. He's seeing her on Monday at 9 a.m.

2 Complete the dialogue with be + going to or the present continuous of the verbs.

Jake: Hey, Sam! How _____ ? (**do**)
Sam: Fine, and you? So, _____ to Lisa's party on Saturday? (**come**)
Jake: I don't know. Do you think she _____ me? (**invite**)
Sam: Sure! Check your email. Lisa _____ invitations tonight. (**send**)
Jake: Well, OK. I _____ my email later tonight. (**check**)
Sam: Um, do you need a ride? Pat and Sue _____ us there. (**drive**)
Jake: No, don't worry. I _____ the subway. (**take**)

3 Look at the examples and write sentences about:

1 your arrangements for this week / weekend;
2 your plans for this week / weekend (not arranged yet);
3 predictions for your future (jobs / marriage / retirement).

I'm visiting my parents this weekend.
I think they're going to have a barbecue.

Well, I'm going out with my girlfriend on Saturday. And maybe we're going to eat out on Sunday.

155

Grammar Unit 10

10A Comparatives with -er and more

Comparative adjectives usually go before *than*.
- Her husband is **stronger than** mine.
- Quito is **hotter than** Buenos Aires.

English is **easier than** Arabic. NOT ~~English is more easy than Arabic.~~

One syllable adjectives + -er	
high	higher
long	longer
short	shorter

- Mike's **taller than** his brother.

One syllable CVC adjectives double the consonant + -er	
big	bigger
hot	hotter
thin	thinner

- Belo Horizonte is **wetter than** Rio.

One / two syllable adjectives ending *y* change *y* to *i* + -er	
friendly	friendlier
heavy	heavier
pretty	prettier

- My mom is **funnier than** my dad.

Use *more* before two-syllable adjectives ending -ed, -ing	
bored	more bored
boring	more boring

Adjectives ending -ing describe things or people.
Adjectives ending -ed usually describe feelings.
- I feel **more tired** today than I did yesterday.
- Swimming is **more tiring** than walking.

Use *more* before adjectives with more than two syllables	
dangerous	more dangerous
relaxing	more relaxing

- New York is much **more interesting** than Boston.

The opposite of *more … than* is *less … than*.
- Boston is **less interesting than** New York.

Irregular adjectives

good	better
bad	worse
far	farther / further

- I think Game of Thrones is **worse than** Modern Family.

10B Superlatives

Superlatives usually go after *the* and before a noun.
- Asia's **the largest** continent in the world.
- Raquel's **the most intelligent** person I know.

One-syllable → use *the … + -est*	
high	the highest
long	the longest
short	the shortest

- Suriname is **the smallest** country in South America.

One-syllable CVC → double the final consonant + -est	
big	the biggest
hot	the hottest
thin	the thinnest

- The Lion King is **the saddest** movie ever!

One / two syllable ending *y* → change *y* to *i* + -er	
friendly	the friendliest
heavy	the heaviest
pretty	the prettiest

- Finland is officially **the happiest** country in the world.

Use *the most* before adjectives with two or more syllables	
difficult	the most difficult
important	the most important

- My mom is **the most courageous** person in my family.

The opposite of *the most* is *the least*.
- He is **the least** interesting person in the room.

Irregular adjectives

good	the best
bad	the worst
far	the farthest / the furthest
less	the least

10C Like

Like has different meanings and uses.
It can be:
– a verb meaning *enjoy* or *want*.
- I really like ice cream. I would like an ice cream right now.

– a preposition meaning *similar to*.
- Your phone's like mine.
- What's Stella like? Creative, just like her father.

Unit 10

10A

1 Complete 1–5 with a comparative and match to pictures a–e.

| dangerous | friendly | large | small | tall |

1. A whale's brain is about six times _____ than a human's brain.
2. Driving at night is _____ than during the day.
3. Dogs are usually _____ than cats.
4. Between the ages of 13 and 18, boys usually grow _____ than girls.
5. It's normal for one side of the body to be a bit _____ than the other.

2 Complete 1–5 with a comparative.
1. Sam is at math than other subjects. (**good**)
2. Carrie is than her classmates. (**organized**)
3. Their math teacher is than their science teacher. (**funny**)
4. Tomas thinks science is than English. (**inspiring**)
5. Marcus's mind is than his friend's. (**active**)

10B

1 Complete facts 1–5 with a superlative.

| far | friendly | high | long | populated |

1. Ojos del Salado, between Argentina and Chile, is _____ volcano on Earth.
2. Scientists believe Chimborazo in Ecuador is _____ place from the Earth's center.
3. The Andes Mountains in South America are _____ mountain range on the planet.
4. California is _____ state in the U.S.
5. The Abyssinian cat is _____ cat in the world.

2 In pairs, use *the most* or *the least* plus these adjectives to describe people a–d.

| annoying | bored | interested |
| talkative | tired | |

3 Find the answers to these questions. In pairs, compare your answers. Are they the same?
1. What's the tallest building in the world at the moment?
2. Who's the most popular singer in your country?
3. Who are the fastest male and female athletes in the world?
4. Where are the hottest / wettest / coldest places on Earth?
5. Which is the highest captial city in the world?

10C

1 Add *like* in the correct place in questions 1–5. Then write the answers.

I look more like my mom than my dad.

1. What's the weather today?
2. Do your look your dad?
3. Is your mom you?
4. Would you a coffee?
5. What's your best friend?

Sounds and Usual Spellings

S Difficult sounds for Spanish speakers
P Difficult sounds for Portuguese speaker

▶ To listen to these words and sounds, and to practice them, go to the pronunciation section on the Richmond Learning Platform.

Vowels

/iː/	three, tree, eat, receive, believe, key, B, C, D, E, G, P, T, V, Z	
/ɪ/	six, mix, it, fifty, fish, trip, lip, fix	
/ʊ/	book, cook, put, could, cook, woman	
/uː/	two, shoe, food, new, soup, true, suit, Q, U, W	
/ɛ/	pen, ten, heavy, then, again, men, F, L, M, N, S, X	
/ə/	bananas, pajamas, salad, minute	

/ɜr/	shirt, skirt, work, turn, learn, verb
/ɔr/	four, door, north, fourth
/ɔ/	walk, saw, water, talk, author, law
/æ/	man, fan, bad, apple
/ʌ/	sun, run, cut, umbrella, country, love
/ɑ/	hot, not, on, clock, fall, tall
/ɑr/	car, star, far, start, party, artist, R

Diphthongs

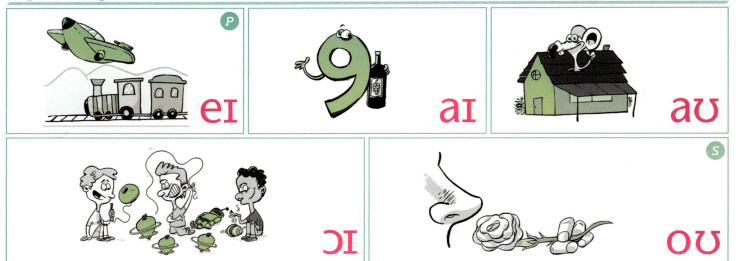

/eɪ/	plane, train, made, stay, they, A, H, J, K
/aɪ/	nine, wine, night, my, pie, buy, eyes, I, Y
/aʊ/	house, mouse, town, cloud

/ɔɪ/	toys, boys, oil, coin
/oʊ/	nose, rose, home, know, toe, road, O

158

Sounds and Usual Spellings

☐ Voiced
☐ Unvoiced

Consonants

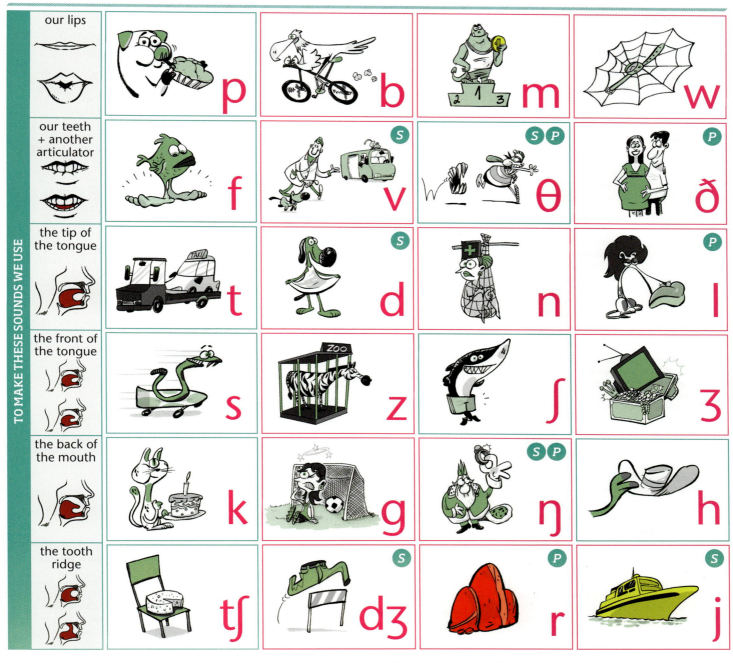

/p/	pig, pie, open, top, apple	
/b/	bike, bird, describe, able, club, rabbit	
/m/	medal, monster, name, summer	
/w/	web, watch, where, square, one	
/f/	fish, feet, off, phone, enough	
/v/	vet, van, five, have, video	
/θ/	teeth, thief, thank, nothing, mouth	
/ð/	mother, father, the, other	
/t/	truck, taxi, hot, stop, attractive	
/d/	dog, dress, made, adore, sad, middle	
/n/	net, nurse, tennis, one, sign, know	
/l/	lion, lips, long, all, old	
/s/	snake, skate, kiss, city, science
/z/	zoo, zebra, size, jazz, lose
/ʃ/	shark, shorts, action, special, session, chef
/ʒ/	television, treasure, usual
/k/	cat, cake, back, quick
/g/	goal, girl, leg, guess, exist
/ŋ/	king, ring, single, bank
/h/	hand, hat, unhappy, who
/tʃ/	chair, cheese, kitchen, future, question
/dʒ/	jeans, jump, generous, bridge
/r/	red, rock, ride, married, write
/j/	yellow, yacht, university

Audio script

Unit 1

▶ 1.2 Notice /ʌ/ and /uː/.
A OK. Let's check.
B Flag 1 is China.
A Yes, one point for you. And country 2?
B That's Spain.
A Yeah! Two points.
B Number 3 is Portugal.
A Right again!
B Flag 4 is the U.S.
A Yes! That's four points now!
B 5 is the UK.
A Correct!
B And 6 is Peru.
A Right! 6 points! And number 7?
B 7 is Canada and 8 is Argentina!
A Yes and yes! That's 8 points for you! Very good!

▶ 1.6 Notice *This_is* connects like one word.
This_is Machu Picchu, it's_in Peru. And number 2 is the Taj Mahal. It's_in India. Number 3 is the Alhambra. It's_in Granada, Spain. Photo 4 is Maroon 5. They're from the U.S. Photo 5 is Drake and Shawn Mendes. They're Canadian. And 6 is Salma Hayek. She's Mexican. Number 7 is Serena Williams. She's American. And this_is Neymar, in picture 8. He's Brazilian.

▶ 1.7 Notice the sentence stress.
1 **Mmmm**! This **pizza** is a**mazing**!
2 This is cool. **Wheeeeeeeeee**!
3 I'm so **pleased**! The **teacher** says my **work** is **excellent**.
4 I **love** New York. It's a **fantastic city**!
5 **Yuck**! This **coffee** is **horrible**!
6 Here's an **important story** in the **newspaper**.
7 I think **Malala** is a **very intelligent person**.
8 **China** is an **interesting country**!
9 This **restaurant** is **OK**.
10 Bill **Gates** is a **very rich person**!
11 This **group** is ri**diculous**!
12 **No**, **no**, **no**, he's a **terrible actor**! **Terrible**!

▶ 1.8 Notice /z/.
1 Oh, yeah, I agree. Neymar's an amazing soccer player.
2 The Taj Mahal — it's a really cool monument.
3 Oh, yes, Serena Williams is a rich person. Very, very rich!
4 Malala's an intelligent person, in my opinion.
5 No, I don't want to go there on vacation! It's a horrible city!
6 I think Japan is an interesting country.
7 I really like him. He's an excellent teacher.
8 I love her movies. She's a fantastic actor.

▶ 1.13 Notice the **stress** in these numbers is on the first syllable.
A A hundred dollars, please.
B OK. That's thirty, forty, fifty, sixty, seventy, eighty, ninety, a hundred. One hundred dollars.
A Thank you, sir. Have a great day.

▶ 1.14 Notice /θ/.
1 I'm eighty-five today. Happy birthday to me!
2 My address is seventy Blue Avenue.
3 I have eleven brothers and sisters.
4 This train ticket is ninety-nine dollars!
5 Hmm, I think it's fifteen miles to Los Angeles.
6 The number after thirty-nine is forty.

7 I have sixteen classmates in my English class.
8 Thirteen hours on a plane ... I'm very tired!

▶ 1.15 Notice the **stress** in the questions.
A **Name**?
B Jack Moore.
A **How** do you **spell** that?
B J-A-C-K M-O-O-R-E.
2
A Good afternoon, I'm Dieter Quinn.
A **How** do you **spell** that?
A D-I-E-T-E-R Q-U-I-N-N.
3
A First and last name, please?
B Rochelle Johns.
A **How** do you **spell** that?
B R-O-C-H-E-L-L-E J-O-H-N-S.
4
A **What**'s your **name**?
B George Wessex.
A Can you spell that, please?
B Sure. It's G-E-O-R-G-E W-E-S-S-E-X.
5
A **Name**, **please**?
B Joy Boscombe.
A **How** do you **spell** that?
B J-O-Y B-O-S-C-O-M-B-E.

▶ 1.16 Notice /m/ and /n/ endings and their spelling.
J = Jonathan K = Karin
J Welcome to Minerva reservations, Canada. This is Jonathan. How can I help you today?
K Hi, Jonathan. Can I make a reservation, please?
J Sure, no problem. I need a little information from you, OK? Uh, what's your name?
K Karin Spalding. That's K-A-R-I-N—Karin—S-P-A-L-D-I-N-G —Spalding.
J Where are you from? Are you Canadian?
K No, I'm not Canadian. I'm American, I'm from California.
J And what's your address, Ms. Spalding?
K 75 Kearny Drive, that's K-E-A-R-N-Y, San Francisco, CA 94133.
J Thank you. And what's your telephone number?
K Um, it isn't a Canadian number. It's American. OK? It's area code 415, then 675-8938.
J Thanks. And what's your email address?
K It's karinspalding@SPDG.com.
J Thanks. Now, what type of room ...

▶ 1.17 Notice /k/ and /t/.
O = officer P = passenger
O Good morning. I'm sorry, ma'am, but we need to check your backpack, please.
P No problem. Here you are.
O OK, let's see. A wallet, a laptop, keys, hmm ... a phone, a pencil, an umbrella, hmm ... what's this?
P Oh, this is a lipstick. Look!
O I see ... Are these glasses yours?
P Yes, they are.
O Right, and what are those?
P These are my earrings.
O OK ... And what's that?
P Come on! That's a sandwich!
O Exactly! You can't enter this country with food, ma'am!!
P Uh-uh. Sorry, it's my first time here.
O I need to take that. Thank you

▶ 1.19 Notice /ɪ/ and /iː/.
R = Rosa J = Jake E = Ed L = Lara
1
R Is this your sandwich, Jake?
J Hmmm ...Yes, it is. It's good!
R And are these your keys?
J Yes, they are, thanks.
2
E Is that your laptop, Rosa?
R No, it isn't. Is it your laptop, Lara?
L Yes, it is! That's my laptop!! It's new!
3
R & J Hey! Those are our potato chips!
L Come on, Ed! These are their chips! Stop eating them!
E Sorry.
4
E Where are my glasses?
R Er ... Are these your glasses, Ed?
E Yes, they are. Thanks. How do they look?
5
J Are these your earrings, Rosa?
R No, they aren't my earrings. They're awful! Are they your earrings, Lara?
L Yes, they are. Hmpf! Thanks.
6
L That's someone's phone.
E I think it's her phone. Hey, Rosa! Is that your phone?
R No, it isn't. My phone's new.
L I think it's his phone.
J Oh, yes, that's my phone ... Er ... Hi mom!

▶ 1.21 Notice /b/, /g/ and /z/.
1 They're big and shiny ... The earrings.
2 They're big and blue. There are two in the picture ... The sofas.
3 They're small and gray ... The glasses.
4 It's not big or small, it's new, and it's on the table ... The laptop.
5 It's small and black, and it's on the sofa ...The phone.

▶ 1.23 Notice /dʒ/ and the sentence stress.
M = Mark J = Justine
M Good evening! **Welcome** to **Conference Registration**. **My** name's **Mark**. **How** can I **help** you **today**?
J I need to register for the conference – your **website** isn't **working**.
M Certainly. I **just** need some **information** about you. First, **What's** your **name**?
J Justine Wallace.
M **How** do you **spell** that?
J J-U-S-T-I-N-E W-A-L-L-A-C-E.
M And **what's** your **address**, Ms. Wallace?
J 18 Jeffrey Drive, that's J-E-F-F-R-E-Y Drive, Denver, Colorado. **Zip** code **80202**.
M **Thank** you, and **what's** your **phone** number?
J **720** is the **area** code and the number is **988-3405**.
M **Thanks**. And what's your **email** address?
J It's jwallace26 at webmail dot com.
M **Thanks**, now, and can I **ask** about your **nationality**? **Where** are you from?
J I'm **American**.
M OK – so, you're all set – you're **registered** for the **conference**.

160

Audio script

1.24 Notice /h/.
A Hi Judy! How are you?
B Good, thanks. What about you? What's new?
A Not much. Things are good.
B So are you ready for the meeting? I hear …

1.26 Notice the sentence stress.
1
A Here's your gift! Happy Birthday!
B Thank you!
A You're welcome.
2
A Excuse me.
B Oh, I'm sorry.
3
A Oops, I'm sorry.
B Don't worry about it.
4
A See you later!
B Bye for now!
5
A We have a great fish special today.
B Excuse me. Can you say that again, please?
A Sure … I said we have a great fish special today.
6
A D'ya wanna order now?
B I don't understand.
C Oh, sorry. Are you ready to order?

Unit 2

2.1 Notice to /tə/ and to a /tu:wə/.
I = interviewer
I When do you go to these places?
A I go to a café every day before class for a coffee.
B I go to church on Sundays.
C I go to the gym after school.
D I usually go home after work.
E I go to a party on Saturdays.
F I go to school Monday through Friday, and Saturday morning, too!
G I go to the grocery store on Saturdays.
H I go to work at eight o'clock.

2.2 Notice stress on days of the week.
1 Sunday, lovely Sunday!
2 Oh, no! Tomorrow's Monday. School! Yuk!
3 Gee, it's only Tuesday – four more days of work.
4 I have an important meeting on Wednesday.
5 Only two more days of work – it's Thursday.
6 Today is Friday. Let's go to a bar after work!
7 Great! It's Saturday! My favorite day! No more work for the weekend!

2.4 Notice /ɜr/.
I = interviewer W = woman M = man
I Hi, I'm doing a survey about sleeping habits. What time do you get up?
W Uh, um, at six in the morning. I go to school at six forty-five.
I Thanks. And what time do you go to bed?
W Hmm. At around ten p.m., during the week. Maybe at twelve midnight on Friday and Saturday.
I So you get about eight hours sleep a night?
W Yeah, that's it … Bye!
I Thanks.
I Hello, we're doing a survey about working hours. What time do you go to work?
M Hmm … I go to work at eight thirty a.m.

I Every day?
M No, no. From Monday to Friday. I don't work on Saturdays and Sundays.
I And when do you get home from work?
M Well, I usually get home at around six fifteen p.m. OK? Bye!

2.6 Notice /eɪ/ and word stress.
Well, I wake up at around six thirty a.m., but I don't get up immediately. I stay in bed for three or four minutes, then I get up and make my bed. Then I exercise for thirty minutes. After that, I take a shower, shave, get dressed and have breakfast – coffee, juice and cereal.
Then I brush my teeth and, finally, leave home at around eight a.m.

2.7 Notice /s/ and /z/.
He wakes up at eight a.m., but he doesn't get up. He sleeps again and then he gets up at 8:50 a.m., but he doesn't wake up. After he wakes up he makes his bed. Then he exercises and he shaves. After that, he doesn't take a shower, he doesn't brush his teeth, and he doesn't get dressed!

2.9 Notice the intonation at the end of each question.
1
A What's your full name?↘
B I'm Miguel Hernandez. But please call me Mickey.
2
A OK. And … are you Spanish?↗
B Yes, I am. I'm from Valencia.
3
A Where do you live?↘
B In Madrid, I work there. It's an amazing city!
4
A Do you live with your parents?↗
B No, I don't. I live with my girlfriend, Monica.
5
A Where exactly in the U.S. do you plan to travel to?↘
B Alaska. They say it's a beautiful place.
6
A Do you know anyone in Alaska?↗
B Yes, my sister lives there.

2.10 Notice the intonation at the end of each question.
M = Miguel W = woman
W Hm … Who's this?↘
M That's my brother, Juan.
W Uh-huh. Does he play soccer?↗
M Yes, he does! He loves soccer.
W And who's that?↘
M That's my sister, Martina.
W So you have a sister! Where does she live?↘
M In Alaska. And, those are my parents.
W Wow, Alaska! And, do your parents live there too?↗
M No, they live in Barcelona.

Review 1

R1.2 Notice /ə/ in the articles and prepositions.
My name's Carla, I'm 17, and I live in La Floresta, a small town in Spain about 13 km from Barcelona. I live with my mom and dad and my six brothers and sisters, so, with me, that's a total of nine people in our house. It's a big family – I have over 40 cousins!

I'm a student and I study at the University of Barcelona. I get up at 6 a.m. every day. It takes me 50 minutes to get to school, which starts at 8 a.m. In my free time, I like watching movies, and my favorite actors are Penelope Cruz and Jennifer Lawrence. I usually go to the movies on Monday night after school.

Unit 3

3.1 Notice /j/ and /dʒ/.
I = interviewer M = meteorologist
I You're a meteorologist, please tell us about the symbols that are used to represent weather.
M Well, when we use weather symbols we try to use symbols that everyone will understand. This yellow circle means the sun, or sunny weather. A cloud means cloudy, obviously, and this symbol means a wind or windy. The gray cloud is for fog or foggy weather. The cloud with these little lines means rain or rainy weather. And the white cloud with stars means snow or snowy conditions.
I So, it's easy to see what the weather is like just from the symbol?
M That's right.
I What about temperature?
M We usually use the words hot, warm, cool, or cold.

3.2 Notice /w/ and /v/.
A OK, in this photo, the weather is warm.
B Yes, it's hot and sunny.
A Maybe it's Cancún?
B And in this picture it's very, very hot!
A Yes, and it isn't raining. It's very dry.

3.3 Notice /d/ and /t/.
B = Bob M = Mary J = Joe
B Everywhere, the weather is … weird! Take the Amazon rainforest, for example. It's usually very rainy there, but now … no rain for three months! The Amazon river is down by 10 meters. It's weird! From the forest to the desert: the Atacama Desert is usually hot and sunny 350 days a year. This year, the days and nights are cool and cloudy. It's weird! And how's the weather in Chicago, the Windy City? Mary, tell us. What's the weather like in Chicago?
M Well, Bob, no wind for us! This month, every morning, it's cool and foggy. It's weird!
B Thanks Mary. Let's go to the Alps. Those beautiful mountains. What's the weather usually like there? It's snowy, right? And what's it like this year? Tell us Joe?
J Uh-huh. It's warm and there's absolutely no snow. Skiing is impossible. It's weird!
B How about Cancún, and the fantastic beaches? Well, tourists go to Cancún to enjoy the hot weather but this summer: it's cold. Really cold. It's weird! What's the weather like where you are? Any weird weather stories? Contact us to tell us …

3.4 Notice s = /s/ or /z/.
M = Maddie E = Eli S = Susan R = Rita
C = caller Mi = Michael
E Hello?
M Eli? This is Maddie. Are you busy?
E Actually, yes. I'm cooking dinner. What's up?
M Oh, no problem. Call you later.
E OK, bye.

161

S Susan.
M Hi, Susan. This is Maddie.
S Oh, hi, Maddie. Sorry, I'm running in the park. I can't hear you. Can I call you later?
M Sure, Susan. Talk to you later.
S Bye.
M OK, uh, bye. Not my day today, is it? Let me try Rita.
R Rita Rogers speaking.
M Hey, Rita!
R Maddie, darling. How are you doing?
M Great.
R Excuse me. Can you tell me where the butter is, please? Sorry, Maddie, I'm buying groceries. What's up?
M Well, I have ...
R Oh, and the milk? Uh, sorry, Maddie.
M Oh, you're busy now. Don't worry. Bye.
R Bye, darling. Nice talking to you.
M So, Rita is busy, too. Maybe Michael? Let me try him. Uh ... the line's busy ...
M Ooh, someone's calling. Maybe one of my friends is finally free now. Hello?
C Gregory Hanes, please?
M Uh, I'm sorry, you have the wrong number.
C Oh, sorry. I'll dial again.
M Humph. Typical! Well, let me call Michael again.
Mi Hi, Maddie.
M Hi, Michael. Are you running?
Mi No, I'm not running! I'm riding a bike and my battery's dying. Call you later?
M Of course ... Bye.

⏵ **3.5** Notice the connections for similar sounds.

M = Maddie S = Sean
M I don't believe_this. One more call. That's it.
S Hey, Maddie. Long time_no see. How are things?
M Good! Uh, Sean, are you busy?
S Um, well, I'm doing_my homework.
M Oh, never min ...
S ... but I'm just finishing. What are your plans?
M I have two tickets to today's game. L.A. Lakers and Houston Rockets. It starts at three o'clock.
S So we have thirty minutes! Let's go!
M Are you saying yes?
S Of course! Why are you surprised?
M You have no idea ... Meet you at the subway station. Let's go!

⏵ **3.9** Notice /n/ and /ŋ/.

J = Jennifer M = Marisa
J Hey, Marisa! Hi! It's great to see you.
M You too, Jennifer.
J What are you doing these days?
M I'm studying.
J Oh? Are you studying art? You're such a good painter.
M No, I'm studying biology.
J Really? And ... er ... where are you living?
M I'm living with my parents.
J Are you still dating Kevin?
M No, I'm not dating Kevin anymore. He's living in New York now. I'm dating a guy called Steve.
J Oh, that's nice. [awkward silence] Well ... it was great to see you.
M You too. Bye.
J Bye, Marisa.

⏵ **3.10** Notice /eɪ/ and /aɪ/.

S = Sammy M = Marsha L = Lucinda
K = KoolKat D = Dadofthree
B = BBBaxter
S What do you think of technology?
M It's dangerous. Social media companies are changing the way we see privacy. Everyone is getting access to our personal information.
L I don't like a lot of the new video games. They're getting more violent and it makes people act more violently.
K People are going out less and spending more time alone with technology. We don't know our neighbors.
D People today are becoming obsessed with things! They want new clothes, new cars, new electronic devices, and they can buy it all online.
B My kids are spending more and more time on their devices and online, especially on social media. I don't know what to do. They panic when they don't have their phone with them. They just want to look at their phones.

⏵ **3.12** Notice have to /f/ and kind of /v/.

M = Mark L = Linda
M Hey Linda, what are you doing? It's one a.m.!
L Oh it's you, Mark. Umm ... I'm working on this report. I have to turn it in tomorrow.
M Ah. Is it a big report?
L Yep, I still need to do three more pages.
M Ooosh. You tired?
L Yeah. Kind of.

Unit 4

⏵ **4.2** Notice /i/ and /ɪ/.

T = Tasha M = Mac
T Today's exciting events at the Olympic Games include basketball, soccer, tennis, volleyball, cycling, running, and swimming ... Wow! Tell us about it, Mac!
M Hi Tasha! Yeah, it's July 2nd, and ... well, what a day of sports at the Olympics! A very exciting morning here at the Olympic complex. First we have basketball at the Olympic Arena. It's the semi-final between Cuba and Russia, at 9:00 a.m. Then, at 9:30, we have tennis, men's doubles, at the Central Courts. At 10:00 a.m. at the Olympic Stadium we have soccer, Uruguay versus Italy. What an interesting game! After that, at 10:30, it's time for cycling at the Igloo. The men's 5,000 meters final! And at 11:00 at North Park we have women's volleyball, the U.S. and Australia going for a bronze medal. And that's just this morning! Tasha, it's hard to decide what to watch!

⏵ **4.4** Notice intonation = speaker's emotion.

I = interviewer W = woman
I Excuse me, miss? Can I ask you a question?
W Yes?
I What's your favorite sport?
W Skiing. I love↗ to ski.
I Nice↗! Thanks.
W You're welcome.

I = interviewer B = boy
I Hi, uh, do you have a moment?
B Uh, OK.
I What's your favorite sport?
B It's golf↘. Absolutely, golf↗. To play and↘ to watch. Best↗ game in the world↘!

W Thanks.

I = interviewer W = woman
W Uh, sorry. Excuse me!
I Sorry, er, hello! Do you have time to answer one question?
W Uh, what question?
I It's for a survey. What's your favorite sport?
W Let me think. It's definitely not↘ soccer. I hate↘ soccer.
I OK, but what sport do you like?
W Er ... is skateboarding a sport?
I Well, yes, I guess so.
W So it's skateboarding↗. I love↗ it.
I OK, thanks then!
W Is that all?
I Yes. Thanks very much!
W Oh, no problem!

I = interviewer M = man
I Excuse me?
M Uh? What?
I Sorry, but, er ... Do you have time to answer one question?
M Uh, I guess↗. But only one↘!
I What's your favorite sport?
M To watch or to play?
I To watch and to play.
M Well, I like to watch baseball↘ on TV↘, but, you know, I don't play↗ baseball. I love to surf↘. I go surfing↗ every weekend.
I Watch baseball, and surf. Thanks a lot.
M You're welcome. Bye↗.

⏵ **4.5** Notice the intonation in yes / no ❓ and Wh- ❓.

J = Janet M = Mark
J Hi, Mark. My name is Janet and I'm your instructor.
M Oh hi Janet. How's it going?↘
J Good. I need to ask you a few questions. Is that OK?↗
M Sure.
J What's your full name?↘
M Mark Swift. S-W-I-F-T.
J Swift, OK. How old are you, Mark?↘
M I'm 23.
J OK. Can you run two kilometers?↗
M Run? No, I can't. I don't think I can walk two kilometers! That's why I'm here.
J OK, great! How about swimming?↘ Can you swim?↗
M Er, yes, I can, but not very well. I need lessons.
J We can help you with that. Let's see ... Can you ride a bike?↗
M A bike? Yes, I can. But I don't like it.
J Hmm. OK. Can you play tennis?↗
M No, no, I can't play tennis at all. I hate tennis.
J I see. Well, so you can run in the gym every day, and our swimming lessons are...

⏵ **4.6** Notice /aʊ/ and the connections.

Let_us pick_up our books_and our pens. They_ are_our most powerful weapons. One child, one teacher, one book, and one pen can change the world. Education_is_the_only solution. Education first. Thank_you.

Audio script

4.8 Notice pronunciation of can in ? and can/can't in + -.
I = interviewer M = man W = woman

1
I   Can you dance?
M   I can't dance very well, but my wife can. She's a very good dancer.

2
I   Who can cook well in your family?
W   Not me! But, my father can cook really well. His food is delicious.

3
I   What about your friends? What sports can your best friend play?
M   Hmmm, my best friend can't play baseball or volleyball. He doesn't like team sports.

4
I   And winter sports? Can you skate?
W   I can skate, but I can't ski at all. Skiing is too difficult!

5
I   Can your friends play soccer?
M   For sure! My friends can play soccer really well. They play every weekend.

6
I   Can you do any martial arts?
W   Yes, I can.
I   What can you do?
W   Tae Kwondo.

4.10 Notice /æ/ and /e/.
J = Joel A = applicant
J   Hello. I'm Joel Clinton. I have your curriculum vitae here and I want to ask you some questions.
A   Sure.
J   There is no information about your language abilities. How many languages can you speak?
A   Er, apart from English, one. I speak a little Spanish.
J   ¿Como estás?
A   What?
J   Yes, I can see you speak very little Spanish. Anyway, I'm also interested in your athletic abilities. Can you play any sports?
A   Uh, a little, yes.
J   What sports can you play?
A   I can play volleyball and tennis, but not very well.
J   Not perfect, but OK. One more question: can you text fast?
A   Yes, I think so.
J   How many words a minute can you text?
A   I don't know – about 40, I think. But wait? Why are these questions relevant? Isn't this a job interview for a position as a babysitter?
J   No, I want a nanny, and I want my son to have the best education!
A   And how old is your son?
J   Two!

4.16 Notice the /t/ and silent t.
S = sales clerk J = Jason
S   The fitting rooms are over there.
J   Thank you.
S   Do you need any help, sir?
J   No, no, it's perfect. What do you think? Blue is Jackson's favorite color. Isn't it, Jackson? Back in you go!
S   And for you, sir? We have wonderful T-shirts, pants, jackets, suits …

Review 2

R2.2 Notice /r/ at beginning of words and /r/ at end of words.
G = Gale R = Ricky
G   And here with us today we have the Paralympic swimmer, Ricky Pietersen. Hello, Ricky.
R   Hi, Gale. It's nice to be here.
G   So, Ricky, what's your favorite sport?
R   Well, I love swimming, of course!
G   How about other sports? Do you like soccer?
R   Yes, I love to watch my team play.
G   Cool! What else do you like doing when you're not swimming or watching your team?
R   Well, I like to help young kids with disabilities.
G   That's great. And a final question: what is your next big challenge?
R   I'm working hard to prepare for the next Paralympic Games. I want to beat my own record.
G   Well, thank you for talking to us today, Ricky.
R   Thank you, Gale!

Unit 5

5.1 Notice /ə/ and /ʌ/.
A = adviser V = visitor
A   Places to go out near here? Well, there's a bar, and a club, and a hotel. And there's a nice museum, and a park. And there's a very good restaurant. And a small stadium, oh, and an old theater.
V   Great, thank you – that sounds good.

5.3 Notice the word stress.
Welcome to Louisville, the largest city in Kentucky! It's a great place to visit. Situated on the Ohio river with a population of about 750,000, it's the City of Parks. There are 122 parks in the city!
Downtown there are seven museums, and three theaters, plus the Louisville Ballet, Orchestra and Opera.
Louisville is home to the famous Kentucky Derby horse race, sometimes called the Greatest Two Minutes in Sports! There's a famous racetrack and a museum at Churchill Downs. There's also a football stadium and a baseball stadium in the city. If you like shopping, there are three enormous shopping malls to choose from. And for readers, there's a fantastic public library with branches all over town. Kentucky is the home of KFC (Kentucky Fried Chicken), but we don't only eat fried chicken! There are restaurants of all kinds here.
There aren't any public swimming pools in downtown Louisville, but there are six pools in the city, so everything is easy. And of course there are bars, clubs, and four multi-screen movie theaters. And seven world-class hotels, just in the downtown area. The only thing you won't find here? There are no unfriendly people – just friends you don't know yet!
So, come to Louisville – for relaxation and fun!

5.6 Notice /i/ and /aɪ/. Notice the position of also and too.
Well, I love playing video games. It's my favorite thing in the world. I also love going out with my friends. I like to shop and I like to eat out. And, um, I like blogging too. And I don't mind going to work. I also don't mind cooking – it's fun with a friend, but I don't like going to the gym very much. I don't like watching TV either, but the one thing I really hate is cleaning. I hate cleaning the house! What about you? Are you similar?

5.9 Notice main sentence stress on content words and at the end of phrases.
N = Natalie P = presenter
N   I'm Natalie and I'm ten years old and I love to sing. I've been singing ever since I was four. I sing at school, I sing at home, I sometimes sing when I'm eating my dinner! I would like to be a singer and a diva and I definitely want to be like Beyoncé.
P   Hello darling.
N   Hello.
P   What's your name and how old are you?
N   My name is Natalie and I'm ten years old.
P   And what are you doing today?
N   Well, I'm going to sing a song called 'No One' from Alicia Keys.
P   OK, yeah – I know that one. Good luck, darling.

5.12 Notice the pronunciation of the -ing /ŋ/ form.
J = Josh E = Emily
J   Let's go on vacation together, Emily. What do you like doing on vacation?
E   Well, I love sunbathing and swimming. How about you?
J   Hmmm, well, I don't really like swimming or sunbathing, but I love snorkeling and kayaking. I sometimes like to take a class or to visit the museums to discover more about where I am.
E   Do you? I prefer reading novels and eating out and dancing, nothing cultural for me.
J   What about sightseeing?
E   I like sightseeing, but not too much.
J   And camping? Do you like camping?
E   Not really. I hate shopping, especially buying souvenirs, and cooking and hiking when I'm on vacation. I just want to relax.
J   Those are the things I love doing on vacation! Hmm …

5.17 Notice the pronunciation of object pronouns in speech.
Hi Lori! Thanks for house sitting for us during our vacation. Hope you don't have any problems. Just a few things to remember. Er, when you come in, please pick up the mail↘ and put it on the table↘.
Um, yeah, please open the windows↘ and close them again every day↘ – oh, and water the plants every day↘. Also, don't forget the lights and air conditioning↘ – turn them off when you go out↘.
Feed Salt and Pepper (that's the cats!) and Chips (that's the dog!) in the morning and evening↘, but please don't give them too much food↘. Oh and, don't forget to give them some water.↘
Please, walk Chips in the morning and afternoon↘. But please don't take him near the road↘. He's nervous of cars. And please, please, don't let the cats out.↘
Call me if you have any questions↘ and please tell us if the cats or Chips escape↘. Thanks again! See you in two weeks. Have fun!↘ Bye.

163

▶ **5.22 Notice st- at the beginning of a word.**

1

M = man   W = woman
M Excuse me.
W H!. How're you doing?
M Oh, hi. Good, thanks, er, where's the mall?
W It's in front of you on Market Street. Cross here at the stoplight.
M Thanks.
W No problem. Have a nice day!

2

W = woman   M = man
W Excuse me. Is there a movie theater around here?
M Yes, there is. Go straight on Market Street and turn right on Fourth Street. Go straight for one block and the movie theater's on the corner of Fourth and Mission Street.

3

M = man   W = woman
M Excuse me. Do you know where the library is?
W Excuse me?
M The library?
W Ah, yes. Um, er, I know! Go straight on Market Street for four blocks. Turn right on Grove Street at the stop sign. Then, um, er, go straight for one block and the library is on the right.
M Thank you.

4

M1, M2, M3 = man 1, man 2, man 3
M1 Um, er, excuse me, are there any …
M2 Sorry, my friend. No time, bye!
M1 Hmpf. Excuse me. Are there any bookstores near here?
M3 Yes, there are.
M1 Good, er, where are they?
M3 Oh yes, sorry. There's one on Market Street. Go straight for about four blocks. The bookstore's on your left. Before the stop sign.
M1 Sorry, can you say that again?
M3 I'm sorry. There's one on Market Street. Go straight for about four blocks. The bookstore's on your left. Before the stop sign. OK?
M1 Er, thank you.

Unit 6

▶ **6.1 Notice /ə/.**

Let's see. We need bananas and chocolate … oil and salt … uh… maybe some spaghetti? Yes, definitely some spaghetti and some tea … oh, and I have to get tomatoes and vinegar.

▶ **6.2 Notice s = /z/ and /s/.**

We need some bread, milk, fish, and chicken … oh, and some apples and carrots, Sandra loves carrots! Then some eggs and lettuce. Oh, and butter and onions. Oh, finally, some cheese, oranges, potatoes … do we need sugar? Oh, yes, and some sugar.

▶ **6.3 Notice the silent letters and /sh/.**

J = Jeff   S = Sandra
S Jeff! I'm home.
J Hi, Sandra.
S What's all this food on the table?
J What do you mean, all this?
S Well, to be precise, some chocolate, tomatoes … uh, some spaghetti …
J Oh, that?
S I'm not finished! There's also some salt, some tea, oil and vinegar here…
J I can explain …

S … and – eleven, twelve, no, thirteen bananas.
J There was a special offer on bananas. We can always freeze them!
S That's true – they make great smoothies! But, Jeff, we're leaving tomorrow. Why did you buy all this food for the refrigerator?
J Just some fruit: apples and oranges.
S I don't like apples.
J But I like apples … and you like oranges. And I got some onions and potatoes, too.
S Potatoes? I don't eat them.
J I also got some chicken and fish.
S Well, we can freeze those. But what do we do with the milk, cheese, and butter?
J Sorry, Sandra … I got some lettuce and carrots for salad, too.
S Hm, I guess I can make a salad for dinner. And all those eggs!!
J Well, I can make an omelet!
S You do make delicious omelets – good idea. So we can use the lettuce, carrots, and some of the eggs for dinner. But, wait – what are these doing in the refrigerator?
J Er …
S Here! Look! You put bread and sugar in the refrigerator! What are they doing there?
J Uh, I don't know.
S You don't know?
J I always put sugar and bread in the refrigerator, I don't know why. My parents and my grandparents did it.
S OK, but it seems weird!

▶ **6.4 Notice the stress in the phrases and /ə/.**

1 a glass of juice
2 a cup of tea
3 some salad
4 a slice of bread
5 a piece of fruit
6 a bowl of rice
7 some meat
8 some fish
9 some eggs
10 some vegetables
11 a bottle of water
12 a piece of cake
13 some carrots or nuts

▶ **6.5 Notice the links.**

So, today is day one_of eating more healthily. I eat too much junk food and sugar. For breakfast, I can have a cup_of tea, a slice_of wholewheat bread, and a piece_of fruit! For lunch, it's a bowl_of brown rice, some meat, some vegetables, and a bottle_of water. In the afternoon, for my snack I get some carrots or nuts! Hmm … or maybe a piece_of cake. No, I don't think so. Carrots or nuts and that's it! Then for dinner, I get some salad, some protein again – some fish or eggs, and a glass_of juice.

▶ **6.6 Notice /ʌ/, /ʊ/ and /uː/.**

M = Maria   T = Tony
M Hi, Tony. Want some potato chips?
T No thanks. I'm trying to cut down on junk food.
M Oh, OK – that's a good idea. How's it going?
T Great. I'm keeping a video diary. It really helps.
M So, what do you usually have for lunch?
T I have some brown rice for lunch – with vegetables and meat.
M That sounds pretty good.
T Uh huh, it is. And I can eat as much as I want. I'm never hungry!

M Now that's important!
T It's pretty easy, actually. I'm learning to cook, too.
M What about dessert?
T I never eat any sugar. But I eat a lot of fruit.
M Oh, come on. Never?!
T Well, OK not at home. I sometimes have a piece of cake in restaurants.
M Do you ever eat bread?
T Of course! I have a slice of bread with my lunch.
M And what about cheese?
T Well, sometimes for dinner. But usually I eat fish or eggs. And a glass of juice. Natural juice!
M Wow! That sounds great – I think I might try it! Forget about these potato chips! Do you want this bottle of water?
T Um … no, thanks. I think I'll have a glass of juice, instead!

▶ **6.11 Notice the dark l vs. normal l.**

J = Joe   S = Sandra
J Hey, Sandra. Ready for lunch?
S Sure. I'm so hungry!
J Come on! Let's go to that Mexican restaurant on the corner. I'm dying for a burrito.
S I don't think that's a good idea. I want to eat something healthy today.
J Burritos are healthy! Look, I'm Googling the nutritional table. We can see what's in them.
S Oh, I hate those lists! They're so out of date!
J What do you mean?
S My grandmother counts calories! The ingredients are important, not the number of calories.
J Exactly! This chart doesn't even show calories. Let's look at the chicken burrito.
S I can't see anything without my glasses.
J Um, let's see. Well, it has five grams of fat.
S Aw! That's a lot.
J There's also a vegetarian burrito. It only has beans and cheese, and four grams of fat.
S Ugh! Beans! But my doctor told me to watch my cholesterol. How much cholesterol does the vegetarian burrito have?
J Only five milligrams.
S And the others?
J The chicken one has thirty milligrams and the meat one has thirty-five milligrams.
S Hmm … that's a lot. Another reason to be a vegetarian! What about sodium? It's not good to eat too much salt.
J Well, let's see. The chicken one has 880 milligrams, the meat one 890 milligrams, and the vegetarian one only 730 milligrams. But they have a lot of protein! The chicken burrito has 18 grams and the meat burrito has 19 grams. That's important, too. And they all have fiber, especially the vegetarian one: 14 grams.
S You know what? I'm having the chicken burrito! I love chicken.
J And I'm having the meat burrito. "Everything in moderation." And they're so delicious. We'll have the vegetarian burrito another day.
S Great! Let's go. It's now one o'clock. I'm hungry!

Audio script

6.14 Notice the the alliteration.
This is Wonderful Weekend at Fast and Fresh! Special savings on our fabulous favorites! Our special starter is the Chopped Chicken: a salad made with fresh lettuce and tomato and topped with grilled chicken. We offer you two choices from our marvelous main courses: Fish Fillet, our delicious grilled salmon in orange sauce. It comes with a baked potato. Or the Special Steak, a succulent half-pound barbecued steak topped with a light cream and pepper sauce. Finally, there's nothing like a light, refreshing dessert: our Seasonal Fruit Salad, which includes strawberry, mango, melon, and pear topped with fresh fruit juice. All for a great price! Come to Fast and Fresh and check it out!

6.15 Notice /ɪ/ and /iː/.
Me = Melissa   P = Phil   Ma = Marie
Me Hi, my name's Melissa, and I'm your server today. Are you ready to order?
P Yes, please.
Me What would you like as a starter?
P I'll have the tomato soup, please.
Me OK. With croutons and parmesan cheese?
P No cheese, please.
Me OK. How about you, ma'am? What would you like?
Ma What's in the chicken salad?
Me The salad is lettuce, spinach, green peppers, red peppers, tomato, and onion. It comes with sliced grilled chicken.
Ma That sounds good. I'd like that, please – but no onion. I don't like onion!
Me Certainly. I'll be right back with your starters.

6.17 Notice /tʃ/ and the connecting sounds.
Me = Melissa   P = Phil   Ma = Marie
P Excuse me?
Me Yes, sir?
P Can_I have some decaf coffee, please?
Me Of course. And you, ma'am? What would_you like to drink?
Ma I'd like some tea, please. What kind_of tea do_you have?
Me Mint_or chamomile.
Ma I'll have chamomile tea, please.
Me Anything_else?
Ma Uh, actually, I'd like some dessert. Can we have the Chocolate Chunk? It's to share.
Me Certainly. It's very good.
P Oh, and can you bring_us the check, too, please?

Review 3

R3.1 Notice voiced th /ð/, and unvoiced th /θ/.
T = Tina   C = Carl
T I'm thirsty. Is there any juice in the fridge?
C No, we didn't buy any juice this week. But, look, there are oranges. Do you want me to make you some juice?
T Yes, thanks. Uh, and did we buy any cookies?
C No, but there are still some cookies in the cabinet.
T Great, thanks!

Unit 7

7.2 Notice /eɪ/, and /æ/.
T = Tom   A = Anna
T This is the living room.
A Hmm ... It's a little small.
T There's a fireplace and a nice TV with cable ... and, er, armchairs, and er, what else, ah, we love this sofa – it's the center of the house.
A Oh, but I never watch TV.
T Oh. This is the kitchen – it has a gas stove and a microwave and you can wash the dishes in the sink here. Here's the refrigerator. It's new. And, er, there's a table and two chairs here if you want to eat in the kitchen.
A Well, it's not very light in here.
T Here in the dining room we have this big table with eight chairs. Good for dinner parties!
A I don't really like to cook very much, though.
T Now for the bathroom – just a toilet and shower, there's no bathtub, I'm afraid.
A Oh ... I really like to take a bath. Especially in the winter.
T This is your bedroom – you can see it's large and it has a large bed and a table and a big closet and plenty of storage space and there is a fan so you don't get hot at night.
A Hmm ... But what's that smell?
T Here's the laundry room – there's more storage space on these shelves here. So, what do you think? Do you like it?
A Well, I need to think about it.
T Sure. Give us a call tomorrow.

7.3 Notice /ɔːr/ and the contractions.
This is my tiny house. Come on in. Just inside the front door I've got these two puffy chairs flanking this little faux fireplace. It's a very tiny fireplace, but it's a tiny house. Closet storage and cabinet space below this desk. Computer storage space and there's a little table down here. When I pull this table out, believe it or not, as long as I have tiny plates, it seats four people. Like that.
Here in the kitchen I've got a bar sink, a double burner stove, a little refrigerator, and a toaster oven.
The bathroom is the shower, so when I want to take a shower the nozzle's on the ceiling and everything would get wet except for I've got these little sliding doors that keep things dry and I can put this plastic curtain in here over the toilet which is right down here.
Above the kitchen I've got access to the loft – that's where I sleep. So the loft is nothing more than storage and sleeping. I've got all the storage at this end and then at this end I've got the sleeping – with the bed. It sleeps two really comfortably. So this is my bed and I've got a window at this end and a fan vent behind the shelves at the other so that if it ever gets hot I can just turn this whole thing into a wind tunnel.

7.5 Notice /ɛ/ and how /eɪ/ is usually stressed.
Hello, my name's Liz Marshall and I'm a party planner. Today, I want to talk to you about how to give a great party. Well, it all starts with the invitation. Send the invitations early – three weeks before the party – and include all the important information. Where? When? What type of party? Now ... what do you need for the party? First, food and drinks: Well, for drinks you need some soft drinks, and always have water. I like to keep it simple: just tea and coffee. You can have fresh juice too.
For food, I recommend chips and one or two other snacks, perhaps a healthy option like carrots. Don't forget the plates, glasses, and napkins too. If it's a birthday party, a cake is essential. And display your birthday cards! Next – decorations – again keep it simple with balloons. You can decorate the house with candles too – this gives a nice atmosphere. And if it's a special occasion, you can even give each guest a small present to take home.
Now for entertainment – music is essential for a good party – make sure there's space for people to dance. OK, so it's time to start planning. Have fun!

7.6 Notice the ↗ and ↘ intonation.
M = Martha   R = Rob
M I was at a great↗ party yesterday, Rob!↘
R Oh, that's nice, Martha. Where was it?↘
M It was at Jane Foster's home. It was her birthday.
R Oh! Were there a lot of people?↗
M Yep, there were about fifty.↘
R Wow!↗ Was there a lot of food?↗
M Oh yes, and there was an enormous↗ chocolate cake.↘
R Hmmm ... And ... was Jane's boyfriend there?↗
M Yes, he was. Rick and Jane make a perfect↗ couple↘!! He's so attractive↘, they were so beautiful↘ together, and the music was great↗ – everybody was dancing, you know.↘
R He sounds nice↗. Were Jane's parents there?↗
M No, they weren't↘. Do you know them? ↗
R Yes. Ummm ... I was Jane's boyfriend before Rick.↘
M Oh, I'm sorry↘ ... I didn't know that↘ ... in fact, the party wasn't that↘ great ... and her new boyfriend wasn't really that nice ...↘
R No problem. It's fine. Don't worry about it.↘
M Hey, there was a great show on TV last night. Did you see it?↗

7.8 Notice /oʊ/ and /aʊ/.
1 Is that ... Cheese? Mm. It is! Where is it? Is it in the box?
2 No ... Maybe under the table ... Hmmm. Where is it? ... People! Oh, no!
3 Now, quietly between the sofa and the table.
4 Slowly, next to the sofa ...
5 Where are the people? Where is the cheese?! OK, let's go! In the bed ...
6 Now on the bed ... and jump!
7 Ah! There they are! OK! I'm across from the people! I'm across from the people! Quick!
8 OK, concentrate, where IS that cheese? In front of the TV?
9 No. Behind the TV? No. Not here.
10 Ah, there it is! I see it. Now. How can I get above the TV? Hmmmm.

7.9 Notice stress to emphasize change.
M See that?
W What?
M There was a mouse under the table.
W Oh no! Where?
M Over there!
W Oh now I see it! It's next to the sofa. It's moving!
M Where did it go?
W Ahhhh! It was in front of the TV now it's behind the TV.
M Let me see if I can get it.
W Ahhhh! It's on the bed. It was in the bed and now it's on the bed!

165

M There it goes. It was **on** the **bed**, but now it's **in** that **box**.
W Quick, close the box and take it out to the garden.
M Good idea!

▶ **7.16** Notice weak forms of **to**, **at**, **for**, and **of**.

1
Ma = Mara Mo = Morgan
Ma Hello Morgan!
Mo Hi Mara!
Ma Scott and I are having a housewarming party on Sunday. Can you and Sandy come?
Mo Oh, I'm sorry. We already have plans for Sunday.
Ma Oh, well, that's OK.
Mo Thanks for inviting us and I hope the party goes well.
Ma Thanks, Morgan.
Mo See you.
Ma Bye.

2
W = woman M = man
W Hi Tony! How about going to the movies tonight?
M Sure. Sounds good. What time?
W The movie starts at 8 p.m.
M Great!

3
C = Carrie T = Tommy
C Hi Tommy! It's Carrie. We're having a barbecue tomorrow. Do you want to come?
T Thanks for the invitation, but sorry, I can't. I'm away all weekend, not back until Monday.
C Oh, well. Maybe next time, then.
T Yes, definitely.

4
W = woman M = man
W Would you like to come to my sister's wedding with me?
M When is it?
W On March 28th.
M What time?
W It starts at 2 p.m.
M Great. I'd love to. Thanks.

5
M = man R = Roz
M Hey Roz! We're having a surprise party for Lucy's birthday. Are you free on Friday?
R What time?
M At about 7:30.
R Sounds great! What can I bring?
M Your favorite snack, maybe?
R OK – sure, see you there.

6
W1 = woman K = Kit
W Hello Kit! We're having a baby shower for Laura and Michael on Saturday. Do you think you can come?
K Of course we can! What time?
W 3 p.m. at Laura's.
K Great. See you there.

Unit 8

▶ **8.1** Notice the silent **e** of most -**ed** endings, and the /ɪd/ after **t**.

1 Maud was born in 1877.
2 She worked in the circus.
3 Gus wanted to go out with her.
4 She agreed to see him.
5 She married him.
6 She studied hard.
7 She learned how to tattoo.
8 She stopped work.
9 Lotteva started tattoo lessons at nine.
10 Maud died in 1961.

▶ **8.3** Notice -**ed** endings are /d/, /t/ or /ɪd/ (never /ɛd/).

Frida Kahlo was born on July 6, 1907, in an area of Mexico City called Coyoacán. Her full name was Magdalena Carmen Frida Kahlo y Calderón, something most people don't know. When Frida was a child, she lived in the famous Casa Azul, or blue house, with her family. It is now the Frida Kahlo museum and a fascinating place to visit! Frida painted her entire life, and was famous for her self-portraits. When she was young, she wanted to be a doctor, but in 1925, when she was only 18, she was in a bad bus accident. She then decided to be a painter, and in 1928, she married the world famous muralist Diego Rivera. Kahlo traveled to the U.S. with Rivera in the 1920s and 1930s, and she traveled in Mexico, too. She enjoyed her time in the U.S., but didn't like some aspects of American society. During this time, she developed her own unique style. Her first exhibition was in New York in 1938. In 1939, Kahlo went to live in Paris for a time. There, she exhibited some of her paintings, and met other artists, including Picasso. In 1943, she started teaching in Mexico City. Sadly, Frida was sick for most of her life. She died in 1954 at the age of 47 in her bed in the Casa Azul.

▶ **8.8** Notice sentence stress.

What did you **do** on your **last vacation**?
Where did you **go**?
Did you **meet anyone interesting**?
What did you **do** every **day**?

▶ **8.11** Notice and imitate the connections.

I = interviewer J = Jay
I So, what's your typical day like, Jay?
J Well, everyone thinks my life_is_exciting, but it can be pretty boring!
I Really? What did_you do yesterday?
J Yesterday? OK, I got_up_at_about 6 o'clock.
I Wow! So_early! That's amazing.
J That's when_I usually wake_up, you know.
I And then?
J I brushed my teeth, and then I made coffee. I absolutely can't start my day without_it.
I And did_you have breakfast?
J Yes, I had_a big breakfast. I love to cook, so then I made_an_omelet.
I That's great! And what did you do after that?
J After that, I turned_on the computer to check my email.
I Do you get_a_lot_of messages?
J I sure do! You have no_idea. I spent five hours_ on the computer yesterday. I answered 100 emails!
I You're kidding! That's_incredible.
J Well, not_all_at once. I_answered 30 messages, and then_around 10 a.m., I went out and ran_a mile. Then I came home and took_a shower. After that, it was time for lunch, so I had_a sandwich.
I And then?
J Well, I finished_answering all the emails. Then_at_about 2:30 p.m., I started to play the keyboard and_experiment with some ideas. I played for three hours ... and I wrote_a new song.
I That's fantastic! And what did you do after that?
J Well, then I went to visit some friends. My day_ ended_at midnight. That's when went to sleep.
I You had_a full day!

▶ **8.14** Notice spellings of /ɑ/ and /oʊ/.

Q = quiz host M = man
Q So has everyone finished? Time for the answers. Number 1 was in fact The Beatles.
M Yes! We got that one!
Q OK, question 2. The first artist to surpass 50 billion streams in 2018 was Drake.
M Another one right!
Q Question 3. Idina Menzel sang "Let it Go" in *Frozen*.
M No!
Q OK, question 4. Eminem wrote the first rap song to win an Oscar.
M That is correct ...
Q A difficult one now. Question 5. Who made the video ...
M I know, I know, I've got it, I know the answer! It was Maroon 5!
Q Well, actually it wasn't ... it was Mark Ronson and Bruno Mars.
M I don't believe it. No. I'm sure it was Maroon 5 ...
Q Well I'm sorry. On to question 6. Enrique Iglesias sang the first song in Spanish to surpass a billion views.
M Hmm.
Q Now on to question 7. Ariana Grande was born on June 26th in Florida ...
M Oh.
Q ... Justin Bieber was born on March 1st in London, Canada, Rihanna was born on February 20th in Barbados, and Shawn Mendes was born on August 8th in Toronto. Now, question 8. Lady Gaga didn't sing at President Obama's inaugurations.
M Really?
Q Yes, really. Question 9. Reggaeton began in Puerto Rico.
M I was sure it was Brazil.
Q And finally ... question 10. Bob Marley told his son "Money can't buy life."
M Well, I got that one right ...

▶ **8.16** Notice sentence stress.

S = sales clerk C = customer
S OK. So **when** did you **buy** this **phone** ex**act**ly?
C Er ... last week.
S And did you **buy** it in **this** store or **another one**?
C I **bought** it **here**.
S That's **good**! Well, did you **keep** the re**ceipt**?
C Yes, I **think** so ... Ah! **Here** it **is**!
S OK. **Great**. Can you **leave** your **phone** with **me**?
C Er ..., but, um ..., **how long**?
S You can **come back** in an **hour**. We **just need** to **take** a **look**.
C Phew! Thanks!
S Can you **give** me your **password**, **please**?
C Oh, well, **OK**. But the **password** is **only** for **you**!

▶ **8.17** Notice **h**.

M = Mike C = Chris
M Hey Chris! How's it going? I tried to call you.
C Hi Mike, I'm not happy at all.
M Why? What happened?
C Well, I was at work at the hotel, right, and I had my phone in my jacket pocket. And my boss

Audio script

says, "Chris, can you clean the bathroom?" So OK, I went to clean the bathroom.
M Then what happened?
C I was cleaning the toilet when ... SPLASH! My cell phone fell in to the toilet!
M Oh no! Did you get it out?
C Yeah, but that phone cost $400!
M What did you do?
C Well, I put it under the hand-dryer, but it still doesn't work.
M Gee! That's bad luck. But at least the bathroom's clean now!

8.18 Notice the connections.
1
M = Mom S = Sophie
M Oh no! Look at this mess. Sophie!
S Yes, Mom?
M Can_you please wash the dishes?
S Uh, sorry, it's Brian's turn today.
M OK, forget it. Brian!!!

2
M = man W = woman
M Excuse me. Uh, could_you open the door for me, please?
W Oh, sure. There you go.
M Thank you so much.

3
W = woman D = Dan
W Dan, there's someone at the door.
D Could_you see who it is? I'm busy.
W Don't worry, I'll get it.

4
W = woman J = Jim
W Jim!
J Uh?
W Could_you please cut the grass, Jim?
J Er, but ... the game ... Come on, I can do it tomorrow.
W Could_you do it this afternoon, please? Your mother's coming to visit.
J Uh, OK, I'll do it now.

5
W = woman M = man
W Could_I ask you a favor?
M Hmmm, that depends. What do you want?
W Can_I leave my son with you this weekend?
M Oh. I'm really sorry, but I can't. I have two parties to go this weekend, so I can't be with your son. Sorry.
W Oh, no problem. Thanks anyway!

Unit 9

9.1 Notice /oʊ/, /ʊ/ and /ʌ/.
Hello and welcome to the Woodbury Music Festival! So, how did you all get here?
1 We rode our bikes. 30 miles!
2 We took the bus.
3 We walked. We live nearby.
4 I rode my motorbike.
5 By car. I drove.
6 I drove the band's truck! The other roadies all came the same way.
7 We took the ferry.
8 We took the train.
9 Some of the bands took a helicopter, I think.
10 I flew. I'm from Canada and my airplane landed this morning.

9.6 Notice /ə/ in articles and non-content words.
B = Brian J = James
B Look at this old picture from school, James! What's everybody doing now?
J Well, you know I'm a cab driver, Brian.
B Yes, you always loved driving!
J And Valerie is a hairdresser. She cuts and styles hair, you know – she loves it.
B And Martina is a firefighter. She was brave in high school.
J I know. What about Chris? What does she do?
B She's a flight attendant. She loves to travel!
J And I hear that Jane is a photographer.
B That's great! She always took fantastic pictures.
J What about Larry? Do you know anything about him?
B Yes! He's a police officer!
J What about David and Amelia?
B David's a cook ... no surprises there. And Amelia's a dentist.
J Wow, and Robert?
B He's a personal assistant to a famous singer! You know how he loves to organize people!
J Yeah! That's Robert! Nice job!
B I know – and I'm a computer programmer.

9.7 Notice the sentence stress.
K = Kelly M = Michael
K What are you going to do when you finish school, Michael?
M Well, first I'm going to go to grad school and then I'm going to be a financial advisor.
K Really? Why? That sounds boring.
M Well, you can make a lot of money as a financial advisor.
K I see!
M But seriously, you help people and you can be your own boss.
K That's cool. Your parents are going to be happy. You can give them financial advice.
M What about you?
K Promise you won't laugh if I tell you?
M Of course not. C'mon, tell me. What are you going do?
K I'm going to be a pet psychologist!
M What? How?
K Stop laughing! You promised not to laugh!
M Sorry!
K Yeah, I'm going to go to grad school and study psychology and then get a certificate in animal behavior. I want to be a pet psychologist. It's not going to be easy, but it's what I want.
M That's great! But, er, why, why do you want to be a pet psychologist?
K Well, first because I love animals, but I don't want to be a veterinarian. I want to work with animals. You can meet lots of people and make them happy. It's going to be fun!
M Maybe ...
K Well, I know I'm not going to be rich, but that's OK.
M OK then ... tell me what that dog's thinking.
K Don't be ridiculous!

9.11 Notice three pronunciations of o - /oʊ/, /ɑ/ and /ɔ/.
Well, Alex, maybe you can learn a few lessons from your dad. I left college in 1975, before graduating. I couldn't wait to get married, so I found a girlfriend immediately and got engaged after just three months! We got married only a month later, and I left home. At the same time, I started a new job as a photographer in a photography studio. And we started a family! But, as you know, things didn't work, and your mom and I got divorced when you were five. So I moved to a new house. Then I lost my job, because of digital photography, so I changed careers and became a computer programmer – boring, but it paid the bills. I finally retired from my job last week and now I think it's time for you to make a few changes in your life – I don't want you to make the same mistakes I did.

9.13 Notice the future verb forms.
C = Carla J = John Ju = Julia M = Martin
1
C Hi Ronnie! It's Carla. My brother's moving to Paris in July. He's going to fly there and he wants me to help him pack all his stuff. Can you help us too? It's going to take us weeks, but you're really good at packing. I hope you can! And I promise to buy you dinner! Thanks. Call me back.

2
J Hi Melissa, it's John. Listen, you know I told you that my parents are going to retire in February. Well, they've decided that they're going to move to a warmer place – so they're going to travel through Central and South America, and I wonder if you could help ... I know you lived in Costa Rica with your parents for a long time. We really value your opinion!

3
Ju Hi Mom! It's Julia. Uh ... Are you sitting down? We have some big news. Guess what! We're getting engaged! We're not going to get married until we finish school, so don't panic. So, uh, call me back when you get this message. Ciao!

4
M Hi Lucy, it's Martin. I got in! It's official! Yeah! I'm changing careers at last. I'm going to study nursing, and I'm going to be a nurse. A nurse! Woohoooo! I just got the news – they accepted me at the nursing school. I'm so excited! Call me back, because we need to celebrate. I'm going to be at work all afternoon, but then I'm going home, so give me a call and let's go out! Love you! Yeah!

9.14 Notice two pronunciations of e - /ɛ/, /iː/.
M = man W = woman
M A civil engineer: an engineer who builds public works, for example bridges or roads.
W A dentist: a person who takes care of other people's teeth.
M A financial advisor: a person who helps people invest their money.
W A market research analyst: a person who studies the reasons people buy certain products.
M A nurse: a person who helps doctors to take care of sick people.
W A software developer: a person who writes new computer programs.

9.16 Notice the connections.
1
L = Len J = Jane
L Excuse me, Jane. Can I ask you something?
J That's fine, Len. What_is_it?
L Could_I take the day_off tomorrow? I need to take my son to the doctor.
J Sure. Go ahead!
L Thanks, Jane. Phew! That's great!

167

2
S = son M = Mom
S Can_I borrow the car, Mom?
M No, I'm, sorry, you can't. I need_it this afternoon.
S Ooooooh! Why not? You never let me borrow the car …

3
M = man W = woman
M Argh, do_you mind_if I turn_on the air conditioning?
W Not_at_all. It's really warm_in here.
M Phew, thanks.

4
A I hate to ask this, but could_you lend me some money? I left my money_at home, and_I need to get something to eat.
B I'm sorry, but_I don't have_any money with me_at the moment.
A Oh, OK, I'll_ask Jeff. Thanks_anyway.

Unit 10

◯ 10.2 Notice /aɪ/, /aʊ/ and /oʊ/.
Well, my job is to get people ready for the camera. I have to think about all these things: first, the hair, then the eyebrows and the eyes, then I quickly check the ears and the nose. Finally, I work on the mouth, and this means checking the teeth and working on the lips. I want people to look absolutely perfect!

◯ 10.3 Notice the connections.
P = police officer A, B and C = witnesses
1
P So, the man who took your bag. What did he look like?
A Hmm … he wasn't short or tall. He was, um_ average height. And he wasn't overweight_or slim, he was_average build_I think.
P And can you remember the color_of his hair?
A Yeah, He, er … He had dark hair.
P Long_or short?
A Er, long dark hair_and he had blue eyes, I think.
P OK. I think_I know who you mean. That's_ Adam. We know where he lives. Thanks! Let's go!
2
P OK, and what does the suspect look like?
B Well, he's short_and slim. And he said his name was Charlie, but, well, who knows.
P Uh-huh? What else do_you remember?
B Hmm, er … he has short dark hair_and brown_ eyes. Like you!
P OK, thank_you. Oh, and don't worry. I'm not Charlie.
3
P OK, can_you describe the suspect, please? You said his name was Mark, right? What does_he look like?
C Well, he's tall_and very_overweight.
P Hmm, OK, and what color_is his hair?
C Er, I think he has short fair hair_and blue eyes.
P OK – thank_you, ma'am.

◯ 10.6 Notice /ə/.
M = Maggie S = Steve
M I need some help, Steve.
S What's up, Maggie?
M Two people have invited me to parties on Saturday.
S Well, which one do you like better?
M They're both nice. Well, Scott is taller than Jake and you know I usually like tall men.
S Yes, so go with Scott to the party!

M But Jake is happier than Scott. Scott's sadder.
S So, go with Jake! That's more important. It doesn't matter that he's shorter than Scott.
M I know, but Scott is more interesting than Jake. Jake is a bit boring.
S Why don't you go to both parties? You can be friends with both of them.
M Good idea. I can go to the first party with Jake from seven to ten and then go to the second party with Scott at ten.
S Problem solved!

◯ 10.7 Notice word stress in the underlined words.
W What do your twin sisters look like?
M Those are my twin sisters, Zoe and Rebecca over there.
W Wow, Brad! They look identical.
M Yes, but they're very different.
W What's Zoe like?
M She's friendlier than Rebecca and she's more generous. She likes to be with other people and she's always giving people presents.
W What about Rebecca? What's she like?
M She's more timid than Zoe, and she's calmer. She likes to be alone, but she's more intelligent and more organized than Zoe.

◯ 10.9 Notice pronunciation of the suffixes.
A Type one is a perfectionist. They're idealistic but sometimes they're critical of other people.
B And what about type 2? What are they like?
A They're generous people but they're also possessive.
B And type 3?
A They're ambitious but they can become arrogant.
B Can you tell me about type 4? What are they like?
A Type 4. Umm, they're romantic, but sometimes they can be moody too.
B What about types 5 and 6?
A Type 5 people are solitary and they try to understand the world but sometimes they feel depressed. That's type 5. Type 6 people are loyal and responsible but also suspicious.
B OK, the last three?
A Type 7 people are spontaneous, happy and fun. But they are very disorganized. Type 8 people are strong and try to do important things. The bad side is that they get angry. And the last one, type 9. They are calm and avoid conflict. The negative side is that they are passive and accept things because they don't want any problems.

◯ 10.14 Notice the sentence stress and the weak forms.
W = woman M = man
W OK, so let's see how we did. Number 1 is true. Scientists don't know why, but your brain is very active when you sleep.
M OK – I knew that one – number 2?
W True. It says that if men don't shave, a beard can grow to more than 10 meters long!
M Wow! What about number 3?
W That's false. Your toenails grow slower than your fingernails because they get less sun.
M Hmm. Interesting. And number 4?
W This is true, because women are smaller than men, so the heart needs to move the blood faster to the different parts of the body.
M Oh! I didn't know that. What about number 5?

W False. The heart needs a lot of space, so the left lung is smaller.
M Really? OK, what about number 6?
W That's false. We can live for a month or even two months without food, but the longest time a person can go with no sleep is 11 days. Sleep is more important than food.
M Wow, this is really interesting! And number 7?
W This is true. When you eat or talk, you are using your tongue so it gets a lot of exercise.
M I suppose so. Blablabla! What about 8?
W This is false – the most common blood type is O.
M I think I'm type O. How about you?

◯ 10.15 Notice the connections.
1
A So, what_do_you think?
B I'm not sure, Chinese_or_Italian?
A Hmm, I prefer the Chinese restaurant, but_it's_ more_expensive than the Italian.
B Yes, but the service_is faster in the Italian restaurant than_in the Chinese.
A I can't decide.
B Well, we're not_in_a hurry, so let's go to the Chinese restaurant.
A OK. Sounds good!
2
C Hmm, which one is best?
D Well, the strawberry is the sweetest and the coconut is more interesting. Chocolate is very popular!
C What do you recommend?
D I like the vanilla best.
C OK. I'll have the vanilla.
3
E So, where do_you want_to go? To the beach_or to the mountains?
F Well, the beach_is warmer than the mountains.
E Yes, but_it's_more peaceful_in the mountains.
F Well, I don't_know. I can't decide.
E OK, why don't we go to the beach? We need_to have some fun!
F That sounds great!

Review 5

◯ R5.2 Notice voiced th /ð/ and unvoiced th /θ/.
L = Laila J = Jenna
L Hi Jenna, how are you?
J Hi Laila. I'm great, thanks. Hey, I got your email. Great news about your trip.
L I know! I'm so excited!
J Listen, Laila. My brother went to work in Los Angeles and his room is empty. You can stay there until you go to Thailand.
L Your brother's room! Really? Oh, that's very kind of you. Are you sure he doesn't   mind?
J No problem at all. But when exactly are you going on vacation?
L Well, I finish school on June 20th and I'm going to fly to Bangkok on July 16th.
J So you need a room for about two weeks, right?
L Umm, let me check … No, about three and a half weeks actually.
J Three and a half weeks. No problem.
L Thanks so much, Jenna. OK, now tell me about you … how are you?